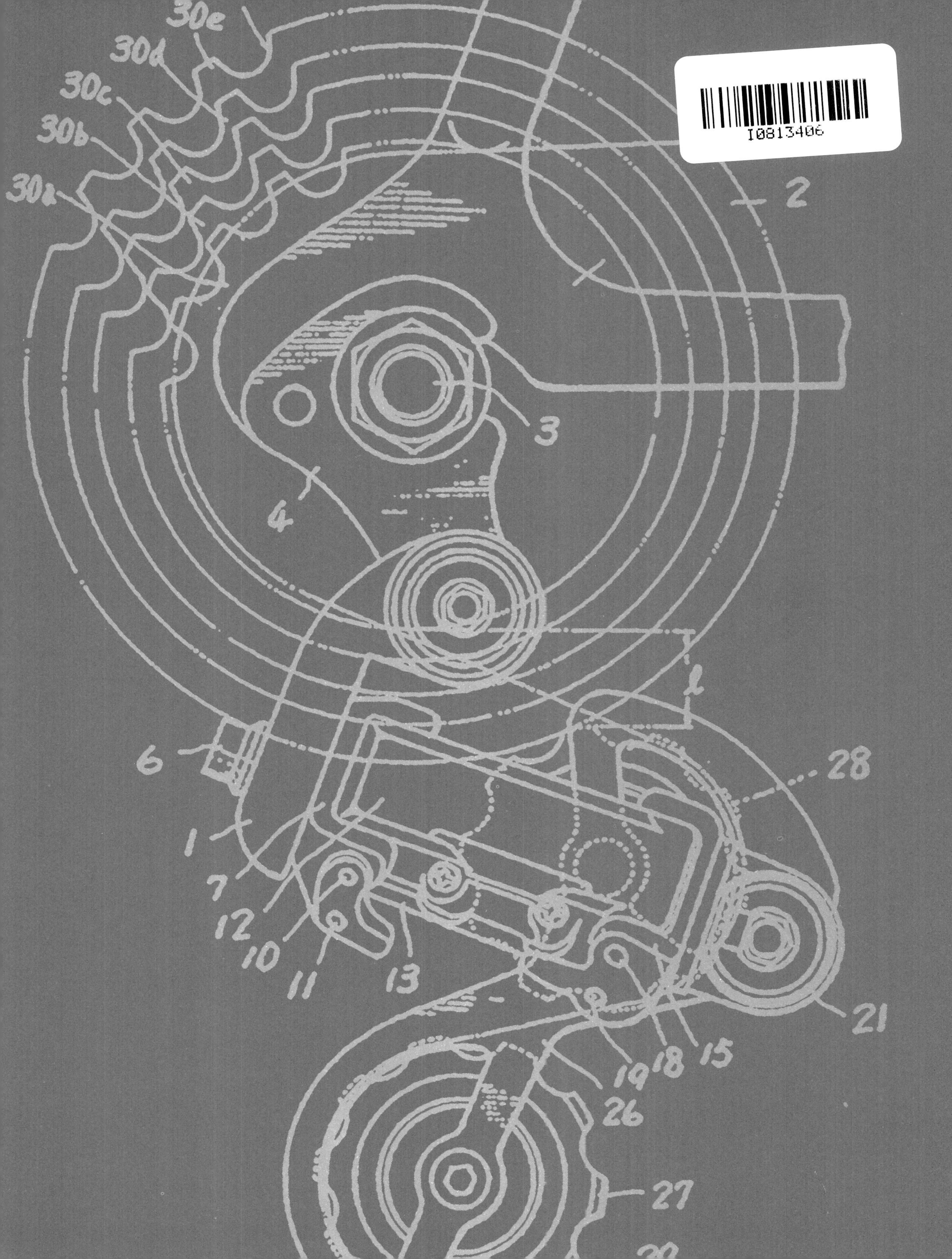
30e
30d
30c
30b
30a
2
3
4
6
28
1
7
12
10
11
13
21
19
18
15
26
27

1964 — 1994

JAPANESE STEEL

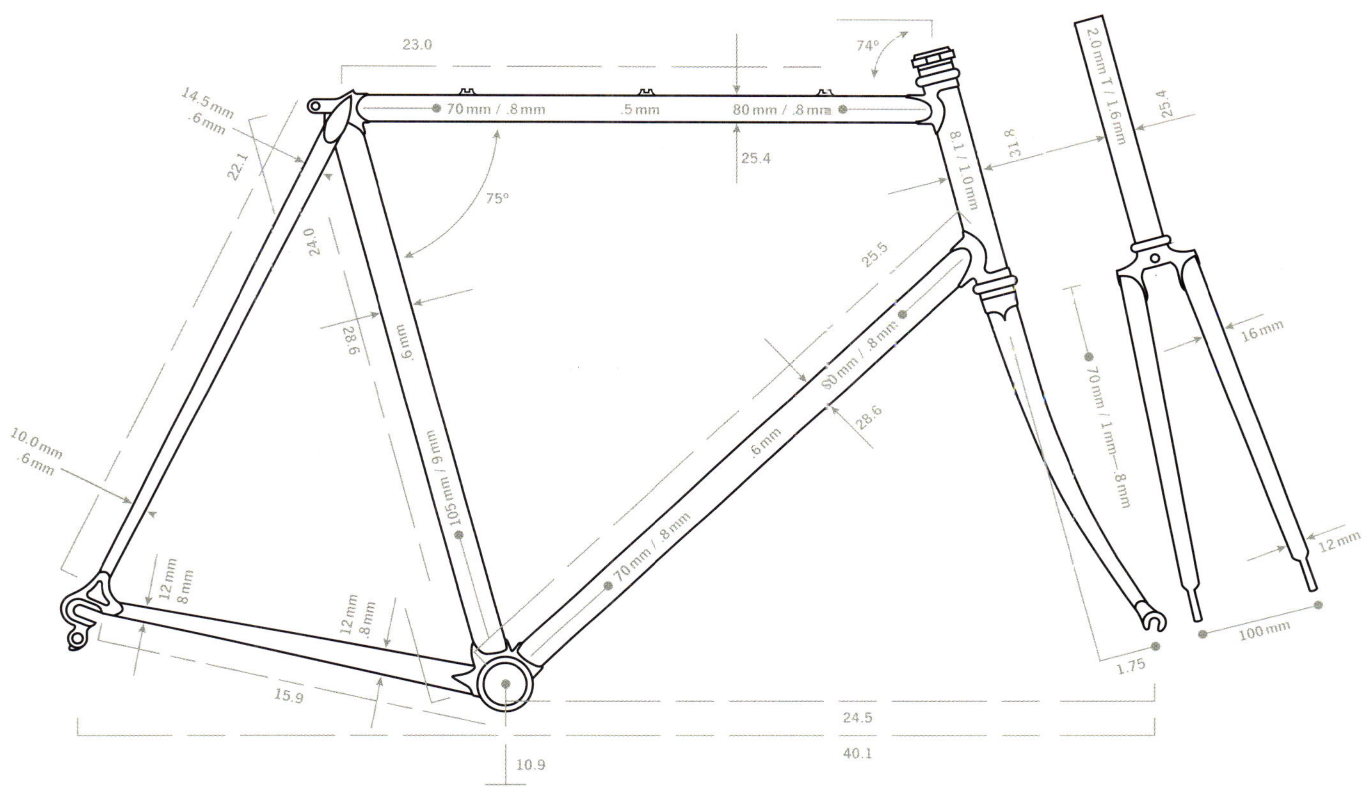

Behold! The bicycle: phenomenon of self-propulsion more efficient than any other human invention. A machine entirely powered by its operator in a delightful biomechanical alliance—communing together for pragmatism or pleasure, for competition or companionship, to improve the self or to minimize one's carbon footprint upon our precious earth.

The synergy between rider and bicycle is an interplay of balance. First, the physical balance of mass and measure, of gravitational and gyroscopic forces exploited to permit the reality of cycling. Next, the balance of geometry and construction to determine the machine's purpose and the rider's posture. Within this balance, the balance of materials—factors of strength versus lightness, flexibility versus stiffness, and comfort and cost versus performance.

Bicycle history presents a showcase of materials in motion. Initially, wood-framed bicycles were supplanted by steel, until steel drew competition from her non-ferrous cousins: aluminum, titanium, even magnesium. Today, carbon-fiber-reinforced polymers, chunky tires, and electronic assist have altered the bicycle landscape. Yet steel, in many alloyed forms, occupies the long, broad center of this history and remains a highly viable material for framebuilding today.

How long will a steel-framed machine last if well maintained? The physics we craftily exploit dictate that even steel will eventually fatigue under usage. However, subject to the conditions most riders encounter (and the number of miles that most will actually not undertake), their bicycle will never fail them. With minimal care, a well-made steel frame will survive—forever.

Many manufacturers still make steel-framed bicycles, and the finest artistry of our day can be seen in the work of a multitude of steel-obsessed custom builders. But new is not the only answer: reach into the rich stream of bicycles that remain in fine form, though they have been jostled about for decades. They're out there in every price range and every configuration. Thousands of these, still resilient, and still plentiful, emanated during the Japanese classic export era—roughly from the mid-1960s until the mid-1990s.

Some are highly collectible, yet most can be snatched up for the cost of an extravagant dinner. And, if they are not fully street-worthy, they can quickly be made so. Each is a testament to the wonders of a road bicycle. All await the chance to prove, with every ride, the enduring properties of steel.

JAPANESE STEEL

CLASSIC BICYCLE DESIGN FROM JAPAN

WILLIAM M. BEVINGTON

SCOTT RYDER
PHOTOGRAPHY

[illegible]ORK

New Y[illegible] · London · Milan

At the onset of the "Japanese Steel" project I merely set out to showcase my collection of extraordinary bicycles. However, as I (and many others) prepared the machines for their moments under the lights and before the camera, I became increasingly fascinated by the brands, as opposed to the individual bicycles.

It became apparent that each brand possessed a kind of DNA, a "style" unique to that brand only. Sometimes this uniqueness was bold, sometimes subtle, but it was always there. The bicycles themselves were speaking about a larger story and many new actors were required to tell the tales that I've shared within this book.

To support this end, exciting examples came from all over the United States, as well as the rest of the world, to represent three "velocipedic" attributes: construction (the frame), composition (the componentry), and aesthetics (the paint, decals, and livery). In the end only a handful of bicycles that came under the discerning eye of Scott Ryder's camera were from my original collection.

The resultant selection is composed of nine brands. These are divided among five major contemporary Japanese domestic manufacturers of the day, in Bridgestone, Panasonic, Miyata, Fuji, and Araya; three non-Japanese owned companies in Nishiki (primarily supplied by Kawamura), Centurion (primarily supplied through H. Tano & Company), and Lotus (of which both examples shown were built by Tsunoda); and 3Rensho (SanRensho), an example of a designer/entrepreneur producing low-volume, high-quality bicycles for a boutique export market.

Each of these brands is handled quite differently in terms of the years covered and models selected—the goal was to present a complete picture of a fascinating era within bicycle history.

The overarching approach is best characterized as "conversational," as if I had the opportunity to have a pleasant lunch with each of you, my readers, and then stroll over to a bicycle gallery show-and-tell. Welcome to the exhibition!

— William Bevington, New York, 2018

The figures provided on the following page are derived from fourteen corporate and industry surveys that illustrate the status of Japanese bicycle manufacturing c. 1980/1981 — the sweet spot within the collection of bicycles presented in this book.

The primary source for this information was obtained from the contemporary trade publication *Japan Bicycle Press* (later, *Japan Cycle Press*) issues *No. 1 through No. 18* (September, 1980 through November, 1984).

The principal citations include a table from issue No. 5, page 3, and reconciliation figures on page 13, issue No. 10.

These tabulated annual numbers, however, often conflict with contemporary industry reports. One example: Matsushita Electric (Panasonic) claims an order from Schwinn in 1981 for 150,000 bicycles (page 1 of Issue *No. 2*, January 15, 1981), this does not align with some annual export trade figures.

The percentage of domestic vs. export production varied significantly depending upon the manufacturer. Fuji had a the highest percentage of self-branded exports respective to production. Conversely, Bridgestone had a very low ratio (although Bicycling magazine, in their January, 1975 issue, noted that Bridgestone exported 200,000 bicycles to North America alone — another high figure).

Some significant manufacturers, such as Marubeni Yamaguchi of Tokyo, did not export. Others, such as Maruishi, the 4th largest manufacturer at the time, are listed here but are not specifically covered within this book.

There were nine (non-sequential) years in which Japanese bicycle exports exceeded a million units. The yearly average, from 1964 – 1994, was about 600,000, about 20 million bicycles in total. That's an impressive quantity of machines.

Of course, it only takes one to achieve cycling bliss! These background figures merely offer the collector a sense of the terrain: the swamps and high-ground of an age that seemed as if it would last forever, but instead faded rather quickly. Fortunately, a plethora of these gems were left behind.

First published in the United States of America in 2018 by
Rizzoli International Publications, Inc.
300 Park Avenue South
New York, NY 10010
www.rizzoliusa.com

Original technical drawings by Talia Cotton and Kris Qiaochu Li
Engineering drawing on page 8 courtesy of Shimano Cycle Development Center Bicycle Museum, Osaka, Japan
Image on page 190, painting by Hajime Kato, by permission of the owner
Initial renderings of tubing decal graphics (pages 232 – 235) by Claire Han

Special thanks to Brian Loudenslager for trade and corporate literature
Special thanks to Scott Johnson for period catalogs and source material
Additional research on Shimano Dura-Ace timeline thanks to R.S. Broderick
Sayoko Yoshida provided invaluable assistance translating Japanese source material

ISBN: 978-0-8478-6170-5
Library of Congress Catalog Control Number: 2018945174
2024 2025 2026 2027 / 10 9 8 7 6 5 4 3

Printed in China

TABLE OF CONTENTS + JAPANESE BICYCLE MANUFACTURING OUTPUT: 1980/81

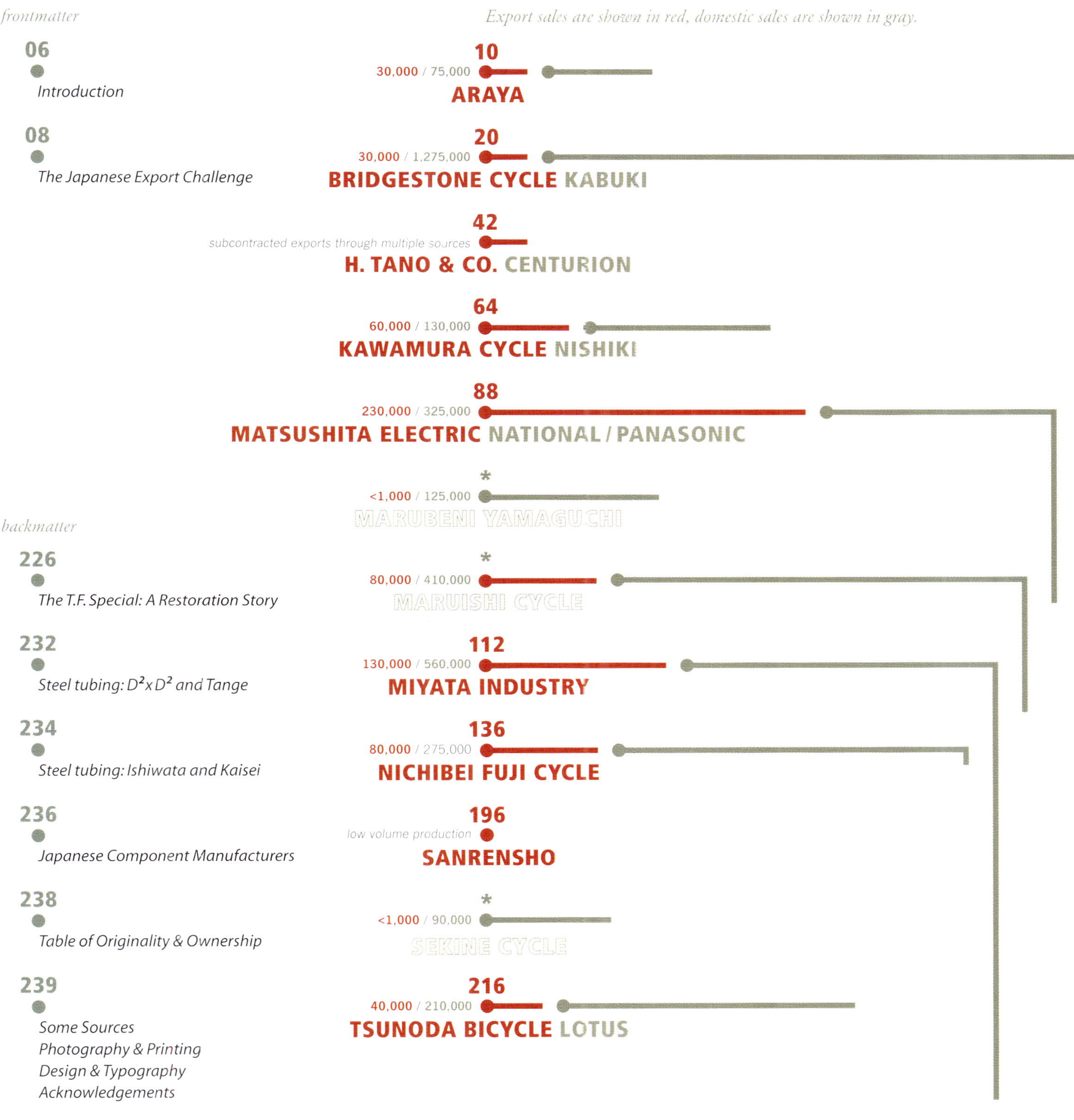

Late 19th c.

c. 1870: The bicycle arrives in Japan; some all-wooden prototypes are constructed.

1890: Eisuke Miyata, a gunsmith by trade, fabricates the first 'modern' Japanese-made bicycle from steel tubing.

1892–1902: Initially stores, and then import firms, rent and sell American models; Chicago is the dominant city of supply, but most concerns survive less than two years as the automobile and trolley car begin to quell the first American bicycle boom.

Stronger brands—such as the Crescent from Western Wheel Works, the Cleveland from Pope Manufacturing, and the Dayton from the Davis Sewing Machine Company—establish robust production and exports.

During this period, Nichibei Shoten, later becoming Nichibei Fuji, is established. They promote the "Centaur" model and decree strict price controls, ensuring a high profit margin for both importer and retailer.

1903

The Tokyo Bicycle Association is formed—joining manufacturers, wholesalers, and (unusual for the time) retailers as well; the retail trade having grown from the expansion of bicycle repair and rental activity into sales.

Approximately 5,000 privately owned and nearly 900 business-use bicycles ply the streets of Tokyo. (A decade previously, few were privately owned—most were either 'for-hire' or business acquisitions.)

Kumakichi Araya creates one of Japan's first dedicated bicycle parts manufacturers, monopolizing the wooden rim market for decades.

1904: At the age of ten, Konosuke Matsushita (founder of Panasonic Corporation) apprentices to a bicycle shop.

1909

Metallurgical and technical advances developed domestically, or acquired from Great Britain during the Russo-Japanese war (1904–1905), are now applied to bicycle-making—domestic production quickly begins to outpace imports.

1910: Premier Cycle Co., of Coventry, England, sets up a branch factory in Kobe; Maruishi Shokai serves as general sales agent (formerly known as Shikawa Shokai, founded in 1900).

1919

World War I causes near-cessation of imports from England, accelerating the need for domestic production; taxable bicycle ownership (calculated by the Ministry of the Interior) exceeds 1.5 million units.

1930s

Japanese firms produce over 90% of the bicycles for the domestic market; however, technical variance, coupled with high, fluctuating tariffs, makes exporting to the United States prohibitive.

1931: Shojiro Ishibashi establishes Bridgestone Tire Co., Ltd.

1940: Pre-war peak annual production is achieved: 1.2 million bicycles are produced.

1943: Bicycles are collected, scrapped, and remelted for the war effort.

Woodcut block print, c.1879, depicts a Tokyo street scene with wooden-wheeled bicycles and tricycles—the art was used by the Japan Trade Center in the 1969 issue of American Bicyclist and Motorcyclist.

A classic bicycle is a confluence of wonderfully diverse components, each distilled to its very essence; deceptively simple in design, yet requiring a substantial and reliable manufacturing base. For its composition the bicycle draws upon elements extracted from the earth, taken from animals, and harvested from plants. And for its power it draws upon you, the rider. At the heart of this machine is the frameset, an engineered sun within the universe of engineered planets: derailleurs, crankset, cogs, chain, and pedals for going; stem, handlebars, saddle, seatpost, and brakes for control; and the wheels (engineering marvels unto themselves) to transfer the rider's energy into forward motion. All these components revolve around the magnificent, enabling, and eminently noble frame.

Today, a wide range of materials may be deployed in the making of a bicycle frame—but none of these materials is as storied as steel, nor ever will be. Steel frames are glorious and this book expounds upon the glories of steel-framed bicycles. More specifically, it's about steel-framed Japanese export road bicycles as they progressed through three decades of triumphs and tribulations.

Although there are earlier milestones, the most profound origin for this 'classic export era' aligns with the impetus and importance of the 1964 Tokyo Olympics (the first held in Asia, and the debut of the *Shinkensen*—'old man thunder's' [Shinji Sogo's] bullet train). It is a period that opens with a delightful admixture of national pride and international entrepreneurship; planning versus the unexpected; expertise versus naïveté; imitation versus innovation. The unheralded end of the journey comes about in the mid-1990s, when challenging economic, manufacturing, and consumer shifts become too great a logistical barrier to overcome. However, for us, the ever-fortunate riders, collectors, and enthusiasts, the story does not end.

November 20, 1948: Keirin track racing begins in Japan. The first race is held at the purpose-built Kokura Velodrome in Fukuoka Prefecture; multitudes attend.

February 24, 1952: Japanese fact-finding delegations are sent to Europe and Africa. One team (Messrs. Asaoka, Takei, and Toriyama) investigates bicycle and component production at ten European firms.

This timeline presents a brief historical overview of approximately one hundred years of the bicycle market in Japan and provides the context for the classic export years featured in this book — 1964 until the mid-1990s.

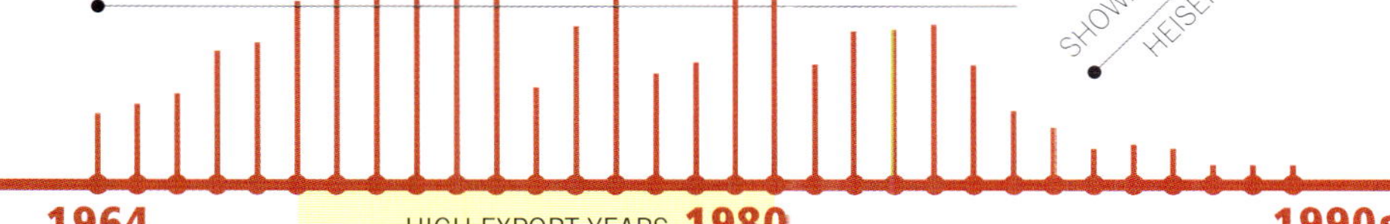

945 **1955** **1964** HIGH EXPORT YEARS **1980** **1990s**

WWII ends in Asia: Japan officially surrenders to the Allied powers on August 14th and 15th; 'Occupied Japan' ensues for nearly seven years, lasting until April, 1952.

The manufacture of bicycles resumes: 18,000 units are produced in 1945; output rapidly grows to 100,000 in 1946, and to one million by 1952.

1951: Japanese cyclists take all four gold medals at the first Asia Games, held in New Delhi. Shoichiro Sugihara wins the opening race; he will go on to earn his Ph.D. in engineering, to coach, and to design bicycle frames for Fuji.

The Eisenhower administration establishes a 22.5% import duty on bicycles; six years later this tariff is raised to 50% by the Kennedy administration. This punitive rate remains in effect until 1964.

1957: The Japanese government updates the 1948 Bicycle Racing Law—revising key elements of the act to raise standards, stimulate exports, assist businesses, and provide direct financial assistance to the industry.

1953–1962: JIS (Japanese Industrial Standards) are developed and implemented for the bicycle industry.

Games of the XVIII Olympiad held in Tokyo, the first Olympic venue assembled in Asia, during which Japan debuts the Tokaido Shinkansen, the world's fastest train—the Bullet Train.

1963–4: Howie Cohen (West Coast Cycle) travels to Japan, selecting Kawamura Cycles to build the American Eagle brand; later renamed Nishiki.

c.1965: James C. Abegglen popularizes the term, "Japan Inc." to bring attention to the spirit of quality, cooperation, and competition at the heart of Japanese business practice.

1969: Western States Imports assumes possession of 2,000 "Gran Prix" bicycles built by H. Tano and Company; originally ordered by Raleigh Bicycles, USA, but not approved by the parent company; rebranded as Centurion.

1970: Schwinn Bicycle Company contracts with Matsushita, and later Bridgestone, to produce third-party, high-quality, lugged-frame bicycles within their product lineup.

1971: Nichibei Fuji, as well as other manufacturers, begin directly marketing their own branded products worldwide and cease producing bicycles under other brand names.

Major manufacturers, assemblers, and exporters again achieve an export level of over one million units to the United States, Europe, and other Asian nations. For the first time Japanese bicycle production surpasses that of the United States—with over seven million units manufactured.

Despite this production milestone, currency shifts, pressure from emerging industrial nations, rising raw material costs, a shift in consumer taste to mountain bikes, a general decline in worldwide sales, stagnation of the domestic market, and growing internal competition—as well as a still persistent bias toward Europe for highest specification racing bicycles—the Japanese industry will see exports steadily decline in the ensuing years.

1981–1983: Aerodynamic bicycles represent the swansong of innovation for steel-framed machines. Tsunoda, founded 55 years earlier, achieves its highest sales figure to date and becomes the preeminent builder in aero-framed bicycles for the next several years.

The yen to dollar exchange rate becomes 80:1, and the second 'oil price shock' occurs, eroding Japan's export advantage. Manufacturers either cease production, finalize exports, move operations to Taiwan Region, form new alliances, modify business models, or continue to produce for the domestic market only.

Post-2000: With the waning of one world comes the waxing of another—following quality traditions established by brothers Hitoshi and Yoshi Konno at Cherubim and 3Rensho in the 1960s, the number of premium builders steadily increases as the steel-framed bicycle tradition witnesses notable growth and recognition in Japan. By 2004 exports again achieve the one-million-unit mark.

Auspiciously, the efforts of the decades-long export drive yielded multiple offspring. Millions of bicycles were constructed and shipped during the period. Even the cheapest were well made, but the best of these machines were truly exemplary—as viable today, decades later, as the day they were created. These bicycles are a testament to real quality, that joyous commingling of form and function. Beyond this, they are depositories of many wondrous invisible attributes; they are the silent soldiers embodying the passion of their creators, conveying the style and spirit of the age in which they were born.

Each embodies something of the faded whims and desires of their once targeted purchasers, reflecting both the culture of origin and the culture of destiny. They tell of the winds and waves of period marketing, and they showcase the method and materiality of the day. Each traveled thousands of miles from its industrial birthplace: Chigasaki, Hasuda, Kashihara, Kobe, Komaki, Machida—but mostly Osaka and Tokyo. Each was a child of multiple parents—entrepreneurs, engineers, factory workers, and enthusiasts, all striving for their offspring—at birth already fated to prove themselves in skeptical, foreign lands.

Many of the bicycles featured in this book have outlived the artisans and assembly-line workers who brought them into existence; outlived the rain-makers who induced the consumers which necessitated their manufacture from the factories and companies that may no longer be. In some cases, even their first owners have left this earth for their next great journey. This is not a sad thing, but rather a testament to the two highest attributes of great design: quality and permanence. In this day, saturated with built-in obsolescence and celebrations of the superficial and ephemeral, these delightful bicycles proclaim: "Simple beauty is timeless and good engineering endures."

THE JAPANESE BICYCLE EXPORT CHALLENGE

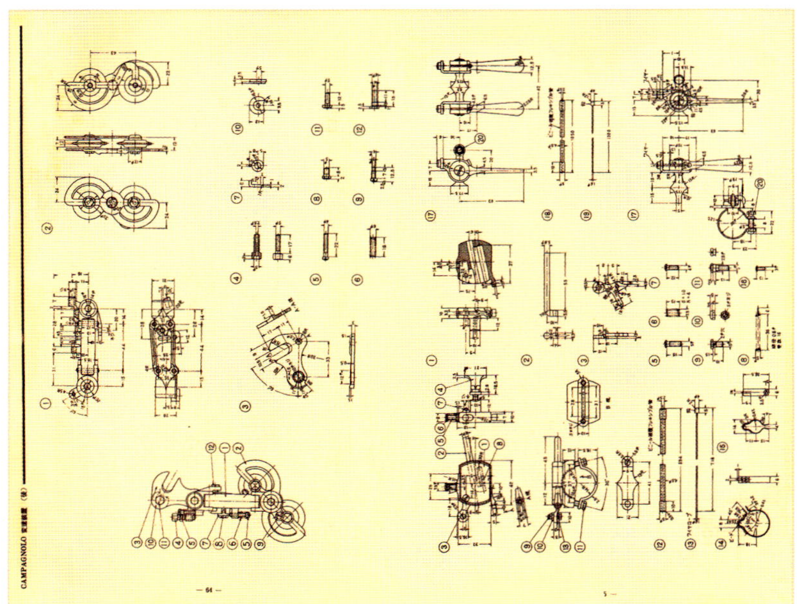

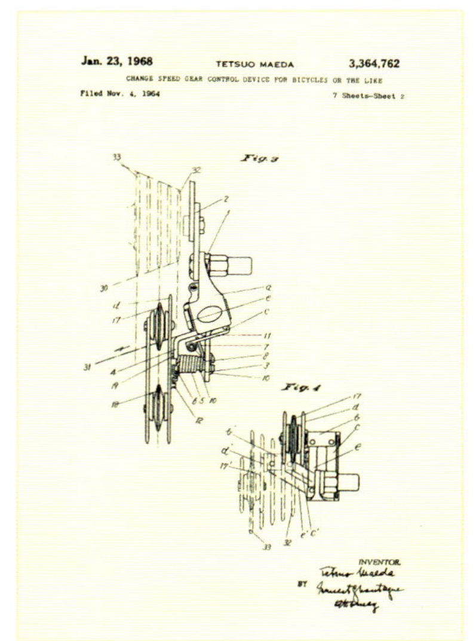

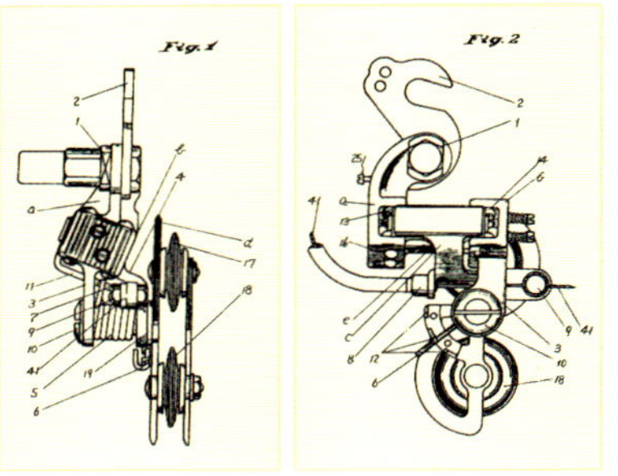

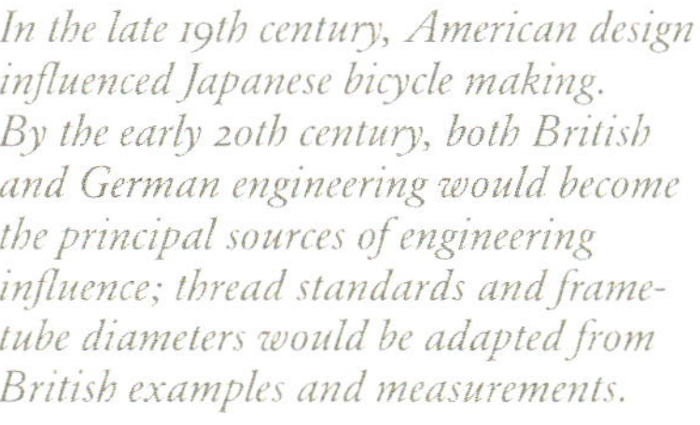

In the late 19th century, American design influenced Japanese bicycle making. By the early 20th century, both British and German engineering would become the principal sources of engineering influence; thread standards and frame-tube diameters would be adapted from British examples and measurements. With the rise of the racing bicycle, the Japanese looked to France, but most particularly to Italy. In February, 1952, three Japanese teams departed on fact-finding missions: two went to Europe and one to Africa. The European team that visited Belgium, France, Switzerland, and Italy produced exquisite technical drawings of Campagnolo and other components. Technical and aesthetic standards would be set by Campagnolo throughout their storied history. However, it would be a Japanese citizen, Tetsuo Maeda, who filed the patent for the slant parallelogram rear derailleur design in 1964, setting a proprietary standard for twenty years.

How priced? How produced? How perceived? These factors determine success for a manufacturer. Initially, the third factor, perception, was the principal challenge that the new breed of Japanese export marketers had to confront. The Second World War was only a generation past, and the products once saddled with the stigma of 'Occupied Japan' still conveyed notions of poorest quality. In reality, the Japanese political and industrial establishment had fully devoted itself to higher quality by the 1960s, but it took many years before the West came to appreciate that commitment.

The foundations for this national quality ethic were threefold. First, Japan was rebuilding much of its industrial base. Second, new ideas of management, based on scientific and mathematical principles, were being advocated—William Edward Deming was the major figure in this movement and his procedures for improving quality were entirely sympathetic to the Japanese notion of competitive cooperation. Third, Japan was people-rich and commodities-poor: the greatest resource of Japan—its natural beauty—could not be exported, nor would it be exploited; raw materials had to be imported, and therefore only avalue-added ethos could generate wealth and rebuild the reputation of the nation. Quality was crucial.

The bicycle was viewed not as a mere consumer product, but as a tool toward expanding industrial breadth in general. Government planners saw the opportunity to nurture many emerging industries by making them a part of the supply chain for bicycle manufacturing. The Japanese government developed policies, rationalized the industry, and encouraged export. During the initial phase of the 'bicycle craze' (early 1960s), Japanese exports would be very strongly positioned on price and well poised with manufacturing capacity. It would take time for them,

The Japanese government establishes the 'Bicycle Industry Promotional Subsidy System' with a first grant of 3M¥ toward 'Improvement of Production Techniques.' One year later, W. Edwards Deming delivers his 'Plan-Do-Study-Act' quality control concepts to Japanese industrial leadership.

Gene Randel and Marion Moore take notice of the 'sting-ray'–style bicycles being cobbled together by San Diego teenagers; they build and sell similar prototypes. Schwinn Bicycle Company, under the direction of Al Fritz, sees a trend and directs the creation of a commercial version. Nearly 50,000 are sold by the end of 1963 and phase one of the bike boom (targeted at the youth market) is underway.

Factory workers at Schwinn Bicycle Company's Chicago plant go on strike. During this period Schwinn contracts with Giant, the Chinese producer established in 1972, to supply the majority of their product line. Giant will ultimately grow to become the world's largest bicycle manufacturer.

Exhibits and events such as the North American Handmade Bicycle Show revitalize interest in classic steel-framed bicycle building. The craft does not fade; in 2012, the Tokyo College of Cycle Design, a Japanese government-authorized facility, begins programs in bicycle design and bicycle manufacture.

1949 **1962** **1980** **2005**

1951 **1964** **1973** THE GOLDEN AGE OF THE 10-SPEED **1990**

The first Japan's Bicycle Guide is produced by the Japan Bicycle Industry and the Japan Bicycle Exporters' associations. These compendiums list all bicycle components and accessories produced by the Japanese industry. They will be published for nearly forty years, serving to present the manufacturers on a united front.

Tetsuo Maeda, with chief engineer Nobuo Ozaki, designs the slant parallelogram derailleur. Maeda files both Japanese and US patents. This gives SunTour a technology lead in derailleur design for two full decades.

The initial boom peaks in 1968, when the 10-speed bicycle reinvigorates sales. Phase two (for the adult market) is now underway. By 1973, purchases are so heated that some bicycles are cargo-shipped via airline (instead of by sea) to meet demand. Total United States sales exceed 15 million; nearly 10% are Japanese imports. The OPEC oil embargo causes a 400% increase in retail gasoline cost, boosting the environmental credibility of bicycling.

All-terrain bikes, mountain bikes, and hybrids begin to displace road bicycles as the lead entries in manufacturers' catalogs. Top road models—relegated to the latter part of sales literature—are less frequentl composed of steel. Instead, titanium, aluminum, or, increasingly, carbon-fiber frames represent the major brands' first-tier offerings.

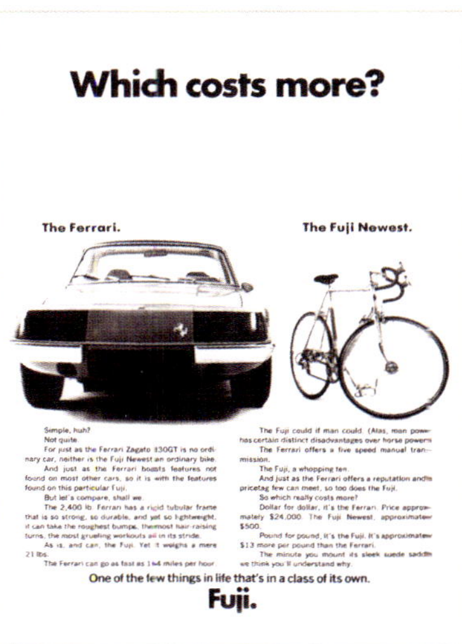

Japan's Bicycle Guides, targeted to manufacturers and importers, were essentially catalogs of bicycle parts and accessories, but the executive editor and creative director, Tanaka Hironobu, produced them with extraordinary care as masterpieces of graphic design.

By the early 1970s, Japanese bicycle manufacturers were shaking off any references to cheapness. Fuji debuted their new three-dot logo (designed by the author at the tender age of fifteen and still used by Fuji today) in this witty and minimalist ad placed in Esquire magazine. The copy compares the Fuji Newest to a Ferrari Zagato 330GT (thereby extolling great Italian design!).

however, to develop marketing savvy. As the bicycle boom unfolded, quality continued to improve. In concert, Japanese manufacturers became commensurately adept at marketing—Fuji even ran an advertisement claiming that their top-tier model, the Newest, cost more than a Ferrari Zagato 330GT. (When priced by the pound, this was true; they also pointed out that, while the Ferrari had only five speeds, the Fuji had "a whopping ten.")

Consumer perceptions of quality were greatly advanced by the efforts of the bicycle component manufacturers, particularly through Shimano and SunTour. Consumer and trade reviewers often cited components, rather than full builds, for their superiority. SunTour was an engineering-driven company that, in retrospect, underpriced their products. Shimano positioned their product line brilliantly, taking advantage of the 'Campagnolo tax.' Importantly, but to the detriment of some of the smaller manufacturers, Shimano developed technically reliable and well-branded groupsets such as the Dura-Ace line, which have become standards of excellent design.

Japan's 'Bicycle Industry Promotional Subsidy System,' initiated in 1948, provided grants of three billion yen covering the production, export, and rationalization of the bicycle industry by 1980. This was a thousand-fold increase from the founding year, but the export market was nevertheless becoming increasingly unprofitable.

Ironically, as consumer perception became increasingly favorable, the bicycle industry changed. The boom was waning, the yen was rising; Taiwan Region was rapidly absorbing the market share that the Japanese firms had nearly secured. The quality laurels had been earned, but it would be other Japanese industrial entities—such as automotive, electronic, and expanding aerospace—that would reap the rewards through the upcoming decades.

ARAYA

1903

In 1903 Kumakichi Araya, a woodworker by training, invests earnings from his lacquerware merchandising business and sets up a shop building wooden rims for the growing bicycle trade; thus establishing one of Japan's first bicycle parts-making concerns.

1909: After six years of wooden rim production, Araya is officially established as a company. Metal rim manufacture begins in 1915; in 1919 the company name becomes New Bicycle Manufacturing Co., Ltd.

1931: TOKYO

Main production plant moves from their founding location of Yamanaka (in Ishikawa Prefecture) to Tokyo—bicycle rims remain chief production focus. In 1944 headquarters are moved to Osaka.

In 1937, the official company name becomes Araya Industrial Co., Ltd., a new facility in Osaka (Kansai factory) is established—it will be Japan's largest bicycle rim-making enterprise.

1946

Postwar production of complete bicycles begins; the first model is named the Araya Swallow.

The original Yamanaka plant is retooled and updated. (Rims and hand-made disk wheels are still being produced at the Yamanaka location.)

1965

ARAYA INDUSTRIAL CO., LTD., OSAKA

Araya begins the manufacture of complete bicycles for export. By the early 1970s lightweight 10-speed models are being produced and shipped; exports will cease by 1990.

In 1973, Araya establishes a presence in Tangerang, Indonesia. Some rim manufacturing moves to that location; in 2012 they take full ownership of this venture. Bicycle building continues in Japan for the domestic market: chromoly steel tubing is used for non-racing models; all bicycles are proudly fitted with Araya rims.

1975

Araya establishes an independent bicycle division. In 1980 they complete both a Kansai and Nagoya factory—developing new lines of hardened alloy rims and initiating a push into aero bicycles for export.

1996

Araya continues to develop a premium touring model, the Swallow Randonneur, for the domestic market. The company continues to innovate in bicycle rim manufacturing, creating a model line for each genre of bicycle typ-

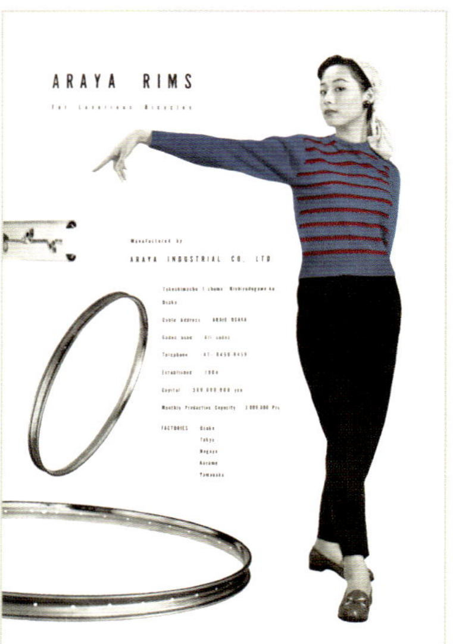

The Araya brand conveyed elegance. Stylish and considered, it commingled taste and technology in a sophisticated manner that other Japanese parts makers would take nearly a decade to emulate.

The 1957 Japan's Bicycle Guide was the only year with a horizontal (rather than a typically vertical) orientation. Araya capitalized on this by securing ad placement that spanned two pages. Models in tasteful, modernist clothing (tossing rims about) exemplified 'the Araya-look.' The well-crafted typography and sense of scale (presented as a miniature poster) made competing advertisements appear old fashioned.

ARAYA®

I was cycling down 9th Avenue, rapidly. In order to add a sense of excitement to the effort I was drafting a New York City bus, closely. Then came disaster. As we proceeded the bus cleared a massive polygon of a pothole. It was far too deep to ride through and I was already upon it. I'd need to jump it. We did this all the time; with our feet well cinched into the toe clips it was a routine matter of arcing our bodies like startled cats and lifting the machine below us up into that just-formed concavity.

The front wheel barely cleared, snagging the outermost edge of the far side of that valley, it flexed disturbingly, recovered, and moved on; but the rear wheel slammed forcibly against the canyon wall, collapsing in anguish. The shock was so intense I heard the rim's fiberglass core snap; miraculously (with vehicles oncoming from the rear) it departed the pit, but, like a drunkard who escapes a minor stumble then succumbs to a great fall, what befell was horrific. I had broken a collective of spokes and the now-ellipsoidal wheel became an enraged vortex, sucking everything into its maw. It grabbed the derailleur, the rear brake caliper, and sundry trash up from those city streets creating a mangled dystopia. The rear dropout bent a full 90 degrees; the bicycle was destroyed. Remarkably, the tubular tire (a configuration that remains intact regardless of its being attached to the rim) stretched out like a rubber band, providing a stabilizing ski of sorts. As the front chainring dug gently into the asphalt, I decelerated to a controlled, post-crisis halt: balance maintained.

If you are hopelessly knowledgeable respecting brand and product trivia, you might surmise from the clues given (fiberglass core and tubular tire) that I was riding on a Ukai rim. I was. It may have saved my life; at least it spared me some broken bones. According to the 1973 edition of *The Complete Buyer's Guide to Bicycles*, "these [rims] are filled

1982 ARAYA AERO 821: ARYL105

ARY: CODE FOR ARAYA
L: MONTH CODE FOR DECEMBER
1: YEAR CODE: 1981 [1982 MODEL YEAR]
05: BUILD NUMBER

The aero age was unveiled with great fanfare. Many in the bicycle industry were confident that aerodynamic design would rule the 1980s; however, the aero movement went into decline after only a few years. The two largest investors in the aero movement, specification-wise, were Shimano, with their components, and Tange, with their frame tubing.

Shimano's aerodynamic groupset was showcased at all the major bicycle exhibitions of 1980–82. The investment in aero design included not only components, but helmets and clothing as well. Through comprehensive wind tunnel testing, Shimano derived a valuable set of research statistics. Using a rapid baseline speed of 50 kph (31.07 mph) their engineering team determined that a rider on a road bicycle encounters resistance in the following manner:

Of the resistance a rider must overcome, 80 percent is air resistance and the remaining 20 percent is ground friction. Of the air resistance, 70 percent is caused by the rider while 30 percent can be attributed to the bicycle. This latter fraction, though nominal, is where component design can work small wonders. Shimano engineers and designers were able to shave 20 percent off of the bicycle resistance through the redesign of the component group in conjunction with an aero frame. Although impressive, this equates to a total of only half of one percent—nothing to write home about for the average rider, but significant when split-seconds count. (Shimano was justified to claim that they shaved component resistance by 20 percent, but some dealers worried about a rhetorical backlash.)

Araya would also play its part in aero development, not only with its profiled rims but with its fabulous disk wheels (still handmade to this day). These would be manufactured in aluminum and carbon. They also used titanium to manufacture their Tita-Ace tubular rim. Unlike Tange's aero tubing and the Shimano aero groupset, Araya's products would become a permanent part of the bicycle scene for time trials, pursuit machines, and standard road bicycles as well.

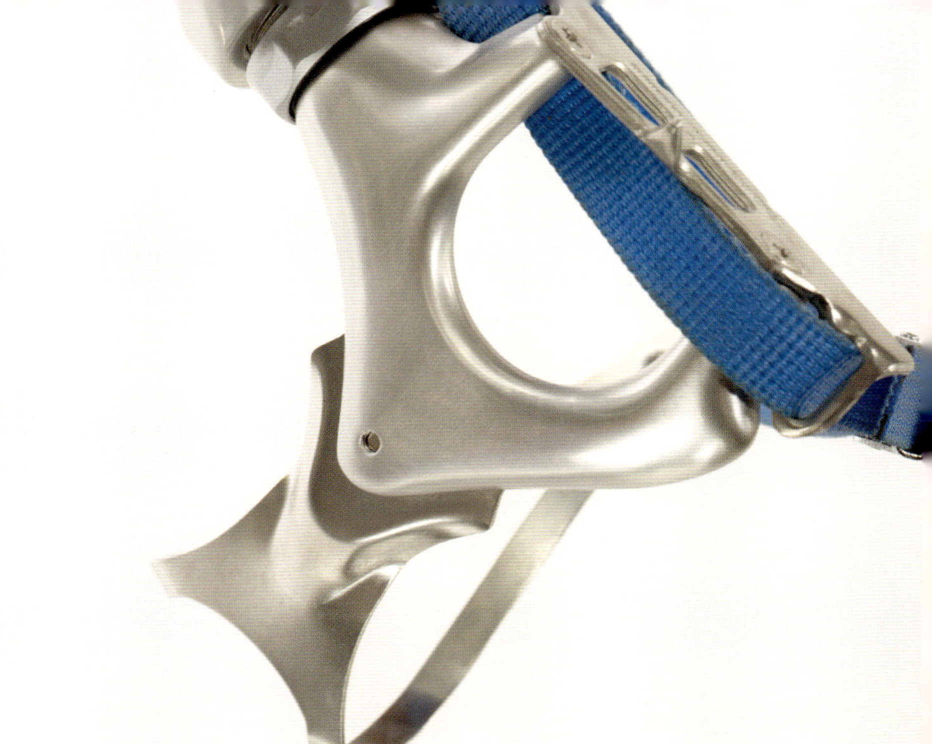

Aerodynamics was only half of the story. The sculptural, windswept look of aero components was the other. Imbued with fluid design qualities as seen in the contemporary work of Denmark's Verner Panton, or the fabulous aerodynamic shapes of Italy's Luigi Colani, bicycle parts were suddenly sexy and fashion-forward.

Protruding elements, such as brake cables, were thoughtfully 'tucked in' or routed internally. More impressively, squared corners of bicycle components became rounded and thinned. Mere functionality was elevated with forms that conveyed speed and excitement, beckoning to their riders: 'Come, let us fly across the tarmac and slice a pathway through the wind.'

In 1965, with the 10-speed bicycle boom just getting underway, Araya was producing five million sets of bicycle rims annually (controlling about 70 percent of the domestic market). At the climax of the boom, c. 1980, its rim production was holding at six million units despite a downturn in bicycle sales. In that year Araya was the second largest parts maker in Japan, following Shimano—yet fully half their size in sales.

Araya was part of the JBM group, which included Shimano, Tange, Kyokuto, Takagi, and Sakae Ringyo. However, unlike its corporate associates, Araya was far less dependent on exports (which represented a mere 20 percent of its sales). For this reason, Araya would be resilient and responsive to the evolving market trends.

with plastic… one of the few that you would dare to ride in the city." Sometimes it takes a near-disaster to encourage an appreciation of engineering details. On that day I developed a very deep respect for bicycle rims. Not long afterward, I learned about a company called Araya.

In the closing years of the 1800s, along the western coast of central Japan, Kumakichi Araya completed his apprenticeship as a carpenter. His fine woodworking talent was bolstered by an entrepreneurial spirit; together these led to Araya's first trade as a merchant in lacquerware articles. When venturing east, toward Tokyo, he discovered that wooden wheels were being imported from America, and the young Kumakichi thought to himself: "Why import these?" Araya decided to use the funds saved from his lacquerware business to set up a shop in order to construct wooden rims, thereby inaugurating one of Japan's very first specialty bicycle-parts makers.

He took painstaking care to create the best product possible, setting a standard for quality that became ingrained throughout the Araya DNA. This dedication paid off; there would be no competitors for sixteen years (until Ukai, in 1919, and Tokai, in 1921). Even so, Araya would never cease to be the major rim supplier in the nation of Japan.

This near-monopoly permitted great focus on quality and development, as there was no competition to undercut his prices. Araya began producing rims in 1903, established an official corporation six years later, and six years after that began the production of steel rims. By 1936, complete bicycles were being made under the Swallow brand. Araya boasted, "we put the effort of building two bicycles into every single Araya." This was an honest assessment of superior quality, but customers joked: "Yes, that is true, but your bicycles cost double the amount of your competitors!" No matter; for Araya it was quality before cost.

Araya even withstood the quality collapse after the Second World War. At that time, western interests could dictate any price for any item; quality and the reputation of the Japanese industry fell precipitously. Recovery took years. Araya successfully argued that lowering the standards for its rims would be dangerous. As a parts-making concern with a long history and demonstrable capability, its quality manufacturing niche was to remain sacrosanct.

In 1967, Araya began exporting bicycles (they *imported* European parts for their builds if domestic items did not meet their standards; an unusual and expensive proposition). But four years later, an entirely Japanese model, the 1971 Swallow Racer, left the factory; the quality standard had been satisfied. The Swallow was representative of that type which would be a dagger to the heart of mid-level European exports. Specifications for these 'racers' were markedly consistent. The frames were constructed with double-butted chromoly tubing and forged ends. They had drop bars and were equipped with 27 x 1¼ inch (wired-on–style) or 27 x 1⅛ inch (tubular–style) wheels. All of the parts across all the varied brands of these (eventually) tens of thousands of bicycles were interchangeable.

The early 1970s pioneers included a roster of about a dozen manufacturers, assemblers, and exporters. In addition to Araya Industrial (Swallow), these included: C. Itoh & Company, exporter for Bridgestone Cycle, Japan's highest volume manufacturer; H. Tano & Company, the original agent for Centurion; Ishibashi & Company (Ishibashi Flier); Kawamura Sangyo (soon to be Kawamura Cycles) who produced Nishiki and Azuki, contracting Kuwahara (Silk) for some of Nishiki's premier models; Maruishi Cycle Industries (Emperor); Matsushita Electric Industrial (National and Panasonic); Miyata Industry (Racer); Mizutani Bicycle (Seraph Super); Nichiebi Fuji Cycle

1982 ARAYA 'SHIMANO' AERO 821: ARYL186

ARY: CODE FOR ARAYA
L: MONTH CODE FOR DECEMBER
1: YEAR CODE: 1981 [FOR 1982 MODEL YEAR]
86: BUILD NUMBER

(the Finest and the Newest); Nissan Cycle (who made the Sky-Wagon, as well as many high-quality Kabukis for Bridgestone); Okamoto Rinken Gomu (Zebrakenko); and Tsunoda (who would soon become the builder for Lotus).

Another dozen companies would soon join their ranks with 10-speed bicycles of similar design, including: Asia Machinery (Eastern and AsiaBike); Deki Bicycle (Tsubaki); Fukaya Sangyo (Racer and Track Racer); Marubeni-Yamaguchi (the Benny); Marui (Orions and Shogun); Marukin Ohshima Industry (Racer); Sanki (the Sanki-Beat); Takeda Bicycle (Uroko); Yagami (Racer); Yokota Industries (Friendly and Lenroza); and Zushi Industrial (Oryx).

The collective output of these companies would alter the landscape of the bicycling world by producing 10-speeds that were comparatively lightweight, tough, reliable, built to close tolerances, and attractive. These were bicycles that democratized long-distance, self-powered travel. What was unknown then, but is now noteworthy, is their uncanny durability. Arguably, these bicycles represent the most sustainable products in the history of human manufacture. This longevity contributed to the demise of the companies themselves: only a handful would survive the close of the bicycle boom. Araya would be a survivor.

Over the years, Araya Industrial had greatly diversified, producing formed steel, aluminum, and, later, titanium parts for other industries. An independent bicycle division was established in 1975. Today, exquisite bicycles—from the Swallow Randonneur (built with Kaisei 022 Speed Galant tubing) to competitive carbon racing machines—emanate from the bicycle division, while the dedication to quality established by Kumakichi Araya well over a century ago guides the company's rim manufacture. Although some production is overseas, many rims are still being produced near Kumakichi's first workshop.

Shimano introduced its full-color, technology-centric advertising campaign in the autumn of 1978. By the spring of 1979, its ad placement would consistently occupy the premium inside-front-cover position of Bicycling magazine. This advertising slot would be held by Shimano for many years to follow.

Shimano's Dura-Ace AX Aero advertising began in April, 1982 and continued until February, 1983. While the aero lines were not the saviors of road-bicycle sales as first envisioned, they set the stage for further innovation in bicycle-parts design. The aero-dynamics line greatly distinguished Shimano from other manufacturers, eventually earning the brand their leadership role.

An Araya aero frameset was chromed and fitted out with proprietary Shimano decaling to showcase the exciting aero groupset. Over the years, the brand continually added to the fleet. No Japanese manufacturer came close to the kind of displays that Shimano mounted.

Shimano's aerodynamic kickoff took place in Germany at the Köln IFMA (International Bicycle and Motorcycle Exhibition) in the autumn of 1980. Seventy Japanese parts manufacturers were represented at that event. By this time Japan had achieved the number one position in parts sales. The new focus was on quality, not the faltering strategy of price advantage. This was a boon for Araya, who invested heavily in research and development.

With each new bicycle iteration Araya brought a purpose-built rim to market. Some rim manufacturing was shifted to Indonesia, which resulted in lower consumer costs, but Araya still maintains its Japanese rim-making facilities.

Post-2015: Bridgestone Cycle continues to manufacture in Japanese facilities. Along witł high-tech carbon and aluminum machines they produce the RNC and XNC models: steel-framed bicycles utilizin, their Neo-Cot, a fluid-forming tube-making technology invented in 199

C. ITOH & CO., KABUKI BICYCLE DIVISION, BRIDGESTONE CYCLE (USA), INC.

BRIDGESTONE

1931 **1949** **1965** **1984** **1994**

Bridgestone Tire Company is founded by Shojiro Ishibashi in the city of Kurume (Fukuoka Prefecture). Prescient of international reach, he uses the English translation of his surname (Ishi = stone, and bashi = bridge) to formulate the company name. Fifteen years later, Bridgestone produces its first bicycle; soon after, it begins experimenting with die-casting techniques.

Bridgestone Bicycle is formed as an independent division; operations begin in the city of Yokohama (Kanagawa Prefecture).

By 1951 the use of rolled tubing and die-cast lugwork is streamlined; innovation is focused on precision and mass production.

C. Itoh & Company serves as principal exporter. The Kabuki brand is introduced. Bridgestone begins sub-contracting to Schwinn; more than 1.5 million bicycles will be manufactured for them.

1980: Bridgestone Bicycle USA is established, soon reformulated as Bridgestone Cycle (USA), one of fifteen worldwide divisions. The Kabuki line is deëmphasized as bicycles are directly marketed under the Bridgestone brand. In 1984, Grant Petersen joins the company, later assumes Marketing Director role; Grant serves as "defacto" product manager, specifying models until 1994, when Bridgestone ceases USA exports.

In those early days, Shimano named its gear-shifting assemblages after significant members of the avian class: the (wood)Pecker, the Lark, the Eagle, and the Crane. The Crane would be the forerunner of the Dura-Ace line; after this, birds would no longer have a place within Shimano's nomenclature.

The Lark was a substantial mechanism weighing in at 350 grams; some models were graced with still another chunk of steel to guard the derailleur against a fall. Another protective option was to use a conical extender threaded onto the rear axle, snug to the wheel's locknut. Enterprising riders realized that by installing such an extender on both sides they could convert their bicycle into a taxi for the transportation of standees.

The Lark came in multiple versions (the SS, the STO, and the twin-cabled, springless 'W' version). The cage and pulley assembly generally followed the pattern of the freewheel sprockets, a design that Shimano called its 'Servo Panta System.' Albeit heavy, the Lark stayed in adjustment, shifted smoothly, and inspired confidence via its robust chromed-steel aesthetic. This Lark is controlled by Shimano's 3.3.3. top-tube frame-mounted shifters, with their distinctive red paddles. They are well suited to the Kabuki Super Speed, a 35-pound 'sportster' in matte black, constructed with Bridgestone's die-cast lug-molding method.

Bulletproof. Unorthodox. Driven. Bridgestone: a company that sought its own way, was obsessed with innovation, and possessed the manufacturing depth and prowess to withstand challenges. In 1949, Bridgestone Cycle broke from its parent, but the offspring was infused with the same independent spirit, and the brand went on to ply its own course. Bridgestone certainly made a lot of bicycles that appeared funky and overbuilt. However, to assure us of what was issuing from the Bridgestone plantation, these words were emblazoned upon the downtube: *"GUARANTEED WORLD'S FINEST BICYCLE PRECISION MECHANISM."* Now that's chutzpah—particularly coming from a culture that eschews braggadocio.

Unique die-casting methods and injection processes figured into Bridgestone's manufacturing methods from nearly the outset of their bicycle-production capabilities; extremely innovative methods are still deployed for the two steel models they currently produce. But let's step back a bit: the original innovative technique used a high-pressure injection process to form joints around accurately positioned tubes. This allowed precise, consistent, high-volume output. This method meant tubes could not distort, because the lower heat used for the cast-lug process was not high enough to do so. The early Kabukis (Bridgestones exported by C. Itoh & Company, Ltd.) utilized the method exclusively. Later, when Kabuki referred to its full model line as 'The Seven Samurai,' all but the *Diamond Tourer* were manufactured via this proprietary method. By the early 1980s, Kabuki catalogs extolled the die-cast process as "light, clean, strong," resulting in "perfect alignment." The registered name for the method was: "Technart."

Ironically, Bridgestone's exclusive process was only available for lower-priced models, such as the *Submariner, Skyway,* and *Super Speed.* The highest-priced models,

1972 KABUKI SUPER SPEED: B284412

B: MONTH CODE FOR FEBRUARY
2: YEAR CODE FOR 1972
84412: BUILD NUMBER

Section 1 of each year's Japan's Bicycle Guide showcased a gallery of generic and branded models. Early exports shared domestic characteristics—equipped with fenders, guards, kickstands, and as much lighting equipment as any bicycle could bear. By 1970, the exports were stripped-down: the realization was taking hold that a bicycle was as much about fashion and lifestyle as about pragmatic transportation. Modernist style had influenced graphic design in Japan and then product design; design was on the march. The cover of the 1968 edition was probably influenced by the pioneering Italian architect and graphic designer Franco Grignani, who created the enduring Woolmark logo.

Bridgestone specified components with discernment—one eye on weight, one on cost. The 1981 Diamond Formula-12 is a playbook example, combining Sakae Ringyo with SunTour toward the best composite of lightness and reliability with economy. Resources thus saved could then be invested in the frame and more competitive pricing.

The result was an incredibly tough 24-pound setup with straight-gauge .9 mm tubes and 73-degree frame angles. (The following year they would leverage double-butted tubing and lighter components to hit the under-22-pound mark.)

There was some weight give-back when it came to wheels. Kabuki was fairly early in foregoing tubular tires throughout its range, nearly ten years prior to other major manufacturers doing the same.

C. Itoh recognized that their customers wanted the look of a racing machine without tubular tire maintenance issues—what Consumer Reports had called, seven years earlier, "a real nagger because the repair procedure is a time-consuming, nerve rasping ordeal."

But the Diamond Formula-12 was still a worthy racing bike, as economy-minded amateurs came to discover when they swapped out its stock 27-inch Araya 20A rims for a set of lighter-weight tubular wheels, thereby saving a pound of unsprung weight—where it counted most.

under the Diamond series (*Diamond Road, Track, Touring,* and *Formula* variants), had to make do with the vagaries of traditional lugwork and brazing. (Highest-priced, low-volume frames that were constructed entirely by hand were typically subcontracted.) All seven Technart Samurai possessed fairly strong 'understeer'—they liked to go straight, pounding the tarmac mile after mile and eating up loose gravel and potholes with the confidence and poise of loyal soldiers. These were hefty, weighing in at 30 pounds. This group also sported the substantial SunTour PUB-10 stem shifters. In a review published in *Two Wheel Travel Bicycling Camping and Touring* (April 1972), Robert Drennan joked that you could use the SunTour levers to "drive in tent pegs." Die-cast Kabukis were workhorses, cruising quite effortlessly (once up to speed—which did take a bit of energy) and needing far less care and attention than any of the imports coming from Europe.

1981 KABUKI DIAMOND FORMULA-12: B113433

B: MONTH CODE FOR FEBRUARY
1: YEAR CODE FOR 1981
13433: BUILD NUMBER

By 1981 Bridgestone's president, Kochiro Ishii, had his "U.S.A. two-prong" strategy underway. The East Coast was still to be served by C. Itoh's Kabuki line, while the West Coast would see the proprietary Bridgestone offerings under their newly formed subsidiary.

For bicycle sleuths comparing the respective models, it is enlightening to uncover how each marque speaks to brand objectives and consumer perception. The 1982 Bridgestone catalog begins with a cordial note by Ishii followed by a line of lovely machines with rather difficult-to-remember, astronomy-based model names: Sirius, Antares L.D.T., Altair DL, Spica, Regulus. All of these models used Bridgestone's proprietary 4130 chrome molybdenum tubing. (The higher specification models used Tange Champion tubing and fork blades). On the East Coast, the Kabuki Diamond Formula-12 also used the 4130, so the same wonderful steel was behind greatly different liveries.

The Kabukis continued with graphically pure colors, but grab-bag componentry. The Bridgestones were clothed in very sophisticated dual color combinations as though the line had taken cues from the contemporary luxury automotive sector (as Fuji had done, their source of inspiration).

Also, the component choices followed the more traditional collections of allied JEX manufacturers: SunTour, Sugino, MKS, Dia-Compe, et al. Bridgestone was also quite honest about emblazoning their name only on things they made. Even parts that were of their own creation, such as their proprietary caliper and disc brakes, were not overtly advertised.

Of course the tires were Bridgestone across the line. By this time some Bridgestone-branded tires were being produced by IRC (Inoue Rubber Co., Ltd., a manufacturer that had been formed in 1926 in Nagoya). Still, Bridgestone's claim, that "We personally manufacture all of Bridgestone products in our own factories," was mostly on the mark.

In 1975, Bicycling! magazine published a brief article by Larry Burke that covered the full range of Kabukis. Burke wrote that Bridgestone manufactured 2.5 million bicycles annually, with 400,000 exported to North America alone. This claim seems very high compared to other contemporary reports, but does reflect the volume of production. The stated goal was to generate bicycles that were "beautiful and durable."

For Japanese exports, beauty was generally achieved via livery, badging, and decaling; while durability was satisfied by the choice of components. Durability, reliability, consistency: these were the initial factors that helped establish the perception of Japanese quality. Europe had produced some masterworks of aesthetic minimalism, such as the Huret Jubilee derailleur (1970). Japanese component aesthetics were more robust in appearance at that time, and were crafted with a heftier equation of form versus function.

By the mid-1970s, however, Japanese component makers were considering aesthetics within the design cycle. The SunTour Cyclone, c. 1975, is a near-perfect blend of form, function, and beauty. But for something a little more over-the-top, graphics-wise, the BL—Blue Line—was created. It was a departure for SunTour, in many respects a throwback technologically, but robust and visually striking. That came at a price, because painted surfaces are vulnerable on transmission equipment (where grease, dirt, metal, and motion are always in play).

SunTour fans appreciate that decades-old 'V' components can be degreased with citrus, soap, and hot water, polished with rejuvenating Simichrome, and put back into service with an increasingly matured patina that adds to the functional glory of the mechanism. In fact, returning a sad-looking machine (even one that has not seen care for over a decade) to near-catalog glory (through tear-down, cleanup, and rebuild) is rarely more than a two-day affair. The fewer painted, plastic, and decaled parts, the better.

The *Submariner* is of particular interest. It was fabricated with 18-8 stainless-steel rolled tubes. These tubes were flared at the ends and then encased and joined within pressure-formed aluminum alloy lugs. The result was a rust-proof 'coastline cruiser.' The *Submariner* exemplified Bridgestone's philosophy to build consistently engineered bicycles that required minimal maintenance and withstood considerable punishment. Of course, the appearance of this integrated die-cast headtube and lug assembly was decidedly funky in comparison to traditional framebuilding. Not surprisingly, classicists were offput by the clumsy-looking headtube and lug composite.

Concurrent with its exports through C. Itoh, Bridgestone began to consider exporting models under its own brand. The company was easily the largest manufacturer on the domestic Japanese front—a powerhouse producing well over a million machines per year in the 1970s and early 1980s. However, its exports accounted for well under ten percent of their production. In 1981, Bridgestone received a contract from Schwinn to produce 150,000 units, but something far more important was brewing under the direction of its president Koichiro Ishii. Ishii established Bridgestone Bicycle USA (November, 1980, in Los Angeles) for the western region of the United States, while continuing to work with C. Itoh for the eastern markets. Within a year they were producing some delightful, high-quality road bicycles with their proprietary chromoly steel tubing, *4130*. In the east, Kabuki continued with the Diamond series bicycles, as well as adding to the line-up the head-turning BMX machines in chrome plate and 'high-bling' coordinated colors. These Kabuki BMX machines are highly collectable today.

Several years into its USA adventure, a thirty-year-old named Grant Petersen joined the company. Japanese

1983 KABUKI DIAMOND FORMULA D — "DFD": YE88318N

Y: FORTNIGHT SEQUENCE FOR 25th FORTNIGHT [EARLY DECEMBER]
E: NISSAN YEAR CODE FOR 1982 [1983 MODEL]
88318: BUILD NUMBER
N: INDICATES NISSAN (ex-FACTORY BUILD)

Top-of-the-line Kabukis were always well regarded for the precision of their build and balanced handling; they were excellent performers for long-distance, high-speed, sustained runs. Bike World magazine noted that the DFD had a "rock-steady but comfortable fast ride." Points were added for precise frame alignment. This inspired confident, high-speed descents.

And that head-badge! If one finds a fairly nice classic bicycle at a jumble, garage sale, or church flea market sans headbadge, there's a fair chance it will be an old Kabuki shorn of its identifying emblem. There are often more Kabuki headbadges for sale on the auction sites than the bicycles themselves. The Diamond series machines were nearly luminous, possessing liveries of chrome and particularly bright colors. The 1970s editions had optionally available black-anodized chainrings and other components, this added a striking counterpoint to the bright colors that predominated.

The model-year pictured here is post-1980. The Soyo #75 tubular tires, Sugino Mighty Compe Custom crankset, and early-generation Dura-Ace brakes (with Crane derailleur) have been supplanted by Araya light alloy clincher rims (700 by 28c) along with SunTour's Superbe components and an Ultra-6 chain. The SunTour New Winner freewheel, however, appeared on both generations.

Generally, SunTour components would be specified with Nitto handlebars and stems, as well as Sugino cranksets, and Mikashima pedals. In contrast, the DFD-12 had SR equipment for the stem, crankset, seatpost, and pedals. The earlier model had been available in Sweet Tangerine Pearl or Super Sky Blue Pearl over chrome; the newer iteration was available in a two-tone blue or a striking full chrome-plated edition, which Kubaki called the DFD-12 CP.

Early on, Bridgestone developed a strong advertising presence following the dominant British model of advocating name recognition over specific product promotion. In general, their graphic style was in synch with the contemporary practice of major national and international corporations.

C. Itoh also championed a brand-building advertising strategy. A stylized Kabuki theatrical 'Kumadori' (the painted-face technique that stereotyped the stage character's persona) dominated full-page advertisements and became the well-recognized trademark for the Kabuki bicycle brand.

Top-tier Kabukis were given the 'Diamond' classification—originally the Diamond Road, Diamond Track, and Diamond Touring models.

As the model years progressed, numbers and subnames were added to the Diamond moniker, such as Formula, Formula-D, or Formula-12. Later, the abbreviations DFD or DFD-12 were used.

The serial number for this DFD-12 seems to indicate a later year, but the delectable duotone blue livery would suggest a beautifully-aged 1981 model. (Beautifully-aged except for the original gum-rubber shifter-lever hoods.)

This DFD featured the first-generation SunTour Superbe derailleur. It's what every racing derailleur wanted to be in the late 1970s. For a friction-based derailleur, nothing outperformed its shifting speed and precision. Added to these qualities were ease of adjustment and cable installation, lightness, structural stiffness, longevity, reliability, and functional consistency.

It's worth noting that there's not a big leap to the Superbe from the SunTour Cyclone. For riders obsessed with weight, who did not mind the worthwhile effort to run the shift cable across the center of the parallelogram, the Cyclone remained the unit of choice.

business owners, along with their higher-level decision makers, favored dedicated and single-minded personnel, no matter their age or background. Consequently, when Petersen joined Bridgestone as a data processor, his bicycle knowledge and gift for pragmatic innovation quickly became apparent. He was a 'Bridgestone' unto himself: opinionated, driven, and ingenious.

By the early 1980s it was becoming more difficult to gain significant market share. Ten years earlier, whatever could be tossed into the gaping mouth of the bicycle craze was eagerly swallowed up; nearly anything that could be brought before the consumer could be sold. Shortages of bicycles were common. One dealer complained: "I don't sell bicycles, I apologize to would-be customers for not having any bicycles in stock." Then, the objective was simply to get the product into the shops. That formula no longer applied; exported bicycles had become decidedly less profitable than those sold domestically. The manufacture and selling of components was a more stable and more profitable venture, so companies like SunTour, and particularly Shimano, were extremely well positioned, while full bicycle manufacturers, though still doing well, were beginning to feel economic and marketing pressure.

Petersen recognized this, along with the obvious fact that most of the people purchasing racing bicycles had not raced, were not racing, and never would race. His design instincts gravitated toward 'unracing bicycles,' a term he later coined to summarize a design philosophy based on comfort, simplicity, longevity, affordability, and technical classicism. He not only influenced a generation of great bicycle making; he oversaw the production of some of the best bicycle ephemera ever made. When snow, driving rain, or bitter cold keeps one from cycling, one turns to bicycle literature to satiate the void, and the Bridgestone

1984 BRIDGESTONE GRAN VELO 2000: E417488

E: MONTH CODE FOR MAY
4: YEAR CODE FOR 1984
17488: BUILD NUMBER

As the 1980s unfolded, the Bridgestone road bicycle line became increasingly sophisticated. The Grand-Vélo, the crème de la crème, had been offered domestically and soon became the top export model as well. It remained the top model until 1987. In the following year mountain bikes moved to the front of the catalog as aluminum-framed road bicycles supplanted the Grand-Vélos.

This Grand-Vélo 2000 was second in command after the flagship Grand-Vélo 3100. Both models were constructed of Bridgestone's Chrome Molybdenum 4130, which now had a fairly long history for the company. The 2000 had triple-butted tubing and lost-wax-process castings for the exquisite seat cluster and fork crown. Traditional craft methods were now being applied to its high-end road bicycles as greater levels of automation, including robotics, continued across the rest of the model range.

Bridgestone literature became increasingly informative, justifying the build logic for disparate component selection. The goal was to balance performance and price point. As the export world became more competitive, research became increasingly scientific, with studies in human metabolism, ergonomics, and muscular function factored into the design of competitive bicycle fabrication. These sciences were conjoined to the art of marketing to best the competition.

SUNTOUR
CYCLONE M-II

As the mid-1980s approached, bicycle component manufacturing was undergoing more rapid change, accompanied by successes and shakeouts. There was both an ever-tightening technical integration of system function (now led by Shimano) as well as an aesthetic and emotional draw to collections and groupsets (still led by Campagnolo).

Campagnolo pioneered the 'gruppo' idea and it took tenacious hold of the industry, particularly in high-end offerings. In 1983 they were still the masters, and they celebrated with the fabulous, but gaudy, 50th Anniversary Edition. This assemblage of components is so collectible that far more remain in their original blue injection-molded suitcase than toil away on actual bicycles. The export pecking order was established by the middle of the decade: Campagnolo Record: gold, Shimano Dura-Ace: silver; SunTour Superbe: bronze.

For this Grand-Vélo 2000, SunTour's Cyclone MK II served as the drivetrain; the following year it would be the Superbe Pro. But the top-of-the-line Grand-Vélo 3100 was spec'd with Shimano's New Dura-Ace 7-speed SIS system. Slowly, yet steadily, Shimano would climb to the apex. As with Bridgestone, it had the depth of resources to take risks while it perfected the increasingly celebrated, race-winning Dura-Ace series.

The Bridgestone RB-1 was just about everything that Grant Petersen, at that time, could have desired for a high-specification road racing bicycle. The frame was to be as purposeful and capable as a true racing machine, yet appeal (even if they did not know it at first) to the greater purchasing audience. In short, a racing bicycle for the unracing, too. The principal factors that permitted this chameleon act were these: clearance for larger-profile tires; and eyelets on the dropouts to accommodate fenders or even racks.

The RB-1 also had slightly more relaxed frame angles than the most aggressive racing machines, and, as always, components were sourced to achieve the very best bicycle at a cost that was eminently justifiable. All these aspects make the RB-1 and the RB-2 fairly ideal as contemporary road warriors. Comfortable, yet bright and responsive; a trifle more energy-absorbing than the lighter and stiffer Panasonics and Miyatas, but once one becomes attached to an RB-1 or RB-2 an addiction sets in. They are not for every rider seeking a mount from the classic age, but they certainly are the choice for some.

The principal structural change over the five-year build period for the 'RB' suite was in the steel. Initially, Ishiwata's 019-E, 022-E, and 024-E tubes were used; for the model's final year, 1994, Tange's Champion No. 1 was deployed. This provides yet another comparison for road feel (and suggests a solid excuse to collect both variants). Components also varied over the brief period, beginning with mostly SunTour and concluding with Shimano's excellent, albeit third-tier, 105 groupset.

Later in that same year, Petersen would establish Rivendell Bicycle Works. I like to think that the Bridgestone RB-1 is the forebear of the road bikes in that collection. Rivendell is the epicenter of where classic bicycle design continues to this day, another tribute to the very rightness of the steel-framed production bicycle when constructed with exemplary technique according to well-conceived specifications.

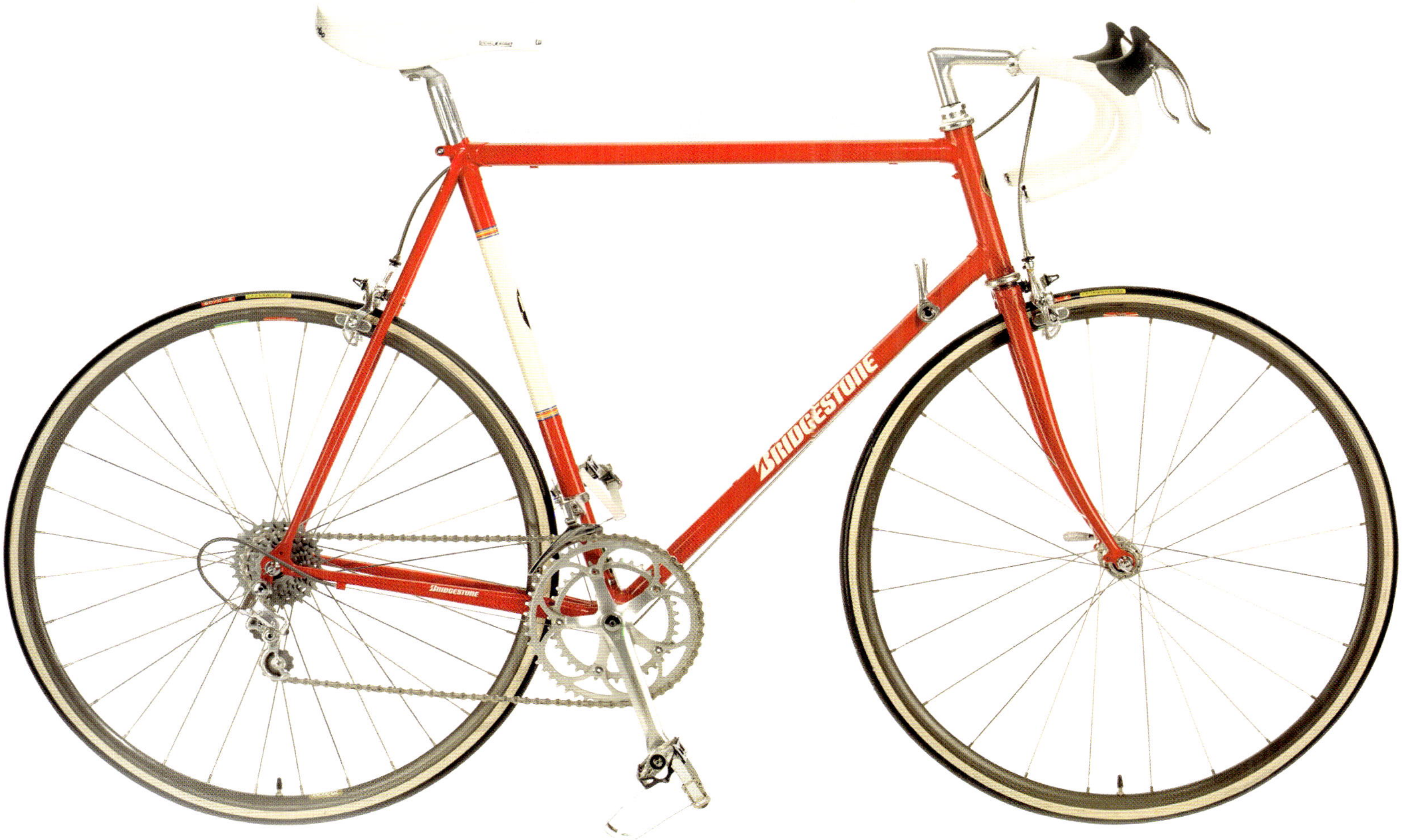

catalogs for years 1992, 1993, and 1994 (the last one they would issue) manage to be both wonderfully erudite and folksy. Exemplary storytelling, charming literary tangents, compelling technical facts, sumptuous illustrations, delicious typography, and unabashed philosophical arguments underpin the products themselves. During these years they offered their steelframed RB-1 and the RB-2, beautifully built road bicycles that could be fitted for serious racing or serious touring. (Seemingly impossible, but it was true.) When Bridgestone ceased exporting in 1994, Grant went on to found Rivendell, where the spirit of the RBs lives on.

Bridgestone Cycles lives on, too, stronger than ever. While it was exporting more traditional bicycles in 1992, the company began working on another injection process which they called Neo-Cot. Instead of forming lugs around positioned tubing, this process injected oil under tremendous pressure into the individual tubes, yielding completely custom forms. The extreme internal pressure allowed for bulge-forming into asymmetrical shaping, tapering, flaring, and molding non-cylindrical tubes. With this process, Bridgestone had come full circle on frame composition—from initially encasing the tubes in formed, die-cast lug composites using external pressure, to lugless construction composed of fitted tubes using internal pressure. Whatever was in the blood of Bridgestonians sixty years ago still flows there today, as exemplified by its current RNC7 Equipe bicycle—magic with steel.

Bridgestone holds the honor of having manufactured the most bicycles in Japan. Some were exported. There are a fair number of Kabuki Diamonds out there, as well as Bridgestone Gran Vèlos, RB-1s, and RB-2s. Seek out one of the many Bridgestones masquerading as Schwinns; perhaps a Submariner, so you can cruise along ocean coasts fearless of salt spray and washouts. One thing you can be certain about: everything Bridgestone made was well made, and made to last. Like a stone bridge.

1994 BRIDGESTONE RB1: H422248

H: MONTH CODE FOR AUGUST
4: YEAR CODE FOR 1994
22248: BUILD NUMBER

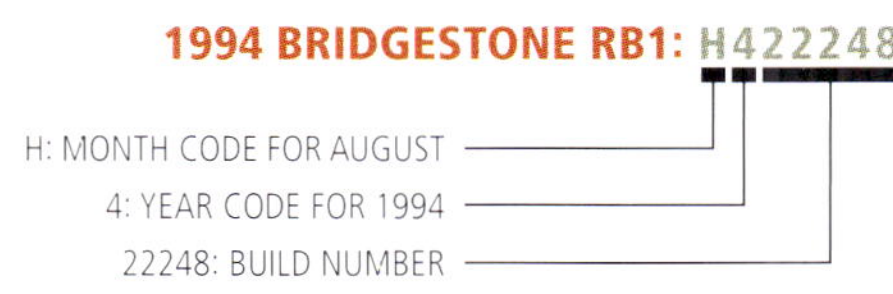

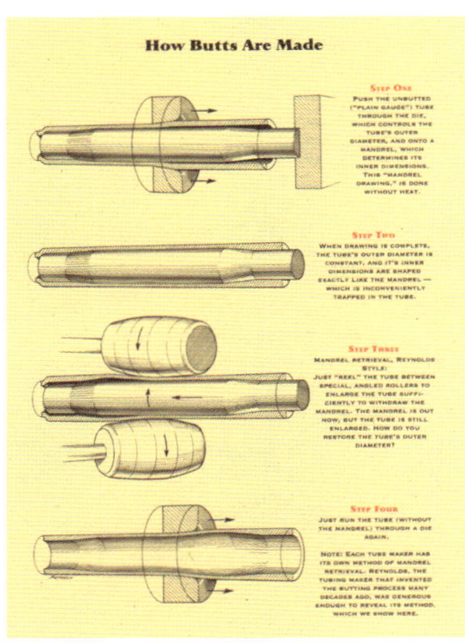

How Butts Are Made

Step One
Push the unbutted ("plain gauge") tube through the die, which controls the tube's outer diameter, and onto a mandrel, which determines its inner dimensions. This "mandrel drawing," is done without heat.

Step Two
When drawing is complete, the tube's outer diameter is constant, and it's inner dimensions are shaped exactly like the mandrel — which is inconveniently trapped in the tube.

Step Three
Mandrel retrieval, Reynolds style:
Just "reel" the tube between special, angled rollers to enlarge the tube sufficiently to withdraw the mandrel. The mandrel is out now, but the tube is still enlarged. How do you restore the tube's outer diameter?

Step Four
Just run the tube (without the mandrel) through a die again.

Note: Each tube maker has its own method of mandrel retrieval. Reynolds, the tubing maker that invented the butting process many decades ago, was generous enough to reveal its method, which we show here.

The 1992–94 Bridgestone catalogs are jewels amongst bicycle ephemera. The series was designed by the Boston firm, DeFrancis Studio (now defrancis carbone.) George Retseck created the compelling and exquisite illustrations; Bob Schenker was the photographer and Grant Petersen wrote the copy in his inimitable style. The "voice" of Bridgestone was continually honed with these well-crafted bicycle catalogs. They were not only unapologetically informative, beautifully illustrated, and typographically astute, they were fun. The 1992 catalog had playing cards of all the models offered, the '94 issue provided technical details on tube making, lug casting, and other fabrication methods.

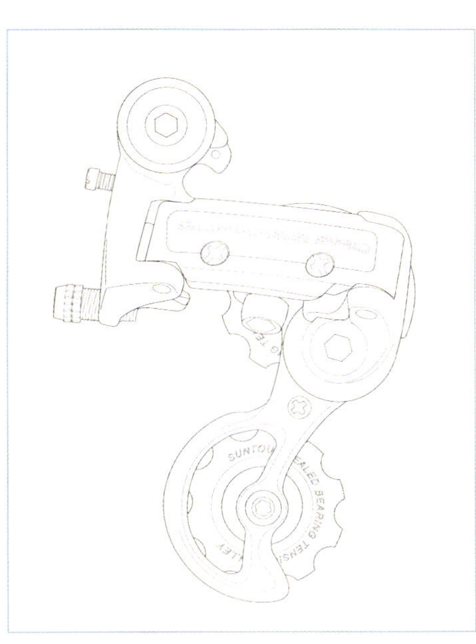

The third and final generation of SunTour's Superbe Pro derailleur graces the business end of this RB-1. Although 1994 may have been a challenging year for Bridgestone (as it accessed the changing export market), it was a disaster for SunTour. Two years earlier, Mori Industries purchased the assets of SunTour when it went into receivership; 1994 would see the last development to the Superbe Pro line, when derailleur model RD-SBOO would be indexed for an 8-speed rear cog.

Several years later, the tooling for this magnificent component would be sold at scrap-metal value. This last generation Superbe Pro derailleur was uncanny in its smoothness and precision, truly the epitome of Maeda's long search for perfection; as beautiful to see and to hold in the hand as it was to operate as part of SunTour's Accushift system. Now that portal to happiness had closed.

Two decades after his last years as president of SunTour, Junzo Kawai died at the age of 94. Three year previously, at youthful age of 91, he helped reëstablish a spiritual successor to the SunTour company called Sun XC-D. The new company was formed in 2011 in partnership with his nephew, Tsugio 'Taki' Takimoto, and focused on cyclotouring components.

SUPERBE PRO
SUNTOUR

Yet another piece of bicycle jewelry to emanate from SunTour's palace of wonders was their famed 'hidden-spring' brake caliper. The caliper made use of an internal coil spring and bearing balls to effect the smoothest and most elegantly progressive brake action, with the shortest amount of throw, that one could fathom; and powerful stopping capability.

By banishing the external spring SunTour had streamlined the caliper brake to its essence. It is one of the last, and most refined, iterations of the 'classic look,' before caliper brakes began to take on the Jules Vernesque 'techno-design' of the road bicycles that followed.

The RB-1 photographed here was obtained as a NOS frame. This provided an excuse to pursue a complete custom build using the full SunTour Superbe Pro groupset. Its owner felt that this was the bicycle Grant Petersen would have built had cost permitted. Of course, the genius of Bridgestone's late builds for export was in the frame and how it could serve both racing and non-racing applications. Components could be mixed and matched to hit more aggressive price-points, and owners could later upgrade as they saw fit.

Very few bicycles, if any, were specified with last-generation, totally complete SunTour Superbe Pro groupsets—the cost would have been high, but moreso, the winds had changed for SunTour and marketing follow-through dissipated. SunTour argued that all the components within its Accushift systems were interchangeable. This ultimately led to compatibility problems. The claim was that superior shifting technology allowed any component of any SunTour groupset to work together.

Shimano was more cautious, and wisely argued that groupsets should be matched (particularly for the drive-train). This was a prudent marketing strategy; more importantly, it allowed focused engineering and development to proceed within specific groupsets.

H. Tano & Company, Ltd., a trading, exporting, and manufacturing concern, is established in Kobe.

In 1976, Wolfgang Renner, famed cyclocross rider, acquires the rights to sell Centurions in Germany; c. 1982, Centurion builds a prototype mountain bike for Renner, who introduces the sport to Germany. In 1986, the flagship Centurion Prestige is produced with Tange Prestige tubing; Western States also imports their first Taiwanese bicycle, the entry-level Signet model.

Hong Kong (Link) Bicycle Co., Ltd., acquires Western States and Raleig America acquires Diamond Back (current spelling Diamondback) un Accell North America (Accell Group)

H. TANO COMPANY, KOBE

CENTURION

Centurion brand transfers to Wolfgang Renner (Stuttgart), predominantly manufactured c mountain bikes to this day.

1885 1905 1970 82/86/90/91 2000

Richard Morris Woodhead and Paul Eugene Louis Angois establish a bicycle workshop on Raleigh Street in Nottingham, England. Three years later, in 1888, Frank Bowden invests in the shop and Raleigh Bicycles is formed–one of the oldest continually operated bicycle brands, currently owned by the Dutch firm Accell Group, Heerenveen, Netherlands.

Raleigh Industries of America contracts with H. Tano to produce the Grand Prix model, which had just been introduced by the Nottingham parent, Raleigh Bicycle Company. At the time, H. Tano is domestically producing and representing the Diamond Racer Model under their Milton brand; they also market the domestic Phoebix and Jump lines.

Mitchell Weiner takes possession of 2,000 bicycles manufactured for Raleigh Industries of America, but not authorized by the parent company. He sells these under the Centurion name. Western States Imports Co., Ltd., is then formed with Michael Bobrick, establishing the Centurion brand. In 1977, Western States introduces Diamond Back, a BMX brand.

Western States Imports Co., Ltd., ceases operations.

The flagship model yields bragging rights. In the very early 1970s, both pride and prejudice would dictate that such a premier offering must be Italian, even if that meant having it built in Mexico at the Windsor factory.

Centurion's 'Cinelli-esque' Professional was constructed by an Italian builder (likely, Remo Vecchi) with Columbus tubing–a North American masterwork. Campagnolo and Universal components completed the de rigueur formula. Most dealers never saw this model, and customers with the means to purchase one likely had the greater means to go 'all in' for the real thing. Years later, Centurion would directly engage Cino Cinelli to help build their 1985 Equipe model.

Finding himself saddled with 2,000 'impostors,' Mitchell Weiner turned an unanticipated situation into one that was unexpectedly fortuitous. He had served as the purchasing agent between Raleigh Industries of America and H. Tano & Company, a builder and exporter located in Kobe, Japan. Raleigh USA contracted for a Japanese variant of the Raleigh Grand Prix, the 10-speed model that Raleigh Bicycle Company in Nottingham had recently introduced under their Carlton line. When the shipment arrived Weiner was informed by Raleigh USA that Nottingham had nixed the sale; the non-British built bicycles had been disdainfully declined by the parent company.

Upon this rejection a bicycle empire would be built. The story goes that Weiner was reading Joseph Wambaugh's *The New Centurions,* just published in January, 1971. Inspired, he decided to cover the Raleigh branding with decals of his own making and sell the bicycles privately.

1973 CENTURION PROFESSIONAL: 1557

1557: BUILD NUMBER

Weiner took delivery of the shipment and rechristened the bicycles with the 'Centurion' name. He even designed a Centurion headbadge that aligned with the rivet holes of the former Raleigh headbadge. The timing was perfect; stores were having trouble keeping bicycles in stock. The Centurions were sold within two months. Michael Bobrick, who owned a shop in Santa Monica, California, retailed some of these 'new' Centurions and saw the potential for selling many more. Western States Imports (WSI) was created to do so. Thus begins the story of Centurion, born in the teeth of a bicycle boom.

The dynamics of a bicycle boom are somewhat formulaic. The recipe requires a fertile alignment of new technology, societal enthusiasm, and prescient marketing. The yield is sales, inspiring more risk taking and innovation. These two-wheeled uproars last about a decade or so; cumulatively they have led to today's diversified bicycle landscape.

Let's take a brief tour of significant bicycle booms. We begin in Germany, with the first steerable walking-bike of 1817; from there, proceeding to the 'bone-shaking' *direct drive* velocipede craze of 1860s France. The next boom will witness the remarkable high-wheelers of 1870s England rolling onto the stage. Next we come to the *indirect drive* safety bicycles of mid-1880s America. Skipping past some smaller spikes within the intervening years, we arrive to find the earliest derailleur-equipped sporting bicycles. These will lead directly to the international bicycle craze beginning in the late 1960s and continuing with furor into the 1970s before stalling a bit. So potent was this '10-speed road bicycle boom' that it birthed manifold bicycle genres: BMX, ATB and mountain bikes, hybrids, city bikes, utility bikes, triathlon bikes, cyclocross, and others.

Having considered the preceding overview, let us now delve into these bicycle booms in greater depth. Let's look

In their second catalog year, 1973, Centurion offered the Professional and the Le Mans. Except for not having tubular tires, the Centurion Professional would represent absolute conformity to current competitive racing bicycle spec's. It was equipped with Campagnolo's Nuovo Record, then the world's most exquisite rear derailleur. This aluminum alloy component was introduced in 1967. It would be standard racing kit for another ten years. Delicate down-tube shifters would control this race-dominating European standard.

Centurion's 'other models' represented 99 percent of their sales, perhaps more. The Le Mans was exceptionally reliable for a mid-entry level bicycle. Other imported 10-speeds in the mid- and lower-ranges were finicky, and quick to go out of tune. The overbuilt Schwinn Varsity was another exception. According to Crown & Coleman, who wrote 'No Hands,' a treatise on Schwinn's decline: "A surly teenager could ride the crap out of [it]…"

Centurion offered their Le Mans with SunTour's VGT-Luxe touring derailleur. Alloy, but still massive, it shifted better than the Nuevo Record. It, too, could take a beating, was easily serviced (you could even snap the chain out with ease), and lasted forever. Centurion chose SunTour's SL front derailleur and substantial stem shifters to complete the shifting ensemble. The result was quality and reliability for minimal dollars.

The Mexican-built Professional was short-lived; few were made. Centurion then focused on their entry-level Sport 3 and their founding Le Mans model. Feature for feature, the Japanese component suite was a persuasive collective. The lower-spec'd European offerings were rapidly losing ground to Japanese finesse or American toughness.

As the sophistication of the Japanese parts-makers increased, Centurion was quick to elevate their models to higher and higher specification. Their well spec'd, high-style machines appealed both visually and technically.

at the ancestry of this Centurion, which has just braved a harsh Atlantic crossing and arrived at a seaport in California with its 1,999 shipmates. The earliest progenitor? German patents confirm this to be Baron Karl von Drais' steerable Laufmaschine (running machine) of 1817. We call these early robust wooden scooters Draisines in his honor. They became popular enough to launch the first 'velocipede craze.' But these original Draisines could not easily travel with the horses, carts, and carriages vying for passage along the rutted streets. The only option was to mingle with pedestrian traffic on the bricked or paved lanes flanking the roadways: a decidedly bad practice for early public relations. Confrontations led to immediate restrictions, even the outright banning of the running machines. Restrictions were enacted even in Mannheim, von Drais' home city, as well as city after city where the velocipedes were being introduced. Stifling fines were levied and publicized to discourage further velocipede usage, even in far-flung places, like Philadelphia. (If the good Baron had only unveiled his Laufmaschine in Japan, where sidewalk riding is controlled and legal…)

The greatest obstacle to the popular adoption of the Draisine was the requirement for balancing, not a common ability in that age. Formal training was required. Today's bicycles are light enough to support when stopped by placing one's foot down as an outrigger. Once a Draisine began to tip, it could not be easily supported due to its weight. Despite this, and the legal entanglements, the popularity of the Baron's running machine did grow haltingly. Ultimately, the wooden running machines, although steerable, were just not practical enough as an alternate mode of transportation upon the roadways of the day. The first bicycle boom foundered, and fifty years would unfold before we would be well underway again.

1976 CENTURION SEMI-PRO: M6H13965

M: BUILDER REFERENCE: MIKI
6: BUILD YEAR 1976
H: MONTH CODE FOR AUGUST
13965: BUILD NUMBER

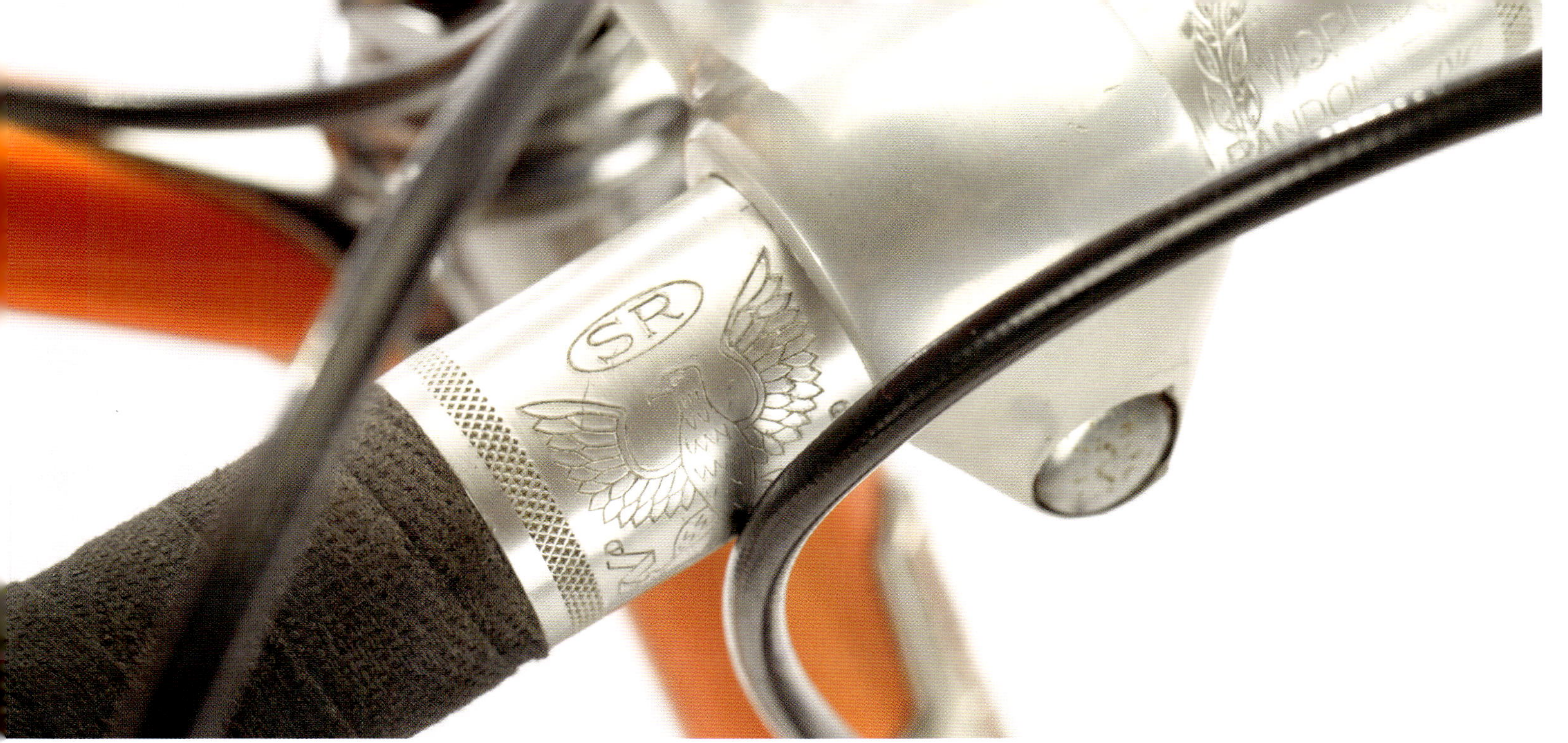

The 1976 Semi-Pro was available in pearlized orange, equally striking baby blue, or silver. This provided the backdrop for black anodized components and chrome-plated lugs. The wraparound lugwork at the seatcluster is particularly compelling. The frame was made from Tange Chromoly double-butted Champion No. 1 tubing, fitted with SunTour GS dropouts.

The Semi-Pro is a lovely piece of moving art, beholden to and possessing the aura of a classic Cinelli—but the entire Centurion line was now purely of Japanese manufacture. The most significant difference between the Professional and the Semi-Pro was the Pro's tubular tires allowing buyers to acquire a premium component suite coupled to a practical wheelset. The Semi-Pro offered the option of SunTour's popular end-bar shifters or their PDL-M downtube version.

It seemed that as long as West Coast sourced their bicycles from Asia, they were successful; their Mexican and Italian forays were, sales-wise, very lackluster. In 1973, they spec'd the Professional, their premium model, with Columbus tubing and Campagnolo Record; it was sourced from Acer Mex S.A., a.k.a. Windsor Bicycles.

Acer Mex was founded by Egon Hessel in Mexico City. Hessel departed Austria in the early years of WW II, when the Nazi regime was appropriating the wealth of European Jews; Mexico City was his destination. His youthful wife, Marieluise (Miss Germany of 1958) would later emigrate to the United States from Mexico; she is a celebrated art collector and philanthropic co-founder in 1992 of the Center for Curatorial Studies at Bard College. Hessel established a European bicycle enclave in the heart of Mexico. He became friends with all the major "movers and shakers" in the bicycle world. His wealth gave him the power to import any materials, even craftspeople, if he needed them. Premium models were built with Columbus tubing. The name Windsor, apparently, is named after the Royal Borough of Windsor, Berkshire, England, in deference to a companion of his.

Centurion

SunTour Cyclone

Piere Michaux began building the next-generation riding machine with front-drive pedals and cast-iron frames in 1867. These velocipedes (called bone-shakers due to their iron-rimmed, wood-spoked wheels) were based on the invention of a fellow Frenchman, Pierre Lallement. The patent, dated November 20th, 1866 (US59915A), was applied for when Lallement was living in New Haven, Connecticut. The application was paid for by a friend, James Carrol. Unable to find a manufacturer, Lallement returned to France where the direct-front-wheel-drive invention became a sensation. Michaux's firm, and well over a hundred other builders, were soon building bicycles in and around Paris. By 1870, Michaux's establishment had over sixty workers. Such output would earn France the distinction of being the world's first major bicycle-producing nation.

The bicycle had truly come of age, advancing from novelty, through fad, to fixture—a staple of Parisian streets and sidewalks, where fifty thousand machines were plying their way with pedals and crank-arms whirling. This boom would rapidly spread to other nations. The bone-shaker, an ugly duckling, would soon transform into an elegant swan—the high-wheeler, whose elegance was fortified by the liberating technical advancements of finely spoked wheels and rubber clad tires.

The high-wheeler (a.k.a.: penny-farthing or ordinary) was the zenith of the direct-drive bicycle. For each full rotation of the pedal and crank-arm assembly, its massive diameter drive-wheel could travel *the ideal distance,* or, *three lengths the height of the rider.* Therefore, a full wheel's rotation of the most towering 19th-century high-wheeler would travel nearly 18 feet. This would compare to the distance covered by a Manhattan bicycle messenger per crankset revolution, assuming a front chainring of 47 teeth, a fixed rear cog of 18, and contemporary wheels.

1977 CENTURION PRO-TOUR: M7A03595

M: BUILDER REFERENCE: MIKI, POSSIBLY: MILTON—H. TANO & Co.
7: BUILD YEAR 1977
A: MONTH CODE FOR JANUARY
03595: BUILD NUMBER

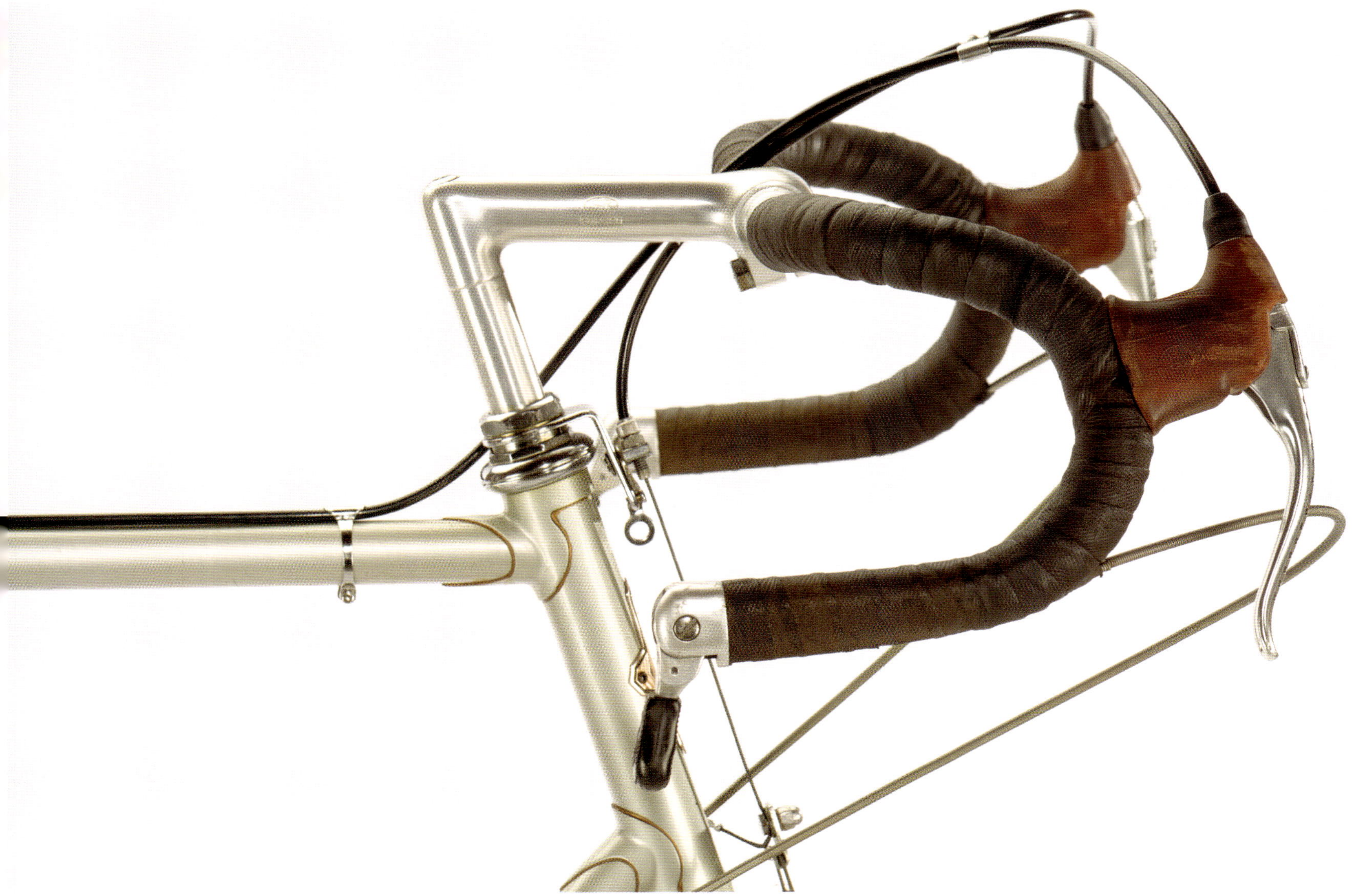

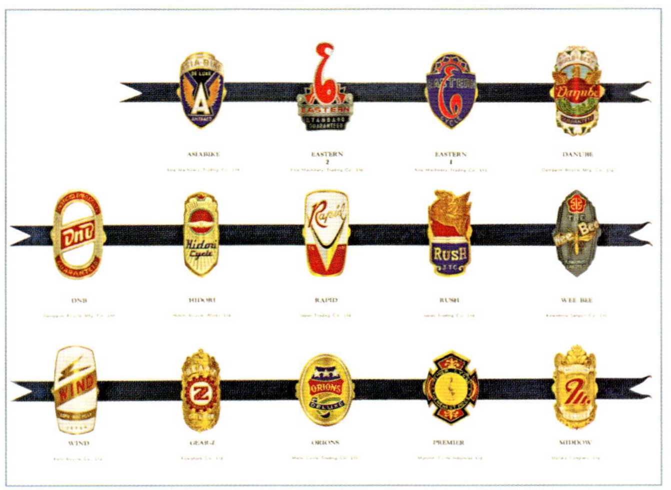

Mitchell Weiner converted an ordering snafu into an opportunity. Having to take possession of 2,000 'misordered' bicycles he saw that the cost of exported Japanese goods, compared to their potential imported retail price, was very favorable. They sold out within months. Turning this opportunity into the Centurion brand would be more daunting.

All the sectors of the Japanese bicycle production system were deeply intertwined. The core participants were manufacturers and exporters. Many so-called manufacturers were actually assemblers, who would gather parts from all over the Sakai region, for example, and merely put these together. In some cases, their only distinguishing contribution would be the headbadge.

Therefore, the knowledge and capabilities of the exporters were all-important. Companies like Asia Machinery (Akibo), C. Itoh, H. Tano, or Japan Trading created essential business connections while facilitating export opportunities.

Generally, these agencies had in-house brands, which could be directly exported (or rebranded). Asiabike and Eastern were brands under Asia Machinery; Japan Trading offered the Rapid and Rush brands; C. Itoh, a major exporter which handled half of all of Japans's exports at one time, represented Bridgestone. Despite having all these available brands to choose from, the 'bike-boom entrepreneur' wanted neither Japanese work bicycles, nor their commuter machines—they sought European styling.

Another agency, H. Tano, offered the Jump, the Milton, and the oddly-spelled Phoebix (which had a phoenix in the headbadge). The Raleigh brand name helped fast-track their relationship for Weiner; Tano handled and produced that initial order, and many subsequent ones. However, none of their existing brands met Centurion's marketing objectives.

Therefore, H. Tano had to find new suppliers to build the kinds of bicycles that Centurion wanted. In retrospect, this makes it difficult to ascertain the precise origin of Centurion's Japanese-built offerings; they can be traced back to at least five different Japanese manufacturers and assemblers.

The Centurion Pro-Tour, designed by Yamakoshi, was constructed with Tange Champion No. 2 tubing. The seat tube and headtube angles were parallel at 73 degrees and the bicycle sported a generous fork rake. These two features resulted in the Pro-Tour's long, relaxed wheelbase of 41.5 inches. Both the front and rear dropouts had a brace of threaded attachment points. This allowed racks and fenders to be securely affixed fore and aft. Centurion even provided a full set of hardware to serve this purpose.

The rear dropout channel was nearly vertical, so despite weight or obscured vision, the rider could easily swing the SunTour Cyclone derailleur back to provide a non-fouling pathway for removing and replacing the rear wheel. This was a most welcome feature that addressed a cumbersome task on a fully-laden, pannier-equipped bicycle.

A really enchanting detail was in the threaded frame-boss fittings (on the fork blades and rear seat stays) that accepted the brake-arm stirrup bolts. This meant that the standard Dia-Compe brakes were always perfectly centered, rigidly secured, and slightly less prone to flex under extreme braking.

Everything about this bicycle was purposeful: the Sakae Ringyo Randonneur handlebars, the Sugino Mighty Tour 36/52 crankset and chainrings, and the SunTour bar-end shifters controlling a Cyclone GT rear derailleur over a very broad gearing ratio of 32 to 100. Centurion even offered the Pro-Tour with a kind of militant, yet tasteful, subdued pearlized silver, along with other brighter options. All these factors contributed to the singularity of its grand touring machine. (In 1979 the Pro-Tour had triple cranksets—34/43/52.)

The Pro-Tour was evidence that Centurion was no longer just another 'exchange rate' importer. This was a bicycle that resulted from copious planning and design considerations. It appealed to riders who entertained no plans to enter competitive events. They were buying a functional fortress: here was a machine purpose-built for exploring the vast American expanse.

One of the joys for the long-distance rider is planning for the impending ecstasy, as well as preparing for the torments. Torments would include not just the physical endurance, muscle ache, downpours, and scorching heat, but also the potential break downs. For this reason, bicycle touring riders always have some mechanical skills under their belts.

The careful selection of tools (chosen by purpose and culled by weight) was a sub-pleasure of the packing experience. As the years progressed, the hex key wrench assumed increased status as the definitive and universal bicycle tool. The hex key applied torque from the inside of the bolt, so it is lighter than, say, an equivalently useful wrench or spanner.

Centurion even had hex-key fittings in the brake-stirrup bolts. This made adjustments easier. As mechanical tweaking was always a part of a grand tour, they appealed. Specification details like these were very seductive to young customers who were about to part with several months' wages on such an important purchase.

To a spectator the parks and byways of London must have appeared otherworldly as these majestic machines glided about, topped by their sophisticated riders. For the rider, the lofty view, the exhilarating speed, and the impeccable sense of balance above that tall front wheel must have been addictive. Despite the danger, they surged in popularity (surpassing 100,000 machines by 1880). The design was so advanced that even though indirect drive had been exhibited and tested for nearly two decades, it had not dislodged these imposing wonders of scale and stateliness. But levers, treadles, pulleys, belt-drives, gears, cogs, and chains were crouching at the door of progress.

High-wheelers also ruled in America until, after a short lull, the late-19th century bicycle craze began in the 1890s. Albert A. Pope, founder of Columbia Bicycle, was an avid American cyclist and ardent proponent of paved roadways. Through machinations both determined and

1978 CENTURION SEMI-PRO: M8D00899

M: BUILDER REFERENCE: MIKI
8: BUILD YEAR 1978
D: MONTH CODE FOR APRIL
00899: BUILD NUMBER

cunning he secured Lallement's patent. Although there were dwindling years of legal exclusivity remaining, the boom was still raging. Pope launched lawsuits, demanding royalties for every bicycle he did not manufacture, while buying up existing and nascent patents. He became fabulously wealthy in the process. In the late 19th century, Columbia was even a major exporter to Japan. Ironically, Pierre Lallement (the original patentee), though not fabulously wealthy, was satisfied with the recognition that he had invented the bicycle. He worked for Pope as a mechanic and even testified as a key witness for Columbia bicycles regarding patent challenges!

Columbia grew to 17 acres of factory floor space with 2,200 employees. Their premium bicycles were built with state-of-the-art nickel-steel tubing. By 1890, United States bicycle sales would exceed 150,000 per year. Pope was tough business-wise, but extremely dedicated to aspects of social wellbeing and to the quality of the nation's infrastructure. Efforts of Pope, and of early cycling advocacies such as the League of American Wheelmen (founded in 1880) fought for paved roads. This literally paved the way for the automobile, and as an ironic consequence, the decline of bicycle sales. By 1900, the boom had ended. Despite this collapse the bicycle industry entered the 20th century with well developed technologies: indirect drive, spoked wheels of uniform size, pneumatic tires, hollow rims, and quality steel-tubed, diamond frames.

Cruisers, service bicycles, ubiquitous town bikes, children's bikes, and a new breed of racing machines emerged. Many of these had multi-speed, internal-hub gearing. Due to an engineering bias against out-of-line (flexing and bending) chains—particularly in Great Britain—external gearing took years to be accepted. Initially, derailleurs and multi-cog systems did present chain alignment issues,

Japanese components were rapidly becoming more refined throughout the early 1970s. This allowed Centurion to shed their European fixation. Centurion's not-so-secret weapon was Junya (Cozy) Yamakoshi, a master at the art of specification. He would select component suites that Weiner would then obtain from suppliers after several bouts of tough price negotiations. (As a significant number of Japanese parts-makers were concentrated in the Osaka region, buyers could literally spend a day canvassing the area, pitting one parts-maker against another, until some company owners succumbed to barely sustainable profitability levels.)

Cozy's frame-angle specifications were generally more relaxed than the competition, yielding a comfortable ride. He aimed for low-maintenance bicycles attired in sophisticated liveries. As a result of his efforts Centurions were both technically and aesthetically beautiful.

It was not until the later Taiwanese builds that Centurions lost their sublime aesthetic, the look becoming more what might be called 'Memphis design'–style (primary colors, geometric shapes, and squiggles). The classicism of the earlier liveries came to an end. Even the final Centurion headbadge graphics convey this Memphis style, which originated in 1982, the house look of the Memphis Group in Milan, under the brilliant Italian architect, Ettore Sottsass.

By this time, H. Tano & Co., Ltd. (first supplier of Centurions), having been instrumental in making initial contacts and even working through areas of export facilitation (the Japanese Ministry of International Trade and Industry actually limited exports in order to prevent trade tariffs, or as a compensating gesture to support other potential export markets), was far less involved in Western State's supply chain.

H. Tano even secured patents; particularly interesting is their pipe-joining technology (US Patent 4,737,047), which uses centrally threaded walls within frame tubes to bolt, rather than braze, tubes at the lugs. Heavy and possibly rust-prone, but practical in that they were easy to ship and assemble.

Semi Pro

The late 1970s set the stage for the strong growth of Western States; their builds were confident and well received. Through good marketing and dealer relations they became the fifth largest supplier in the United States. They took chances and diversified their lineup, even introducing a new BMX brand, Diamond Back (the two words later combined into Diamondback).

They still had their missteps. One would be the later marketing of their road bicycles under Diamond Back; another (prior to this branding snafu) would be their second attempt at Italian bike-building. In 1984, Western States contracted with Cino Cinelli to build their second 'Cinelli-Centurion.'

The effort was led by Alan Goldsmith, the savvy entrepreneur who had founded the highly successful bicycle mail-order company Bikecology in the 1970s. (Goldsmith had consulted with Western States earlier and established a great track record.) Cino had sold the Cinelli concern to A. L. Columbo several years earlier, so this would be a kind of 'unofficial' Cinelli—albeit built with the latest precision-alignment equipment at the factory. The Equipe was released in 1985 with Cinelli markings to prove its pedigree. One odd feature was the use of the then-dated Campagnolo Record—not Super Record—rear derailleur. Other components were mostly Ofmega, beautiful Italian componentry that could be had without the so-called 'Campagnolo-tax.'

It's likely that only 150 Centurion Equipes were built, as that quantity would have filled a single shipping container from Italy (and it was the only model to come from Europe). Goldsmith worked hard to position the Equipe below the one thousand dollar price-point; it was a great bicycle at a highly competitive price. But Western States had not learned their lesson from a dozen years earlier; if buyers wanted a Cinelli, they would buy a Cinelli. Later, the cost of the Equipe was dropped to $750. Like the 1973 Professional it was a one year only model. Today, the Equipe has reversed its fate and has become quite collectible. They also offered the Prestige and the Ironman models in 1985, two superlative machines which more than compensated for the Equipe's poor sales.

but competitive advantages outweighed these concerns. Chains were also being designed with more flex. The modern derailleur, connected through cables to a shifting lever, was introduced by Simplex in 1930 (which had begun derailleur manufacture two years prior). Simplex ruled the derailleur world until the mid-1960s. Not surprisingly, Raleigh Bicycle Company's first Grand Prix came equipped with Simplex derailleurs and all European parts.

The first Centurion had SunTour derailleurs and all Japanese parts. Look, there's one sitting on the showroom floor of Rick's Bike Shop, here in Reno, Nevada. The shop is owned by Richard Bulis. Previously, he had offered French imports at the mid-entry level. It was common for those bicycles to come back two or three times for adjustments within the thirty-day free labor and servicing period. Chainguards would rub the front derailleurs, cables would rapidly stretch causing brakes to lose effectiveness, wheels would quickly lose their true; things like this were common issues for bicycle shops of the day.

Then came the Centurion Le Mans. At first, when the Centurions did not come back for any kind of adjustment within the first thirty days, Rick was worried: "something's wrong...." To his relief, he learned upon a chance encounter with a customer that they had no reason to return their Centurion for service—it just stayed in tune. Rick's bicycle shop ceased ordering mid-tier European bicycles and he became one of their highest volume dealerships. Centurion had found a home in the desert.

Western States never manufactured a bicycle. But they had the pulse of the West-Coast bicycle scene, where changes were happening. They saw derelict Schwinn Sting Rays become BMX machines, witnessed the unfolding mountain bike scene, and capitalized to great effect on the Triathlon market with their Dave Scott endorsement.

1984 CENTURION TURBO 12: N4H8700

N: BUILDER REFERENCE: Unknown, possibly NATIONAL [PANASONIC]
4: BUILD YEAR 1984
H: FORTNIGHT CODE: WEEKS 15 AND 16
8700: BUILD NUMBER

What a difference a decade made. Centurion now had unmitigated confidence in their all-Japanese models, their sales literature even teasing: "You'll be saying 'Ciao' to the competition," when showcasing the magnificent Turbo 12.

The heart of the machine was Tange Champion No. 1 with SunTour Superbe dropouts, thinned lugs, and an aero investment cast with sloping fork crown. Oddly, they did not exceed 73-degree angles for the build. With similar practicality, they specified clincher tires, choosing Araya 20A hard-anodized rims in the bronze finish. The Araya 20A was of very narrow width (under 20 mm) and weighed 430 grams.

One of Centurion's marketing pitches was their no-time-limit warranty—such was their confidence in the line-up. The Turbo 12 represented the high-water mark of their Japanese imports; by this time their entry-level machines were coming from Taiwan Region.

Ironically, even though the Centurion brand was conceived as a result of Raleigh's rejection (at the time the world's greatest single exporter), it would become a competitor. Centurion would also grow to be a thorn in the side of Schwinn, then the world's largest manufacturer. Western States would sell 250,000 bicycles in 1990; yet, like a bicycle boom unto themselves, Weiner and Bobrick had reached a plateau together and were ready to sell. In a complicated arrangement that nearly involved Schwinn, Western States was ultimately acquired by Hong Kong (Link) Bicycles. Shortly thereafter, Raleigh had the last laugh, acquiring the Diamondback brand. Today, Diamondback and Raleigh are both under the Accell Group N.V., located in Heerenveen, the Netherlands.

And Diamondback's elder sibling? The Centurion brand is now owned by Wolfgang Renner, Germany's high priest of mountain biking. Renner was an invincible cyclocross rider who needed more than a cyclocross machine for the type of rugged mountain riding he was doing in the late 1970s. He designed and had Centurion make a prototype in 1976 for the punishing courses he rode. Impressed, he licensed the Centurion brand in Germany that same year. At the time of the sale of Western States, Renner acquired full ownership of the Centurion brand, and the road bike was reborn as a next-generation mountain bike.

Nurtured by Renner and like-minded German enthusiasts, top-line Centurions epitomize the coolest mountain bikes on earth and are respected worldwide. Most charmingly, Centurion's home is now in Magstadt, Germany, a mere 90 minutes from Mannheim, where bicycle boom number one began—where Baron von Drais' Velocipede was unveiled precisely two centuries prior. Centurion, born smack in the middle of a bicycle boom, is a story of historical elegance and the generosity of good timing.

Ichisuke Katakura begins silk-making in Nagoya. A mill is established by his son, Kanetaro, 5 years later. A munitions factory during the war, then a 'converted maker' post-war, Katakura chooses Silk as a brand in deference to its former, peacetime operations.

Leo Cohen Senior and RosaBelle Cohen, parents of Howie Cohen, open a retail bicycle shop in Minneapolis, Minnesota.

West Coast Cycle Supply is founded by the Cohens in 1958; the retail store sold by 1960.

By 1992, Kuwahara shifts production out of Japan; all models are built abroad under their own brand, with design undertaken in Osaka at their Kuwahara Bike Works. In 2007 they fabricate an all-steel MTB frame using Kaisei Nickel-Chromoly. This model is fully built, once again, in Japan. Kuwahara celebrates the 100th anniversary of the company's founding in 2018.

KATAKURA CO., LTD, TOKYO; KAWAMURA CYCLE, LTD., KOBE; KUWAHARA CO., LTD., OSAKA

NISHIKI

Katakura builds bicycles for Japan's 1964 Olympic road and track teams.

Cohen supplies Steven Spielberg with Kuwahara BMX models for the movie "E.T. the Extra-Terrestrial."

'99, Katakura Silk ceases productio[n] Katakura Industri[es] Co., Ltd., continue[s]

1873 **1918** **1939** **1958** **1964** **1981** **late 1980s** **late 1990s** **201[...]**

Sentaro Kuwahara begins business as Kuwahara Shokai, selling bicycle parts locally; by the 1920s sales expand to Russia, China, and Southeast Asia. In 1927, the Kuwahara family (Sentaro and eight children) establish a manufacturing facility, and in 1946, Kuwahara Co., Ltd. is officially established.

In 1960, Kuwahara's eldest son, Masao, becomes president and oversees construction of a major new plant in Osaka. In 1979, Takuo Kuwahara assumes leadership; production will be focused exclusively on private -label exports for Azuki, Takara, Puch, and Schwinn, as well as Nishiki. In 1972, Kuwahara begins producing BMX bicycles under its own brand.

Howie Cohen, representing West Coast Cycle Supply, meets Yukio Kawamura and contracts to build export bicycles under the name, 'American Eagle.' These are marketed by the mid- 1960s, but are soon to be rebranded under the Nishiki marque by 1970.

The Nishiki brand is acquired by Norco (Canada); manufacturing is fully transferred to Taiwan (China). Derby Cycle AG (Germany) buys Nishiki in 1989, licensing USA rights to Dick's Sporting Goods in 2010. Kawamura is acquired by Mizuno (Japan), and Kawamura Cycles is reformulated in 1995 as a wheelchair and medical device maker for domestic markets.

"Three times pays for all." So goes the old Yorkshire aphorism, and so it was for young Howie Cohen as he ventured out to build a new brand for his family's West Coast Cycle Supply. For adult riders in the 1960s, bicycles had three emotive values: every bicycle, in some manner, conjured childhood memories; racing bicycles evoked ideas of competition and human endurance; touring bicycles beckoned riders to adventure and exploration. All Howie knew were bicycles. He practically lived at his parent's old bike shop in Minnesota while growing up. The prospect of earning one's living while bringing joy, competition, and adventure to thousands of people—what could be better? Bicycles were, and would remain, at the epicenter of Howie Cohen's world.

The seeds that would grow into the Nishiki brand would begin when Howie's parents sold that bicycle shop in the Midwest and moved to California. Their dream was to establish a new brand, expanding their business and creating a wholesale empire. Sadly, with the sudden death of Howie's father, increased responsibility came sooner and was more keenly felt than expected; it was time to travel, to build the necessary partnerships, and to seek one's fortune "in this dark world and wide..." First stop, England: but this was the mid-1960s. British bicycle manufacturers were at the pinnacle of their bicycle output capabilities. Factories in England were churning out all the bicycles that could be churned out. At that time the overwhelming majority of bicycles that were imported into the United States came from England, and the majority of these came from Raleigh. A *youthful* (euphemism for inexperienced) American–cum–export partner did not appealt to the British manufacturers. Perhaps the feeling was mutual—Cohen penned this in his notebook: "The labor force over here take too many tea breaks."

Cohen returned to the United States, and to his mother, empty-handed. Perhaps, she thought, we should go west instead of east–so she suggested a new angle: an angle 180 degrees in the opposite direction. RosaBelle Cohen sent Howie on a mission to Japan: "Find a factory to build bicycles for us." This was 1964; direct flights to Japan were just beginning from the West Coast. The close of the Second World War was still within the generation, the American dollar was all-powerful, and (for most buyers and merchandisers) the thought of quality control was at best ill-formed and at worst insignificant. The emerging post-war Japanese industry was quite exploitable. Anything would be built to a price. Cohen was young, naïve; he had a different tactic in mind. His goal was simply to push for the very best he could get while traditional cost versus quality ratios did not yet apply. Instead of exploiting for smallness, he wanted to explore for greatness.

On the first voyage he set up as many meetings as possible. With each hard-won contact, he made his request the same, and it was disarmingly simple: "Build me the very best you can, regardless of the cost." Surprisingly, this was a radically unusual request, and it found no receptive ears. Again, he returned to the United States, and to his mother, empty-handed. Like all good mothers she persuaded him to try once again: three times would pay for all—West Coast Cycle Supply would become a fifty-million-dollar company within the next twenty years (well over double this amount by today's valuation).

On the next trip, Howie stayed for weeks, purportedly visited over fifty factories and workshops on that crushing phase-two tour before he met the man that would co-create the Nishiki brand. His name was Yukio Kawamura; his company would ultimately grow to become the seventh largest bicycle-manufacturing facility in Japan, and

1972 NISHIKI PROFESSIONAL: KE22777

K: KAWAMURA CONTRACT: KATAKURA "SILK" BUILD
E: MONTH CODE FOR MAY
2: YEAR CODE FOR 1972
2777: BUILD NUMBER

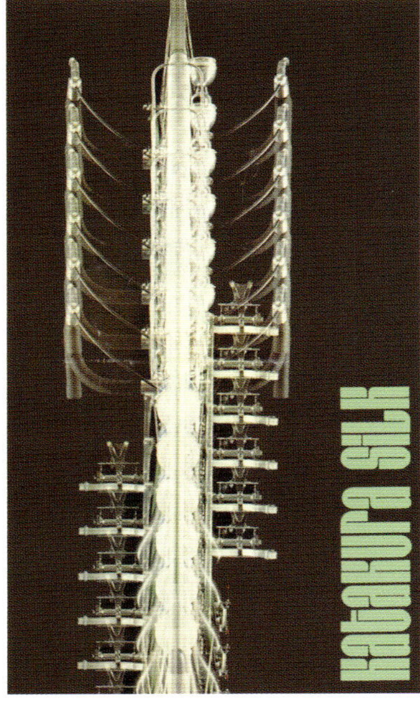

The post-war reconstruction period would yield two kinds of bicycle manufacturers: pre-war companies which resumed production, and a new breed of builders called 'converted makers.' Converted makers were former munitions facilities that had not been destroyed during the war; these were left with tools, machinery, personnel, and raw materials. Some were given manufacturing directives (by MacArthur's General Headquarters); others pursued peacetime manufacturing opportunities.

About ten of these converted makers began building bicycles. They were not attached to past methods and looked to Europe and America for design inspiration. Most shifted to non-bicycle production within a decade but Katakura Silk (one division within Katakura Industry Co., Ltd.) proved to be a fascinating exception.

Katakura's facilities had once been a silk mill, so that name was adopted for the brand. The Japanese cycling team used both Cinelli and Katakura Silk bicycles for the Olympic events of 1964, which brought considerable prestige to the firm. Many great Japanese craftsmen became associated with the Silk brand. By the mid 1990s, however, Silk rationalized their production under the Sanwa Bicycle group. In 1999, Sanwa discontinued bicycle making, their Hasuda factory was sold, and the storied Katakura Silk division closed.

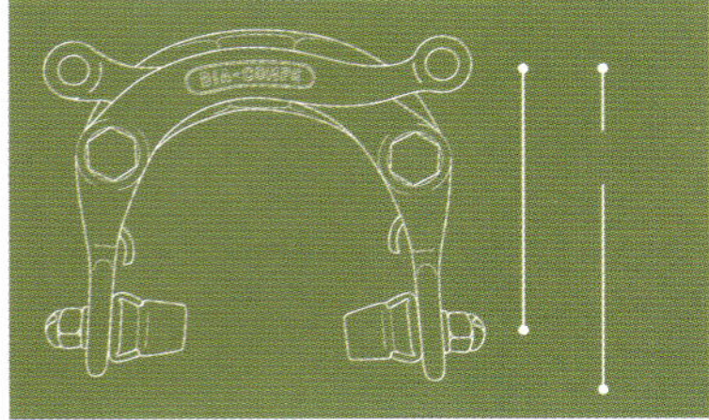

Derailleur-wise, the SunTour V was king of the mountain. If emerging notions of Japanese innovation, performance, and the look of pragmatism could be traced back to a single source, the SunTour V-series would be it. The SunTour was a little unstoppable machine that said 'Japan-brand,' and one could argue that every modern derailleur can trace some of its genome to this stalwart gem.

Only one bicycle component was more ubiquitous, and that was the (Weinmann designed) Dia-Compe center-pull brakeset that was on every racer that emanated from the Japanese archipelago in the early 1970s. Originally Dia-Compe assembled Swiss-made components; the earliest examples sold in Japan had the Vainqueur name on the forward arm. Dia-Compe licensed the design, then acquired it, pumping out examples by the tens of thousands—a slightly modified model is still being produced today, sixty years after they were first developed by Weinmann. The length of the brake arm determined the model number.

the fourth in exports. Of all the Japanese-American partnerships, none beat with the heart, the entrepreneurial passion, and the dedication for quality as did West Coast Cycle supply and Kawamura Cycle, Ltd. Their owners' working relationships would be matched with a friendship sparked when they first met, in 1964. Mr. Yukio Kawamura even allowed the young Cohen to refer to him by his informal name, 'Higesan,' meaning 'man with a beard.' Cohen later described Kawamura as "a wise gentleman [who] took me under his wing and taught me much about the production of bicycles and philosophy of life."

During the formative years of West Coast's expansion their bicycles would be produced by Katakura, Kuwahara, and Kawamura (a serendipitous alliteration of suppliers). Katakura made the Silk model. This was a forward-thinking firm that began manufacturing bicycles soon after the war. Katakura had been responsible for creating the entire fleet of machines for the Japanese road and track cycling teams' efforts at the 1964 Tokyo Olympics. They would be one of the first firms to build export bicycles at high-quality standards for third-party labels. The 'Silk' decal is an indication of their manufacture (the label appears on fork blades or seat tubes in conjunction with whomever they built for.) Later, they would be boutique domestic constructors.

Another sub-builder for West Coast would be the famed Kuwahara brand. Kuwahara built numerous models for Cohen over the years; unquestionably the most important were the E.T. BMX models for Speilberg's E.T., The Extra-terrestrial in which the bicycles played a most pivotal role in the movie. Kuwahara will celebrate their 100th anniversary in 2018.

The principal player, by a massive margin, would be Kawamura. Their factories would provide a continuous pipeline of bicycles issuing forth in impressive quantities.

The charming Nishiki headbadge came onto the scene already full of history and symbolism. The eagle remained from the brand's founding name, American Eagle. The eagle, within this crest, was itself wearing a crest of three colors. This represented (three) threads of color and quality: Nishiki.

The logo would go through multiple iterations over the years. The most indicative of the Nishiki name was the variant with a stylized 'N' and five strokes of color. This representing five threads of interwoven silk, in reference to one idea of Nishiki: the complexity and refinement of highest quality, colorful Kimono thread.

During some months this number would exceed 6,000 units. The good times would last into the 1980s, when Giant Bicycles (Taiwan Region) would break the spell through their labor cost advantage. We will follow the dynamics of Kawamura, as they were the manufacturing muscle behind West Coast, initially producing the American Eagle model.

Yukio was the grandson of the founder of Kawamura. He and his brother were third-generation bicycle builders. The bicycles were painstakingly built in their small shop. Afterward they were carried out into the surrounding yard, primed, and painted, there to be dried under sustainable solar power. Unexpected rainstorms would necessitate re-priming and repainting. The facility grew to a fair level of prosperity, was heavily damaged during World War II, and rebuilt afterward. When Cohen visited the facilities they were new, and despite the modesty of their technology they were highly productive under Mr. Kawamura. They began producing export models according to Cohen's specifications (which were really Kawamura's specifications based on the best 'racers' of the day.) The first models arrived in California by the late 1960s. Cohen later exclaimed, "Kawamura could not build enough of them."

If you recognize the brand name American Eagle, then you know the story of how a potential dealer felt that a Japanese bicycle with the name American Eagle was both deceptive and disingenuous. Howie took this to heart. His solution to the problem was a marketing masterstroke. He asked if Kawamura would engage teams (or individuals) at the factory to come up with a new name for the brand. He offered a one thousand dollar prize to the winning team—a very considerable sum in that day. The rules were simple: "Something Japanese that the non-Japanese will be able to pronounce." Cohen reviewed the list of candidates and chose the name Nishiki. A brand was born.

1979 NISHIKI SUPERBE: KI00225

K: KAWAMURA

I: YEAR CODE FOR 1979

00225: BUILD NUMBER

The word 'brand' is an ancient one, of Germanic origin; etymologically it means to *mark with fire*. A thousand years ago, brands were effected by burning an indelible insignia into a piece of wood, or more ominously upon skin or hide. The resultant mark signified irrevocable permanence. A good brand is ownership; it appeals to the human psyche. It captures the past, speaks to the future, and outlasts its origins. When the Nishiki brand was born, who could have known that it would persevere under many national owners: American, Canadian, Dutch, German, and Luxembourgian (even a short stint of Japanese). It was a smart brand, seeming to know exactly when to find a new owner. With each transition there is some upheaval. Sometimes this is cause for celebration, sometimes commiseration. Sometimes a brand is excitedly purchased by new owners. Sometimes a brand dies, is divested, or liquidated. Every brand possesses a story.

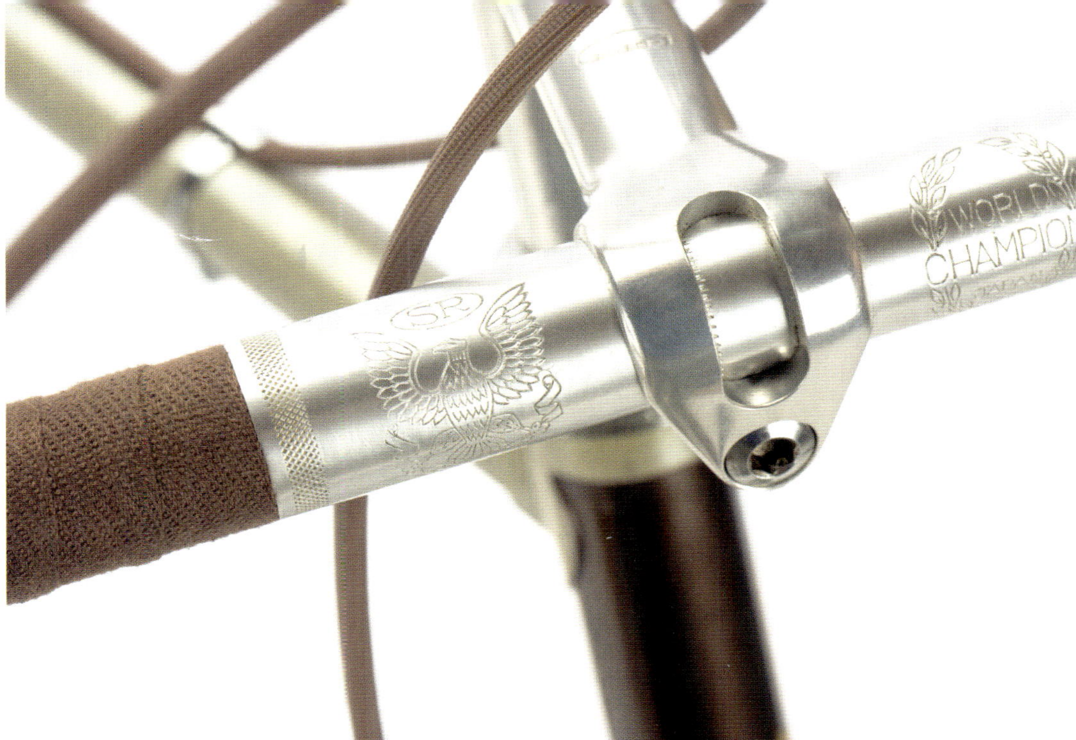

You know Kenny. He's the National Biathlon Champion this year. And last year. And the year before that.

His secret? "It's pretty simple," he explains. "A 40-minute 30K bike split and a couple of 15-minute 5K runs. Nothin' to it."

Having the world's fastest bike doesn't seem to hurt, either. With stock features that would be considered "custom" on any other bike.

Like a special R. Cunningham Design. 75° seat angle geometry. Airfoil shape down tube. Wickedly fast TriSpoke carbon composite wheels.

With Kenny's help, we've swapped the fork over to lightweight alloy and changed the bars to Modolo X-Kronos cowhorns (with Profile Clip-Ons, natch). Extended the top tube. Even upgraded the frame to Tange Concept ultra light tubing.

All designed to move your bike split a little closer to Kenny's. Or, if you're on anything else, to move Kenny's a little farther out of reach.

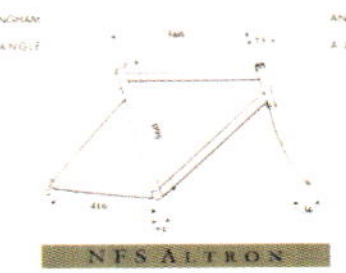

NFS ALTRON

• Richard Cunningham Design frame with Tange Concept tubing • Prologue alloy tapered fork • Shimano Ultegra components • TriSpoke composite wheels

What a difference a dozen years can make respecting production and consumer perception. When considering the quality of a high-specification classic road machine, such as the Nishiki Superbe model (of the very late 1970s and early 1980s), there is a simple standard for comparison. At the pinnacle are handbuilt, custom-made examples made by a respected craftsman; all lesser machines try to emulate some aspects of the handmade machine.

Then came the 1970s and 1980s—exciting decades in bicycle design, epochal years of change as bicycles were adapted to emerging alternative cycling sports from traditional road and track functions. The components and the bicycles themselves were functionally reconfigured for motocross, mountain biking, and other non-road and track purposes. Although many of these could be advantageously handmade as well, the look was more high-tech and 'machined' in nature. State-of-the-art technology was required to produce some of the more intricate components, such as hydraulic shock-absorbers.

Ultimately, technologies developed for these repurposed machines found their way back to road bicycles. The Richard Cunningham–designed Nishiki 1992 NFS Altron is a case in point: the lugless construction and TriSpoke carbon-composite wheels reflect a robotically generated product. Consumers were less drawn to tradition and hand craftsmanship as they once were. The NFS Altron was built with the recently introduced Tange Concept, an ultralight heat-treated steel tubing.

Identifying a bicycle by the components it featured was not an uncommon practice. There were many models called 'Record' or 'Super Record' named after so-equipped Campagnolo groupsets. In 1974, Fuji named their Ace model in recognition of equipping that bicycle with the early Shimano Dura-Ace line (when the Shimano Crane was still part of that groupset).

Sometimes the model name would continue even though the parts were no longer specified for the model in question. The Nishiki Superbe, toward the end of its run, was actually equipped with SunTour Cyclone derailleurs, not Superbe. Many Superbe models also did not include the brakeset (being fitted with Gran Compe 400s) because the SunTour Superbe brakeset was fairly expensive (although less than half of its Campagnolo counterpart).

The release of the SunTour Superbe groupset in very late 1976 deserves a special mention in bicycle component history. It was an effective cross-corporate effort and marketing endeavor–the component parts book issued by Maeda Industries was an event in itself and the line of components was unrivalled in performance, lightness, and appearance,

The Nishiki Superbe, draped in chocolate and champagne hues, is heightened by the beautiful warmth of the polished Superbe groupset. Even the brown o-ring of the caliper-brake cable's adjusting screw joins in the pageantry. The result can be described with a single word: delicious!

Nishiki carries its own stories directly, and in an abstract way carries the story of the entire bicycle industry from those years of initiation, through periods of transition, to this day (where it resides in America as well as Europe, but is a German-owned entity). The Kawamura employees who chose the name were proud of what they were doing because they took a word associated with tradition, quality, and richness, and applied it to industry. The name refers to the highest levels of craft and intricate use of color. It references the luxury of delicate, multicolor threads in a silken Kimono, or the complicated excellence in multi-stage Ukiyo-e production (through multiple color block printing). The term had never been used for those who made bicycles. (Bicycles were factory things, not objects made within an atelier.) Nishiki indicated: meticulously produced, luxurious, labor-intensive, highest quality and multi-colored.

That Cohen displayed such trust in the workers must have been very meaningful. He did not turn to a Madison Avenue firm, nor his friends or family; he turned to the Kawamura workers, sought their advice, and was willing to pay for their efforts. (As to how such a fee was distributed within a culture that eschewed glorifying one over another within a cooperative environment, there is no record. My guess is that Mr. Kawamura distributed the funds equally, or modified the rules so that all the workers were engaged.) In 1971, the last of the American Eagles flew off into the sunset and the Nishiki brand set sail for the golden coast. It would be a great decade.

Kawamura—as a private-label constructor, a.k.a. "ghost-builder"—knew that they had to build the majority of their orders to a defined cost. Something in the blood of the company, however, had an ardent striving for quality. After all, the director and two of his brothers were

1980/1981 NISHIKI ULTIMATE: KJ0 2938

K: KAWAMURA *also* K: USA EXPORT MODEL *or* K: KATAKURA

J: YEAR CODE FOR 1980 (KAWAMUA) *or* J: MONTH CODE FOR OCTOBER *if* KATAKURA

0: YEAR FOR 1980 *if* KATAKURA [1981 MODEL YEAR]

02938: BUILD NUMBER (KAWAMURA) *or* 2938: BUILD NUMBER *if* KATAKURA

Both Kawamura and Katakura used the 'K' prefix in the serial number protocol and debate surrounds the provenance of this machine—the tip-top specification Nishiki Ultimate.

One indication of a Katakura build is the Chrome Molybdenum Double Butted sticker used by that firm. However, the bicycle does not carry the telltale Silk, decal, which would guarantee a Katakura build.

The Ultimate is the rarest of all Nishikis and is built to similar frame specification as some of their professional models. In addition to Campagnolo Record component specification, it sports the lovely drilled ferrule of the SR World Champion handlebars.

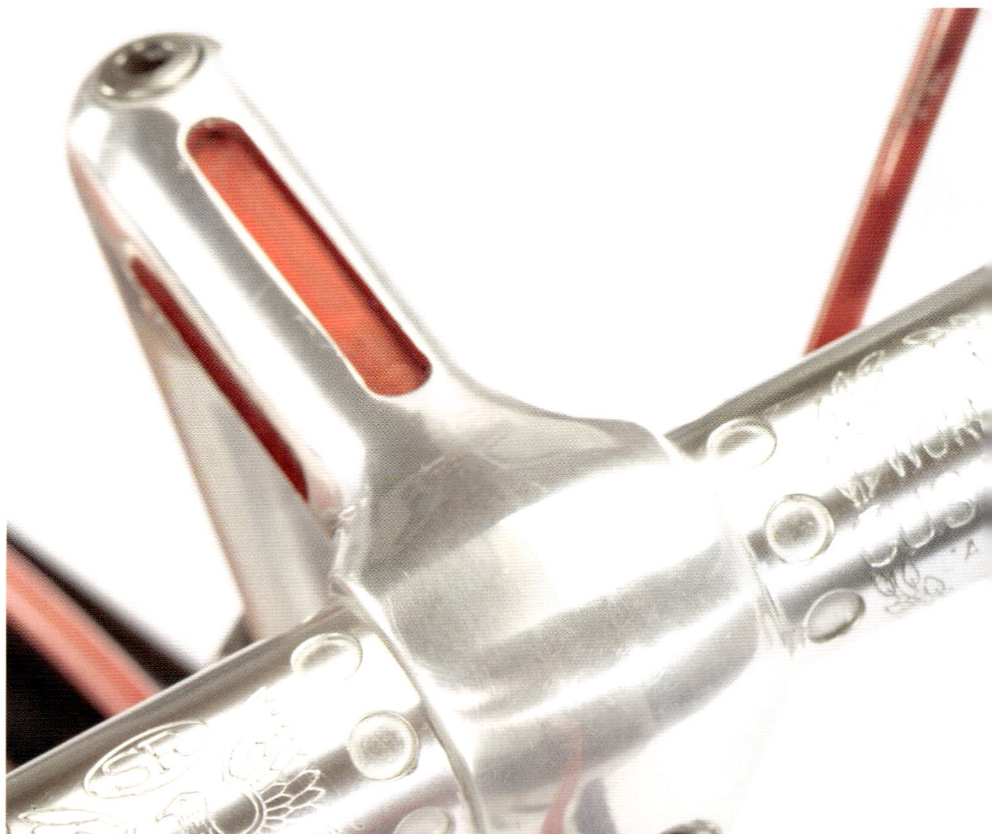

NISHIKI

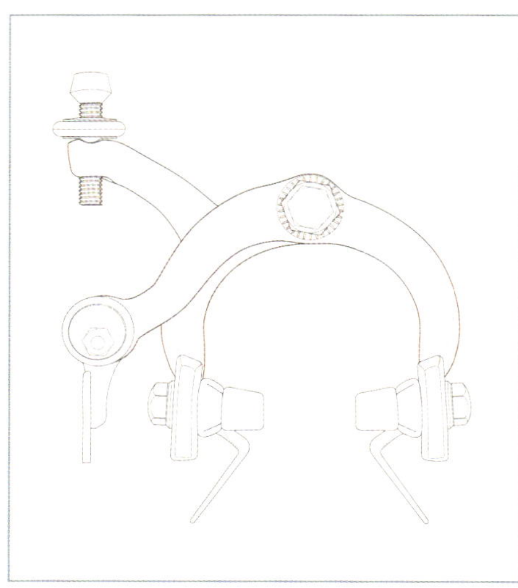

It's not possible to heap enough praise upon the Campagnolo Record caliper brake. Every accolade is well merited, except "inimitable," because it is probably one of the most closely-copied bicycle components ever made.

Everything about this lovely sidepull gem was an inspiration: its exquisite appearance, its straightforward functionality, its ease of adjustment, and its longevity. Little known today is just how radical the design was when first released in late 1967; it flew in the face of engineering precepts of that day.

At that time everyone knew that centerpull brakes were the superior design and that sidepull calipers were cheap and ineffectual. Then came these; they were not only lighter than every centerpull on the market, they also did away with the requisite brake cable housing stop-hangers that centerpulls required, saving yet more weight. More than this, they were far easier to install. They were a grand slam of merging engineering with beauty.

The Campagnolo Record groupset was a tall order to be approached, matched, and then overcome by competing brands. It took a long time to happen, and by the time some brands had done so, many others had gone out of business. The prestige and the quality alone were major barriers for competitors. It was high cost, and ultimately lack of innovation, that would first permit the breaching of castle Campagnolo.

"This bicycle combines the finest Japanese frame craftsmanship and technology with the most respected components from Europe." So claimed Nishiki in their 1981 catalog when describing the Professional, the sister bicycle to the super-scarce Ultimate model. The Professional had TTT Record handlebars with a matching TTT stem; the Ultimate was specified with SR World Champion handlebars and a lovely fluted and painted stem.

The catalog writers took special pains to describe Campagnolo parts on Japanese frames (or Shimano and SunTour parts on European frames) because they had to be cautious to temper the praise in respect to their full line of offerings. They were careful not to call the components the "very best" or the "highest quality," because that would then conflict with descriptions of their other bicycles.

Nishiki (as stated above) used "most respected" for Campagnolo. Fuji placed the prejudice back upon their customers, stating, "those very few riders who insist that each separate component of their bicycle be recognized as the very best of its kind in the world." (This was part of the text promoting their 1981 Fuji Professional Super Record).

Nishiki equipped their Professional and Ultimate with the Campagnolo Record and not the available Super Record components. By 1980, Japan had lowered their absurdly high (300 percent) import duty on foreign bicycle components (another protectionist legacy of the post-war years) and manufacturers or importers could now begin to specify this equipment on these loss-leaders.

Regardless, sales of these bicycles were miniscule. To make matters worse, in terms of surviving examples, the unfortunate likelihood is that many of these bicycles were stripped of their parts previous to sale. The reality, then and today, is that the a 'parted-out' bicycle is worth far more than a happily intact example–particularly in the case of premium and super-premium components. With some recognized classics this is thankfully beginning to abate and intact machines are surviving.

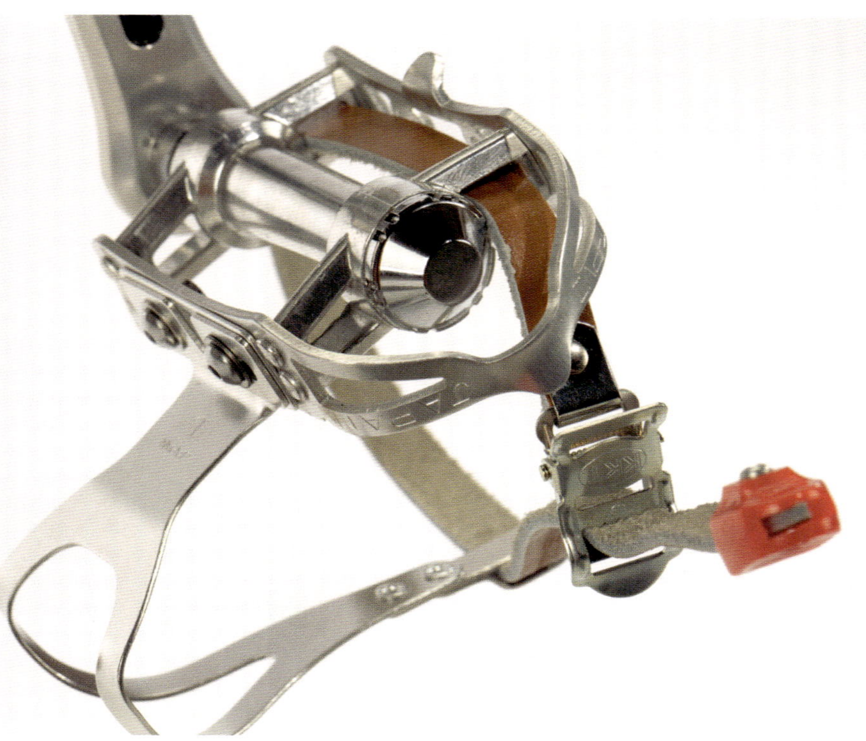

once frame makers. In 1974, they initiated the construction of a special region within the factory. Here they intended to build the highest-quality bicycles available in Japan, if not the world. They assembled a team of eight craftsman, the best they could find: all master framemakers who would build frames under the ONP line—this stood for 'Order Nishiki Pro.'

If, during your bicycle hunting forays, you happen upon a Nishiki with a serial number beginning 'NP,' you will be in for one of the finest riding machines ever produced during the golden age of steel. Nishiki built these frames to road-racing or criterium-racing specifications (or by request to any purpose the rider desired). Richard Jow reviewed a Nishiki Professional frame in the August 1976 issue of *Bicycling*. When the frameset arrived he spent three days trying to find something, anything, that was wrong with it. After a brief introduction, he gets to the

1981 NISHIKI COMP II: KAC05297

K:

A: YEAR CODE FOR 1981

05297: BUILD NUMBER

The Nishiki Comp II was a smartly spec'd machine and one of the most balanced road-going bicycles ever offered by West Coast Cycle Supply. Built with Tange Champion No. 2, it was perfectly capable of being a long-distance day tripper while being virtually race-ready. If one merely swapped out the clincher wheelset for tubular tires, one would be ready to go racing. These were the waning years of the fabulous relationship that had existed between Kawamura and West Coast Cycles; Nishiki's sales had reached nearly forty-five million dollars annually by 1981.

Most of the models were being built by Giant of Taiwan Region, however, and not Kawamura of Japan, as the yen had appreciated and other options were required to stay competitive. Within two years West Coast Cycles would be sold to Medalist Industries (and thence to Derby International in 1988). These Japanese-built, highly-affordable, everyday classic steel racing machines were seeing the last of their days.

The Italian temptation never appeared to be satiated. The sirensong of Columbus and Campagnolo would draw assemblers onto the rocks again and again. No matter how many times non-Italian manufacturers attempted to build a profitable 'not-Cinelli' superbike, and no matter the number of times this proved a marketing failure, there would always be another attempt on the horizon. Emulating was good, but claiming the provenance less so.

Nishiki offered the Cervino, built by the famous Italian builder, OLMO, which were founded in 1929. The pedigree was impeccable, with a wholesale dealer cost just under 1,000 (1983) dollars. They sold a fair number, but, as was always the case, an enthusiast who could afford the Italian premium went with the real McCoy (or the real Colombo). The next model in line, the Comp II, was one-third of the cost, built with Tange No. 2 tubing, and offered better shifting with the Cyclone derailleur system.

quick of the issue: "Nishiki has achieved another 'first.' They've brought to America a top-quality handcrafted frameset sure to rival such well-known names as Masi, Colnago, Jackson, and Hetchins." Then follows the search for a flaw ("Out came the dial indicators, string gauges, and micrometers..."). The conclusion? "Everything was perfect." The frame was constructed with the lightest offering from the Tange arsenal: their paper thin, double butted, Professional tubes with a 0.6 to 0.3 to 0.6 millimeter wall thickness. The entire affair was 2.8 pounds. (Based on his calculations, Jow suspected that the tubing may have had an even thinner wall thickness.) The review is extensive and the author ticks off every concern, praising the Nishiki on *every* single test point—tight, yes; alive, yes; choppy, no; flexy, no; sure-footed, yes; responsive, a resounding yes; numbness to hands, none; cornering, perfect; whippiness, none. Jow even admits to breaking his cardinal rule of never using an untested bicycle for an extended ride—after all the delicate measuring analysis and brutal road testing come these words: "The Nishiki Pro has it." All this in 1976—absolute parity with the finest frames available.

Cohen certainly made a a superior choice when he chose the Kawamura brothers to ghostbuild a quarter-million bicycles. It would be an exciting decade. Like most major Japanese-generated brands, however, Nishiki would grow up, reach adulthood, and move to Taiwan Region. For Kawamura, the story is something of a Greek tragedy.

In 1978, Howie Cohen started up a BMX-centric company called Everything Bicycles. His relationship was then far more biased toward Kuwahara, the manufacturer that focused on BMX models and leapt to fame when their E.T. The Extra-Terrestrial model debuted in the 1982 ultra-popular film. By that time Howie Cohen's brother,

Leo, was directing West Coast Cycle where the relationship with Kawamura had continued; but sunny days had clouded over. A full page of *Japan Cycle Press* (July 1981, Issue 4) noted the dual threat of the rise of the currency and the fall of the sales of "high-specification sports cycles"—the headline read, "Image damaged in West Coast USA." Essentially, the highest-quality Kawamura exports were facing a "precipitous" drop in sales.

For their lower-end models, Kawamura contracted with the new Taiwanese upstart, Giant Bicycles, to fill the void. Giant had launched ten years earlier, but their bicycles had not yet consistently reached the requisite quality standards. The article noted: "Production in Taiwan Region is being done by Giant, which supplies about 60% of the company's Nishiki cycles. The problem here lies in the inferior quality of the Taiwanese products, leading to a high rate of rejects by West Coast Cycle (WCCS)." It was simply part of the Giant learning curve, as they are one of the highest quality manufacturers today, and the world's largest bicycle company. This was back in 1981.

Matsushita (Panasonic) and Bridgestone had supplied Schwinn with tens of thousands of bicycles, but through a series of meetings they had in the mid- and late-1970s, it was determined that the price advantage of doing business in Japan was beginning to evaporate. Soon it would. Schwinn began pouring money into Taiwan Region, sending engineering know-how and doing everything possible to get Japan's competitors up to snuff. Schwinn went all in to ensure Taiwanese success. By the mid 1980s, Giant would be manufacturing 80% of Schwinn's products—exceeding 750,000 bicycles in some years.

Ironically, this would further decimate the Japanese price advantage by encroaching upon the Japanese quality advantage. Ultimately, yet sooner rather than later, the

1983 NISHIKI INTERNATIONAL: KC07624

K: KAWAMURA *also* K: USA EXPORT MODEL
C: YEAR CODE FOR 1983
07624: BUILD NUMBER

American advantage would dissipate too, and Schwinn would go into receivership in the very early 1990s, just as the Japanese manufacturers had ceased exporting (or ceased altogether). West Coast Cycles would sell and merge with Medalist Industries, which, in 1986, would become part of the Derby Cycle Corporation (a just-formed division of Derby International Corporation S.A., a Luxembourg entity). Kawamura Cycles would reformulate in 1995 as a high-quality manufacturer of wheelchairs.

Nishikis have been built at Giant Bicycles for many decades now, far longer than their formative years in Japan. Many areas have had their bicycle giants: Great Britain would have Woodhead, Angois, and Bowden; America would have Pope and Schwinn; Japan would have Miyata and Shimano; and Chinese Taiwan would be gifted with King Liu and Tony Lo, founders of Giant Bicycles.

In 1971, as Kawamura was building their first Nishikis, Lo was tending to his eel-farming business, situated along the coast of the South China Sea. As Japanese 'Racers' were storming foreign shores, a typhoon swept into the Chinese island of Taiwan and Liu's eel business was gone.

Liu had spent considerable time touring Japanese bicycle manufacturing facilities, and saw the opportunity to establish this industry in his home country. In 1972, he was joined by Tony Lo, and Giant was off to the races. Giant Bicycles will easily reach its fiftieth birthday as the largest bicycle manufacturer in the world. They support the latest slice of the Nishiki story: a brand conceived in America; born in Japan; owned by a German firm under a Luxembourg entity; and now a brand of a major American sporting goods firm. Nishiki will likely endure for many more years to come, the single offspring of many parents.

The Nishiki International was born in the early 1970s and gracefully, as well as technically, matured through the years. Early models were equipped with convenient features, such as stem mounted shifters, 'suicide' brake-lever extensions, and downmarket components (the three-arm Sugino Maxy crankset and the Taihei padded saddle). During successive years the model saw astute specification upgrades, the most important being the cold-forged five-arm Sugino crankset. SunTour derailleurs followed the International along for the ride, the last iteration being the Cyclone II model allied to the self-trimming aero–style top-mount downtube shift levers.

The International paralleled the Fuji S10-S in both build specification and ride character. Both of these bicycles sold in significant quantities, with their straight gauge chromoly tubes and robust components. The International and the S10-S were two of the most popular production models of the 10-speed age.

The International remained a tough, steel-centric model throughout its long evolution. Initially it was built with straight gauge chromoly, then double-butted Tange No. 3; from there to No. 2, and then in a burst of contrarian build logic (for the very late 1980s) with over-sized Tange No. 1 tubes. The nature of the bicycle shifted considerably with each steel upgrade: the International is a case study in product and brand survival.

In 1952 the Panasonic bicycle division is established—currently known as Panasonic Cycle Technology Co., Ltd.

Japanese Olympic cycling teams (1972, 1976, 1980) select Panasonics for the Munich, Montreal, and Moscow events. The Shimano/ Panasonic racing team is formed in 1979; Panasonic sponsors the Dutch professional cycling team, 1984–92.

In Japan, Panasonic continues to build steel-framed bicycles using Tange heat-treated Prestige or Kaisei 8630 Nickel Cromoly tubing, through production techniques established under the PICS program (now called the Panasonic Ordering System, 1996 sees the introduction of battery-assist models, including lithium-ion power in 2002.

MATSUSHITA ELECTRIC COMPANY, LTD., OSAKA

PANASONIC

1918 1925 1935 1951 1971 1987 1996

In 1918, Konosuke Matsushita establishes Matsushita Denkikigu Seisakusho (Electric Housewares Manufacturing Works) in Osaka. In 1923 he creates a battery-powered bicycle lamp to replace inefficient oil-burning models then in use.

Matsushita registers the name 'National' and products are marketed under this brand shortly thereafter. Seven years later, in 1935, the company becomes Matsushita Electric Industrial Co., Ltd.

National begins the manufacture of bicycle frames; a year later, tires. The Panasonic brand name is introduced in 1955. The National Tire Company, Ltd.; is formalized in 1957.

Panasonic begins export initiative under a private label for Schwinn. They also export under their own brand using the newly redesigned logotype created with the Helvetica typeface.

PICS (Panasonic Individual Custom System) is created. The program uses computer aided manufacturing and robotics for a completely automated build sequence as custom bicycles are produced under lean and just-in-time manufacturing processes. Still, the yen revaluation, liability insurance costs, and eroding profits convince Panasonic to cease exports to America in 1989, and to Europe about six years later.

Be assured that one becomes commensurately philosophical with increased exposure to bicycles. They sneak up on you, they work their way into your very being. When you first learn to ride, bicycles bestow a leap of independence. When you make that initial repair you discover the enduring gift of restoring things to rightness. As you become more brave, and, say, rapidly descend a mountain pass or transit great distances alone, you touch the metaphysical. Bicycles make you set goals, such as long-distance touring (you against yourself), or racing (you against others). As you revel in the joys of human potential, you face the agony of human limitation. With each ride you see something new. In revealing to us the magnificent interconnectedness of things, bicycles make philosophers out of us all.

In April 1989, at the age of 94, a major industrialist and bicycle lover, passed on. His name was Konosuke Matsushita. He was a prolific author, an advocate for peace, and an inspiring teacher. He founded one of Japan's most formidable companies, now called *Panasonic*. Matsushita always had a place in his heart for bicycles and his company would honor this: life's journey made him a great philosopher.

In 1904, at the age of nine, young Konosuke left home for an apprenticeship at a bicycle shop. In those years, Japanese apprentices lived at the establishments they worked for; he'd rarely see his family. In one of the many books he authored, *My Way of Life and Thinking,* he tells the story of laboriously turning the workshop's lathe by hand. After 45 minutes of this he would tire and the lathe would slow. At this point the machinist would gently rap him on the head with a small hammer. Matsushita later observed: "[In those days] everyone was still accustomed to this notion of its being quite natural to take some pounding in the process of getting to be a full-fledged worker." Continuing on, he concluded: "No one even noticed it."

1982 PANASONIC PROFESSIONAL 7000: 2B15380

2: BUILD YEAR 1982
B: MONTH CODE FOR FEBRUARY
15380: BUILD NUMBER

The second generation Panasonic Professional 7000 was released in 1980 with a Royal Silver livery, replacing the Gold of the previous 3 years. The model was always equipped with Shimano's Dura-Ace groupset. Originally, Panasonic anonymized Tange's Champion Chromoly tubes under their '4130' reference. Later they noted Tange in their specification tables. The final iteration of the Professional 7000 (1984) was offered in Imperial Red and proudly wore Tange 'Champion No. 1' tubing decals. The Professional was bumped off the podium in 1985, when Panasonic expanded their Team series and the Team Europe 1 became the premier model.

During their prime bicycle export years, Matsushita's marketing slogan was: "Panasonic–just slightly ahead of our time." The campaign was initiated in 1969, but would not be mainstream until the late 1970s and into the 1980s. Use of the word 'slightly' within a marketing program was unexpectedly modest, but it brought the necessary focus to Panasonic's emphasis on research and development.

Although the ad claimed that their line of bicycles was built "by fanatics for fanatics," it was a fanaticism not of passion, but of precision. Panasonic was always obsessed with engineering tolerances, and the depth of their organization meant that quality-control standards could be brought to bear across manufacturing divisions.

The "ahead of our time" slogan, coined by a New York agency, did help to synthesize the divergent philosophies that prevailed across all the various divisions under Matshushita. For the bicycle division, being "slightly ahead of their time" meant drawing on the muscle of the parent company for something completely new. By the late 1980s, robotics and advanced automation would set the stage for the final generation of Panasonic's bicycle manufacturing.

The AR6000 represented Panasonic's brief and only foray into aerodynamics. The model was offered in 1982, 1983, and 1984. (Reportedly, less than 100 were sold into the United States.) The frame was built with Tange Aero 25 tubing, a unique and somewhat weighty option within Tange's four aero tube range. Aero 25 was a double-walled chromoly plain-gauge design. It was specifically engineered to "correct for the imbalance between vertical and lateral forces caused by the 'teardrop' shape." Manufactured as a 'non-round,' high-quality, drawn seamless tube, Aero 25 required special lugs as well. Panasonic, ever engineering-forward in their thinking, specified Tange's Aero 25 because it was the most innovative aero tubing available.

He never forgot those lessons, nor the joys of that apprenticeship. If not for these origins Matsushita Electric Industrial Company may never have produced bicycles. Once they began production they never ceased—even though, at their peak export level, bicycles purportedly made less profit than did the sale of Panasonic's 'D' cell batteries.

Matsushita Electric began building bicycles under their *National* brand in 1951; in 1954 the Panasonic name was created. Arnold Schwinn & Company went to Japan in 1965 and established an exclusive contract with Asia Machinery Trading Company (now Akibo Corporation) for the purchase of parts and accessories; even the packaging was contracted through Asia Machinery. Subsequent to this aftermarket effort was the importation of complete bicycles; by 1971 Matsushita Electric would be producing a large volume of units for Schwinn (while simultaneously exporting a limited number under the Panasonic banner.)

No matter the brand name Panasonic wore, each bicycle was a testament to quality. This was Mr. Matsushita's guiding edict. Schwinn, the mightiest bicycle manufacturer in the world, demanded consistency, volume, and high quality. They knew that quality and labor cost advantages would stave off the competition. Schwinn saw that Matsushita was already building solid, pragmatic machines. The next step would be to make these bicycles lighter and faster. The DNA of this storied bicycle-maker was thus forged: Panasonic blended corporatism with craftsmanship, fastidious engineering with product innovation.

Panasonic's exports poured into an unprecedented age of American competition—not only competition from other manufacturers, but legal competition in the form of lawsuits, government competition in the form of regulations, and new forms of that old bugaboo—international trade tariffs and restrictions. (Schwinn themselves would even-

tually succumb to this onslaught, filing for bankruptcy in 1992—but prior to that time there would be many exciting years and millions of bicycles produced, many of these built by Panasonic.)

In 1965, while Schwinn had first come to Japan, Ralph Nader's *Unsafe at Any Speed: The Designed-In Dangers of the American Automobile,* was published. Nader would become America's principal advocate for consumer protection and corporate accountability. The courtroom would be his theater of war. Nader's advocacy reached national proportions: his notoriety allowed him later to campaign for the United States Presidency.

Nader is often credited with initiating America's 'age of consumer litigation.' Fifty years after writing *Unsafe at any Speed*, Nader opened an unconventional museum in Winsted, Connecticut: the American Museum of Tort Law. The exhibits commemorate consumer litigation milestones, revealing a transition from the practice of *caveat emptor* (let the buyer beware) to today's system of powerful retaliatory consumer rights.

The expansion of litigation in the United States coincided with the import bicycle boom, fueling the belief that America had become the world's most litigious nation. This perception was exacerbated by media reports of outlandish court rulings. Fear that courts were becoming a lottery for the aggrieved certainly affected the design of consumer products. The ever-increasing legal muscle of the 'common man' was not lost on Japanese corporate leadership.

Another noteworthy aspect of American jurisprudence involved governmental challenges to corporate activity. A case that impacted Schwinn's unfolding relationship with Panasonic was *United States v. Arnold, Schwinn & Co.,* litigated from April until June, 1967. Schwinn was accused of setting prices, attempting to control their

1982 PANASONIC AR6000: 2B17047

2: YEAR CODE FOR 1982
B: MONTH CODE FOR FEBRUARY
17047: BUILD NUMBER

products post-sale, and reallocating dealership sales territories. Ironically, these were the kinds of things the Japanese government was *assisting* domestic companies with.

Additionally, 1960s America was a car-centric culture. Adult bicycles were ubiquitous in Europe and Japan for travel and business purposes; in the United States, the automobile had usurped these roles. Bicycles were for children. Except for Schwinn, most manufacturers were not prepared for the 10-speed boom, nor the quantity of imported bicycles that were soon to breach American shores. When these 'toy makers' began to manufacture full-sized machines there were unwelcome 'trickle-up' design influences taken from their overbuilt children's bicycles.

As a mechanic, toiling away in the recesses of a bicycle establishment, one amusement was servicing the variety of two-wheeled wonders brought in for service. Occasionally, a thoroughbred would grace the repair stand, but most specimens were mediocre. We called them 'gas-pipe specials.' These bicycles tipped the scales at nearly forty pounds. They heaved and creaked and squeaked about as we struggled mightily to bring them back to 'nearly in tune.' The very scariest of these had a curious red, white, blue, and gold decal identifying 'BMA/6' certification. From a mechanic's point of view, this distinction was actually a mark of shame—the scarlet letter of the velocipedic village.

BMA stood for the Bicycle Manufacturers' Association of America, a private, non-profit organization formed in 1916. By the late 1960s, BMA represented nearly every domestic American manufacturer—except Schwinn. They held community safety clinics at local police stations, summer camps, and other civic venues. They were a Washington DC-based trade and tariff, government relations lobbyist group. With the rise of imports, and Schwinn's shocking decision to 'fraternize with the enemy,'

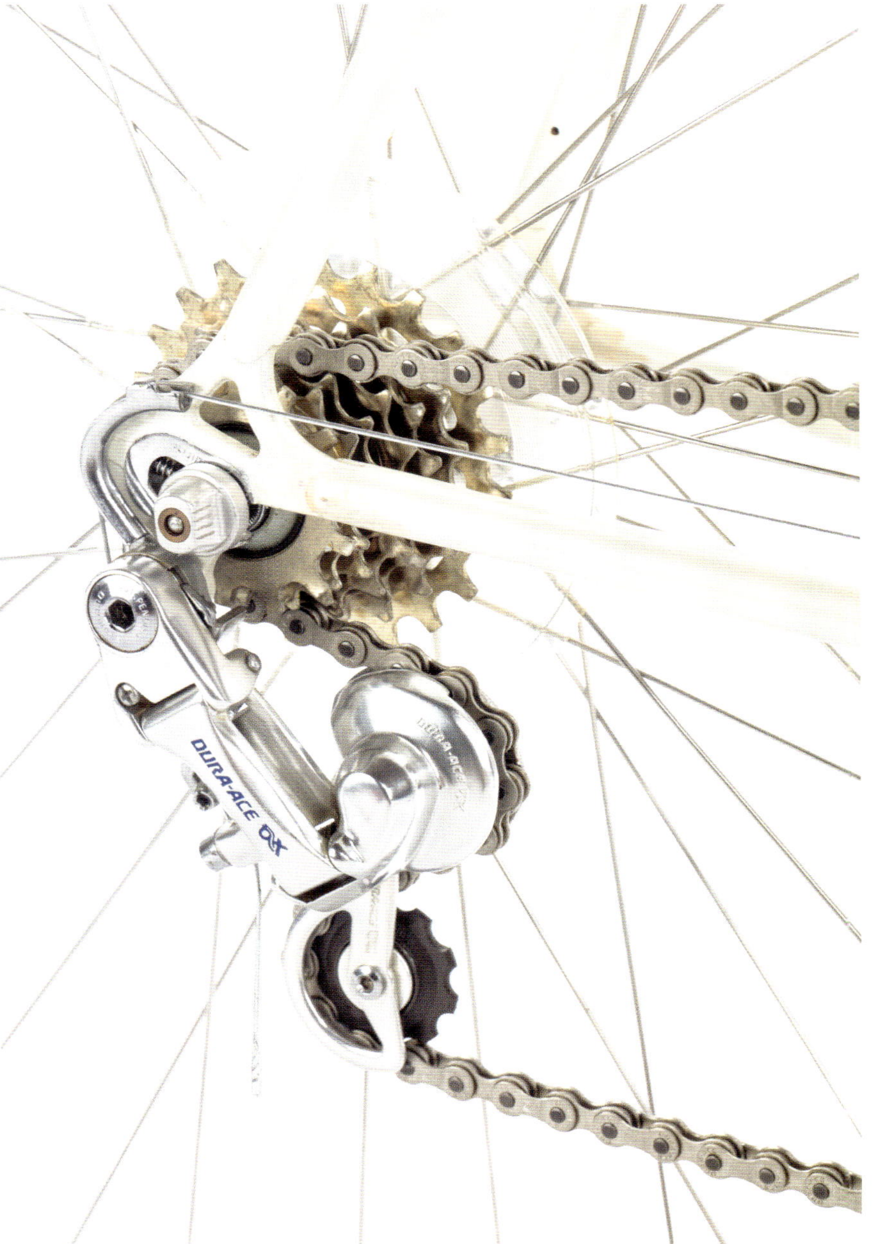

Panasonic employed a naming protocol that, at best, was only mildly consistent throughout their export years. Generally, single-letter designations were abbreviations for full words. The 'R' designation stood for 'Road Bicycle'. To this a prefix of 'P,' indicating 'Professional,' or 'D,' indicating 'Deluxe,' or 'T,' indicating 'Touring,' might be added. In some cases (premium models) the letter combination was followed by a series number in decreasing increments of 1000. (Later double letters [such as 'DX,' for 'Deluxe,' or 'TK,' for 'Track'] were utilized).

Amid all the permutations the most satisfying variation is the two-letter combination followed by the numeral designation. An excellent example of this arrangement is the AR6000—Aero Road 6000.

In 1985, in a burst of nomenclatorial distinction, the 'Team' series became Panasonic's flagship line. The top three were built with Columbus SP/SL or Columbus chromoly tubing and named the Team Europe I, the Team America, and the Team Europe II. The AR6000 was no longer offered. The Team name continued on under various guises, but when Panasonic left the United States and concentrated on exports to Europe they also returned to their older naming conventions.

BMA had the impetus to formalize trade barriers. They stood up their Safety and Standards Committee, who compiled a standards document by 1971 to which the members agreed to abide. It was called BMA/6. Purportedly the standards would "protect the consumer from possible injury and property damage." For enthusiasts, who actually *rode* adult bicycles, the standards seemed capricious, malicious, ridiculous. When *The United States Consumer Product Safety Commission* (CPSC) was formed in 1972, their first undertaking dealt with bicycle safety. As one might expect, they relied heavily on the self-serving standards of BMA/6.

Overcoming these legal, design, and trade obstacles might have meant that Panasonic's voluminous output would have become uninspired, cookie-cutter commodities. Instead, they were understated gems. Panasonic's focus on quality supported by their modern equipment and engineering precision turned out 'quintessential machines.' Panasonics were neither romantic nor emotive; they were classic and rational. Even the Panasonic logotype conveyed this. It was set in Helvetica, the typeface of the corporate world (designed in 1957 by Swiss designers Max Miedinger and Eduard Hoffmann). Helvetica was the embodiment of modernism, internationalism, logic, and functional purity. Panasonics possessed these attributes as well as high-level craftsmanship when it came to the lugwork and brazing on their flagship models. They had more than proved themselves as the world's premium third-party builder. Ninety percent of their output was third-party branded, but this was about to change. It was time for Panasonic exports *all to be* Panasonic exports. A radical marketing plan was underway for 1985.

Until that time Panasonic export catalogs had been mostly small-format brochures or fold-down posters. In 1985, they produced a full-sized catalog and introduced their

What really added to the panache of aero bicycles was their component sets. Shimano's brave development effort into an aero groupset may have been disheartening because the aero was a short-lived phenomenon; but the engineering effort pushed Shimano to new heights, underscoring their commitment to innovation. Shimano, in a deft stroke, became the leader in groupset design. Of particular interest was the center-pull 600 AX *brakeset. The design was not only aesthetically bold in appearance, but radically more efficient in stopping power, particularly in wet conditions. For mechanics the ease of adjustment and the self-centering attribute was appreciated.*

premium *Team* series. The top three models were constructed using Columbus SP/SL tubing. This was a prodigious specification, and they were exquisite. Each was built with lost-wax cast and thinned lugs, sloping fork crowns, and meticulous low-temperature silver brazing. Atypically, they came in extravagant colors: Salmon Pink, Ocean Blue, and Grape Dust. Yet the biggest change for 1985 would not be found in the pages of their catalog. Panasonic was undergoing a critical production shift, turning from a majority of third-party builds to manufacturing exclusively under their own name. The ratio of 90% ghost builds to 10% self-branded would reverse in four years.

In a letter to dealers dated October 1986, Panasonic's National Sales Manager, John Campanella, stated: "Even in these tough times, you enabled Panasonic to have another record-breaking year." Panasonic would introduce Tange's new heat-treated Prestige tubing in 1987. The Prestige tubeset would be used for the DX-6000 (equipped with a SunTour Sprint groupset, another first). The bicycle was cataloged without fanfare, but was one of the finest production models that Panasonic ever made. After testing and comparing Tange's Prestige tubing material, Panasonic's engineers dropped Columbus. The Tange steel appealed to their sense of superior, consistent tolerances—100 sets of tubes met specification for 100 bicycles; purportedly the ratio with Columbus was 92/100. Tange tubes would become Panasonic's premier material again.

The drive to end third-party exports was nearly realized by 1988. However, industry-wide price cutting, waning sales, insurance costs, and Taiwanese competition dulled the milestone. It was time for a bold stroke. Panasonic would lean on their technical depth and innovation to create something big—they would break from tradition and succeed, or withdraw from the export market.

1985 PANASONIC TEAM EUROPE: 5D08078

5: YEAR CODE FOR 1985
D: MONTH CODE FOR APRIL
08078: BUILD NUMBER

By the mid-1980s the great majority (as high as ninety percent) of Panasonic's export machines became private-label bicycles, mostly under the Schwinn moniker. Then, Panasonic began to reverse their ghost-builder status. By 1990, nearly everything they built wore the Panasonic brand. During the transition they were driven to create the highest-quality production bicycle made. To do this, they fell into a 'if you can't beat them, join them,' mentality.

With this goal in mind, in 1985, 1986, and 1987, Panasonic imported Columbus SP and SL chromoly tubing to build their premier Team series offerings. The 1985 Team Europe 1, in the bravely-liveried Salmon Pink, was the highest iteration of this brief disloyalty to Tange. The Italian theme was underscored with Campagnolo Record, Super Record, and Nuovo Record equipment, along with a Selle Italia saddle for this top model.

SunTour supplied the New Winner 7-speed freewheel (and the Superbe narrow-link chain). A Nitto 55 handlebar and Pearl stem, along with Araya rims fitted with Panasonic's own Panaracer Record tubulars completed the build. The larger-sized (61 and 64cm) frames were constructed with dual 74° seattube/headtube angles. All smaller sizes had far more relaxed headtube angles to prevent toe-clip overlap. The Team Europe 1 is painfully rare; they probably number in the single digits or low teens at best.

Campagnolo

With the technical support of multiple divisions, Panasonic introduced 'PICS,' the *Panasonic Individual Custom System.* In one stroke Panasonic would change the bicycle marketplace: everyone would get a custom bicycle! There would be no need to have bicycles on the floor, nor in a warehouse. Every bicycle would be individually ordered, built, and shipped within three weeks. Panasonic would launch an early, lean manufacturing process with total robotic frame-making production capabilities. Initially there would be nearly 12,000 possible build permutations.

The program was announced from Long Beach, California, on January 7, 1988. The ordering side required dealers to set up a 'PICS Center,' within their shop. Here the program was promoted via banners, posters, and illuminated signs; a video of the high-tech production facilities was presented on a Panasonic PVM2028 monitor. These retailer tools were supplemented by a collection of painted tube samples and copious literature. The heart of the display was the Frame Measuring Gauge, an adjustable bicycle of sorts.

The Frame Measuring Gauge allowed dealers to tailor a bicycle to the buyer's specific dimensions. Once measured, the customer would select from one of four different models, and then choose a one-, two-, or three-color paint scheme. The owner's name could be silkscreened on the toptube or engraved into the stem. Orders were faxed to Japan and processed via bar codes, computer aided design, and robotics—truly state of the art.

The flagship Team America (now built with Japanese steel in the form of Tange Prestige tubing) could be purchased through the PICS program or through the standard catalog. What would happen if you could go back in time and order both ways? Your catalog-spec'd Team would be entirely hand-built by two craftsmen and meticulously silver brazed with a thinned-lugged construction.

The crowning advancements within SunTour's second-generation Superbe equipment were their epochal pedals, debuted in 1979. In consultation with engineers from MKS (Mikashima) came a radical break from the 'Campagnolo look.' Features included a burnished 'X-body' with interchangeable cut-away cages (road, track, and later BMX and MTB style) and sealed bearings from Nachi-Fujikoshi Corp. The offset-bearing load and cage design allowed for an additional 5° of cornering lean, a noteworthy advantage in road racing. Mikashima still produces the pedal, as it is a NJS-approved design for Keirin racing (where toe clips and straps, versus clipless designs, are required).

1986 PANASONIC TEAM JAPAN: 6B07937

6: YEAR CODE FOR 1986

B: MONTH CODE FOR FEBRUARY

07937: BUILD NUMBER

In 1986 the build logic for Panasonic's series of Team machines was rational and elegant. The premier Team Europe used full Columbus SP and SL chromoly with Campagnolo 1010B dropouts. The Team America was built with Shimano's Dura-Ace groupset and Shimano EF dropouts. Third place was the Team Japan; for this model Columbus tubing was allied with Tange fork blades and SunTour Superbe dropouts.

In this manner, a fully integrated groupset, down to the dropouts, was specified for each model. Price-wise, Panasonic recommended a retail range from $800 for the Team Japan and up to $1,400 for the Team Europe (in 1986 dollars).

Once again, SunTour made the podium, but only took the bronze. By this time the Superbe line was in its second generation, referred to as Superbe Pro in their literature, but still engraved with Superbe (or just a stylized 'S') on the components themselves.

With the exception of the pedals, the second generation components had neither the classicism of the initial Superbe lineup, nor the technical artistry of what would soon follow. But the groupset was outstanding in both responsiveness and reliability. This made the Team Japan one of the most pragmatic super- bicycles that could be had, the most you could procure from Panasonic for the least amount of money. The Team Japan was only produced in 1986, a one-year wunderkind.

JAPAN
SUNTOUR

There are literally thousands of extant pages of patent documentation claiming innovation in derailleur- and bicycle drivetrain-design. (The author would estimate the number to exceed 4,000.) Bicycle-related patents reach back 150 years, but it was during the 1980s when there was an exponential increase in patent filings, many presenting intellectual property rights respecting bicycle drivetrain technology.

SunTour achieved an early patent milestone with their famed slant parallelogram derailleur. Yet ill-timed innovation would sometimes be their downfall. Although they developed indexed shifting in 1969, they abandoned the idea when initial reviewers were unimpressed.

Shimano had taken multiple stabs at index shifting; but when they released their 'SIS' (Shimano Index System) they were fully invested. SunTour, having once been stung, was then late to reënter the indexing game. Technically, the early-1980s were atypically conservative years for SunTour.

Shimano took the lead in innovation during that lull, fortified by their depth and commitment to research, development, and respect for marketing. Panasonic was drawn to Shimano's innovation as well as their growing corporate clout; the Team Japan would be one of the last higher-specification bicycles that Panasonic equipped with full SunTour components.

You would have three color schemes to choose from and take delivery of your prized Panasonic in about two months. Or, you could have your Team America built by four robots and delivered within three weeks. The robots charged a bit more but offered 35 color patterns to choose from: a dramatic livery was encouraged. One robot assembled the main triangle, another attached the rear stays, a third reamed and prepped the seat tube, and a fourth applied flawless coats of paint and sealant. Humans assisted, but the robots took responsibility to construct your cherished steed within a stunning .001 millimeter tolerance.

The beautiful craftsmanship of the hand-built machine would be evident in a side-by-side comparison against its robotic stablemate. What could not be compared was unseen. The robots, oblivious to their working environs, brazed with multiple torches guided by precision thermo-sensors. From a metallurgist's standpoint this was a higher beauty. In a 1988 *Bicycle Guide* review, Doug Roosa wrote: "A PICS frame may be robot-built, but it rides more like a product from a master framebuilder."

1989 would be the second year of the PICS program. Titanium and aluminum frames would be offered, a first for Panasonic. There would be nearly 60,000 ordering options. Unfortunately, Panasonic was *just too far ahead of their time.* Their paltry bicycle division profits could no longer justify continuance in the American marketplace. In April of that year, Konosuke Matsushita quietly passed away. Some say that with his passing the debt of honor had also been fulfilled—five months afterward, Panasonic terminated bicycle exportation to the United States.

Although American exports ceased, Panasonic was still sending bicycles to Europe and sponsoring a racing team they had supported since 1984. The team was registered in the Netherlands and managed by Peter Post, a Dutch rider

With Panasonic's imminent departure from the United States marketplace, the Team name would be retired and the Pro Road, or PR designation, would be used (again) for top road-bicycle models. More importantly, there would be a return to Tange's Prestige tubing. The entire main triangle would be composed of 1.12 inch- (28.6 mm-) diameter tubes. Panasonic also returned to all Japanese components except for the 'Rolls' saddle from Selle San Marco, Mavic Rims, and, most ironically, Clement Criterium tires (bypassing their own Panaracer brand). They billed the PR6000 as the "best hand built racing bicycle in the entire 'cycling' world."

1990 PANASONIC PR6000: 0D03823

0: YEAR CODE FOR 1990
D: MONTH CODE FOR APRIL
03823: BUILD NUMBER

1989 would see the discontinuation of Panasonic's exports to the United States. Floor models were presented in their 1989 catalog, or bicycles (or framesets) could be ordered through the innovative Panasonic Individual Custom System, or PICS, program. Nearly 60,000 configurations were possible with a three-week turnaround. Panasonic ended their American export operations on a high note.

The PICS program would only reach its second year for the American market. However, this automated bicycle ordering and manufacturing process would be continually refined for the domestic market under the name POS, or the Panasonic Ordering System.

The Shimano Dura-Ace groupset achieved world-class racing recognition through the development of the 7400 series. Unlike SunTour, a company that extolled interchangeability of components across their full range of products, Shimano always advocated for consistency within a product line. This permitted greater engineering control, as well as the ability to innovate within one model range. The 7400 series was introduced as a 6-speed system and was then upgraded to 7- and 8-speed versions. Innovations included the reintroduction of the freehub with casette-style rear cogs; indexed shifting; and integrated brake/shifter dual-control levers ('brifters'). This leap in component innovation would establish design and control standards for decades to follow.

PRESTIGE
CR-MO
DOUBLE BUTTED TUBES
TANGE
Panasonic

Companies like Schwinn contracted with outside production to not only supplement their in-house manufacturing, but to overcome union uncertainties and create "off-line" profits. However, large companies were not the only buyers from manufacturers willing to serve as ghostbuilders.

Panasonic, and many other builders, also produced bicycles (and frames) for companies that had zero internal manufacturing capabilities (such as Centurion). For Centurion outside production was their lifeline. Today, searching back to the late 1970s and '80s to fully unwind the criss-crossing of buyers and private label builders is extremely challenging. So much information is no longer extant; much was intentionally suppressed even then.

During the most volatile periods of growth and production one needed a scorecard to know exactly who was building what for whom. Even companies that had no brands of their own, such as Sumitomo Heavy Industries, were producing precision specified framesets for third parties—some of these were then sold on to other third parties!

By the late 1980s exports were cooling; many manufactures were finally producing products exclusively under their own brand. Panasonic was one of these—by 1988 almost all of their exports were wearing the Panasonic brand name.

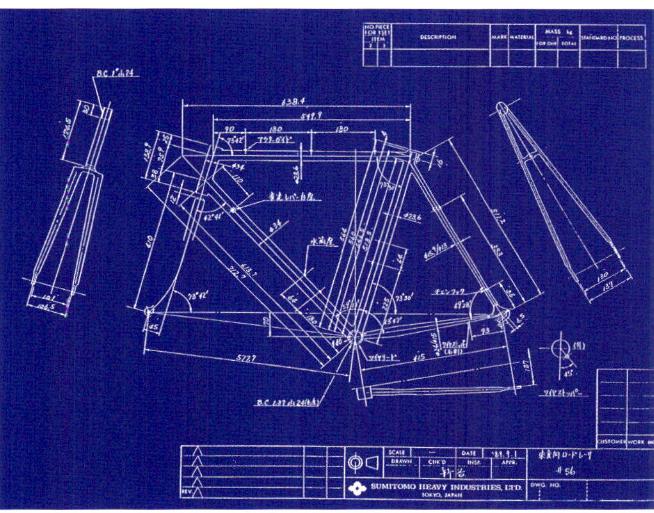

of renown who had been nearly unbeatable during that fabulous era of the six-day races. When Panasonic began their sponsorship, seven Dutch riders came over from the former Raleigh team. One of them, Henk Lubberding, was known as the 'master of the peleton' for his capabilities as an indispensable support rider. (Among his many other achievements were multiple stage wins in the Tour de France, wearing the Yellow Jersey during a 1988 stage.)

Originally, the Panasonic Racing team was used to promote their electronics division, not their bicycles. However, headquarters, impressed by the 1990 World Championship races held in Utsunomiya, Japan, then shifted their marketing focus to the bicycles themselves. Panasonic engineers became deeply involved. The result was the PR6000, a bicycle that Lubberding extolled by proclaiming it "the most favorite bike of my career." The tubes were Tanges Prestige. At first, riders were skeptical due to its thin wall thickness. However, after the celebrated Dutch framebuilder Jan Le Grand built the PR6000s for the team, the skepticism was immediately displaced by admiration.

Lubberding noted that the PR6000 was such a great frame that it was also raced in Colnago livery. And so, Panasonics were being raced in the famed Tour de France as well as the the gruelling Paris–Roubaix. This was victory unto itself, for at long last the Japanese had bested the Italians at their own game. They'd overcome the final challenge. The PR6000 was, perhaps, the ultimate bicycle of its age.

In Japan, the PICS program (there called the *Panasonic Ordering System*) has continued to evolve to this day. Prestige tubes (now from Tange Taiwan, China), brazed at low temperatures (550 celsius) are still being used to make superior custom frames—a PR6000 for everyone, exactly as Matsushita would have wanted it. The spirit of young Konosuke must truly smile with every Panasonic made.

In the Spring of 1881, Eisuke Miyata establishes Miyata Manufacturing Co., Ltd, in Kyobashi (Tokyo Prefecture). Although principally engaged in the trade of gunmaking, the company begins repairing imported bicycles in 1889.

During the height of the First Sino-Japanese War, Japan allowed open importation of guns, diluting the industry. Eitaro decides to cease gun fabrication, concentrating all efforts on bicycle manufacture.

In 1907, Shosaku Morita establishes a fire protection company that will eventually grow to become Morita Industries, a conglomerate building fire engines, fire suppression equipment, and systems and vehicles for recycling and environmental conservation. Morita corporation will invest in Miyata, acquiring majority ownership by 2001. Thereafter, fire extinguishers are built under the Miyata brand by Morita Miyata Industries.

MIYATA INDUSTRY CO., LTD., CHIGASAKI

MIYATA

Motorcycle production terminated.

In 2012 Miyata Cycle Company celebrates their relaunch by producing the 'Miyata Japon,' a handmade road bicycle built along classic lines with their proprietary 4130 S.S.T.B. steel; the premium model is painted in Legendary Blue.

1890 **1900** **1913** **1937** **1950s** **1964** **1972** **1979** **2010**

Eisuke Miyata establishes Miyata Gun Works in Sumida (Tokyo Prefecture); later in the year he and his son, Eitaro, fabricate the first 'modern' Japanese-made bicycle from steel tubing. Eitaro builds a bicycle for Crown Prince Yoshihito two years later, in 1892. Miyata introduces their Asahi brand in 1902.

Under the Asahi brand, Miyata builds bicycles as well as motorcycles (introduced in 1913, the first motorcycle under Japanese manufacture).

In 1937, Miyata produces a two-cylinder front-wheel-drive automobile.

In addition to innovations in their bicycle manufacturing (flash welding, electrostatic painting, and infrared drying), Miyata develops powder-based fire suppression.

In 1959, Panasonic invests in Miyata. In 1964, Miyata occupies a new facility in Chigasaki City. Here they build their '10-speed racer,' for export (1972). In 1979, a partnership is formed with Koga B.V., a Dutch cycling firm, creating the Koga Miyata brand.

Miyata becomes Japan's 2nd largest exporter of bicycles, gaining credentials when Peter Winnen takes the 17th stage of the 1981 Tour de France on a Koga Miyata. Exports continue until the late 1990s; Panasonic divests in 2008.

2009-2010: Morita Miyata Industries reestablish Miyata Cycle Co., Ltd.; Merida Bicycle, Taiwan (China), acquires a 30% stake. Koga and Miyata end their relationship after three decades.

"Swords into Ploughshares." I was too timid and too self-conscious to raise my hand and ask the question; fortunately another student bravely did so. "What's a ploughshare?" Our fifth-grade class was scheduled to go on a field trip the following week and tour the United Nations Headquarters in New York City. Mr. Lukasz, the history teacher and coordinator of the event, was prepping the selected deportees: informing us of what we would see, what we should know beforehand, and, most importantly, how we were to behave.

As soon as the multitude of students was fed the tour would begin in Ralph Bunche Park, across the street from the imposing Secretariat building. There, flanking a curving staircase, was a massive wall faced with 66 imposing granite tiles. Graven into the façade was this inscription (chiseled in fine, Roman Majuscules): "They shall beat their swords into ploughshares, and their spears into pruning hooks, nation shall not lift up sword against nation, neither shall they learn war any more." Mr. Luckasz admonished, "These words are so profound and sagacious that they occur not once, but three times in scripture."

In that day our suburban enclave was assaulted every Wednesday at precisely six o'clock in the evening by an air -raid drill. Its piercing wail rended the entire community asunder for one agonizing minute. To intensify the effect we'd run *toward* the siren, tightly covering our ears as we did so while the force of the sound waves coursed through our vibrating bodies. Each morning we would trudge off to school, ever-aware of the precarious, existential 'great game' between the world's two superpowers. All of the televised spy series defined these adversaries with boolean precision: the USSR (and the East Germans) were the bad guys; the USA (and the British) were the good guys. This was the immutable reality of the Cold War.

1982 TEAM-MIYAYA: J784969

J: YEAR CODE FOR 1981 [1982 MODEL YEAR]

784969: BUILD NUMBER

Miyata had something of a cult following for their premium blue and gold, or blue and black, machines. The Team-Miyata models, from 1981 until 1986 (first blue/gold, then blue/black) exemplified the striking livery, magnificently set off by the semi-polished aluminum of the Shimano Dura-Ace EX components.

The debut for Miyata's signature color would be the GL model for 1977, under their Koga-Miyata affiliation. GL stood for 'Gents Luxe.' (This was a carry-over from Japanese naming conventions going back to the 1940s, generic frames being identified under 'Gents,' or 'Ladies' configurations). The name was a one-year aberration, but the color would set a standard for a decade to follow.

The rich, French blue color was reminiscent of vintage racing Bugattis. This blue would be used in combination with black or gold sections on the seat tube or head-tube. There would be a fair range of hue and value throughout the years, along with naming alterations (it was generally called Bright Blue), but it quickly identified Miyata's top models.

The color is now retroactively referred to as 'Legacy Blue' and identifies the ten-year run of professional-grade Miyatas built with tubing of their own manufacture. By identifying with a single color (as did Bianchi) and producing catalogs that expounded upon their proprietary tubing, Miyata build a strong brand presence for their premium models.

The week passed, the field trip commenced; our group huddled tightly before the wall as a chilled and swirling rain, anguished by winds driven across the East River, swept about us. We were in Turtle Bay where the United Nations headquarters had risen in 1952. This wall, with its prophetic statement, was an ebenezer (a memorial and touchpoint) for our teacher's staunch anti-war stance. "Do you understand?" Mr. Lucasz thundered, "these words sum up the whole purpose of the United Nations. The great inventions of war must be converted into instruments for peace."

To my juvenile mind, his logic seemed to indicate that civilizations needed war in order to come up with good inventions. I smiled impishly, and to my horror he noted my countenance and singled me out. "William, can you name something and someone who turned implements of war to good and peaceful purposes?" I froze, as silent and petrified as the wet stone wall behind him. Moments later we crossed 1st Avenue and began the tour, but for me those brief searching seconds seemed eons in duration as the universe looked down, frowning at my abject ignorance. Prior to my inquisition he had cited some of the peace dividends extracted from war: the trench coat, the radio, stainless steel. How could a boy of twelve know more?

For those who are verbally confronted, yet lost for retaliatory words, there is often a desire to go back in time and avenge their unjust attacker with 'well-tuned words.' If I could now relive that drizzling, distant morning, I'd bravely respond: "Of course I can Mr. Lucasz—the famous Miyata family, who turned their gun business into the making of bicycles." Oh, how I would be the hero of that day! At first, nonplussed, he'd soon recover, and with a condescending stare demand yet more: "Who are these Miyatas? Tell us how they turned guns... into bicycles..."

The beautiful Team Miyata ran with Shimano's Dura-Ace EX groupset until 1984 (a year prior to the 'New Dura-Ace' line being introduced). In 1984 they also offered the Team SL, which featured Campagnolo Record and Super Record components, but this would prove to be a 1984-only model.

By the early 1980s, Shimano was taking an engineering-forward approach. Their components were being constantly modified and refined. By this time the Shimano Dura-Ace EX line introduced hubs with their 'Direction 6' feature. The spokes on Direction 6 hubs were all laced from the inside (so all the spoke heads were on the inside of the flange). This helped to equalize spoke tension, resulting in a stronger wheel that would purportedly remain in true for a longer period of usage.

The Direction 6 rear hub could accommodate six-, or seven-speed clusters or Shimano freehubs. By this time in bicycle evolution the rear fork distance was generally 126 mm wide (no longer 120 mm); EX hubs permitted a standard width chain to be utilized.

Miyata was the only Japanese exporter routinely to list frames as standalone offerings within their catalogs. As they fabricated their own tubing this was a profitable proposition, as well as an opportunity to showcase this impressive capability.

Although variations of chromoly-butted tubes were used across the top range of framesets, the premium specification was their S3B designation, drawn in their own steel-milling facilities. S3B represented: 'S' for 'spiral' and '3B' for 'triple-butted.'

Later, when Miyata introduced their titanium and carbon-built bicycles, these were also offered as standalone framesets. This permitted buyers to equip their frames in any configuration they desired; a particular advantage if one had a well-spec'd bicycle and desired to swap over parts to a new frame.

Buying all new parts individually and creating a custom-equipped bicycle from scratch in that day was prohibitive, because the cost would exceed a factory stock bicycle by nearly double. For collectors today, the Miyata frame option means that then-available models can be equipped with any period-correct groupset, or an eclectic assembly of parts, and still be considered 'authentic.' The frame-only offerings followed the standard serial numbering protocol.

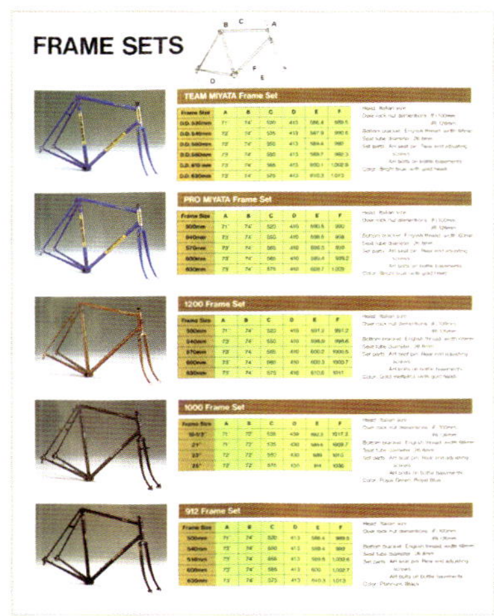

I would begin the story on November 9, 1867. Eisuke Miyata was 27 years old on that pivotal day in modern Japanese history. The Tokugawa shogunate family line had ruled Japan for over 250 years, initially seizing power during the Battle of Sekigahara in October, 1600. Prior to their hegemony, Japan had suffered through a hundred years of bloody civil wars, but this great battle eclipsed all that went before and an enduring peace, under the steely sword of military dictatorship, followed. The Tokugawa lineage had prospered through fifteen successive family members, but the end of that epoch was at hand. The last shogun, Prince Yoshinobu Tokugawa, would cede all power to Japan's reestablished authority under imperial rule. This coup, the centerpiece of the Meiji Restoration, was a political movement that reactively grew and intensified after the coerced trade treaty exacted by Commodore Matthew Perry (US Navy) fourteen years previously.

The Japanese, although historically xenophobic and isolationist (sakoku), also possessed a fascination with the innovative and expansionist nature of world powers. The Meiji restoration embodied a philosophy of strength and was ready to enter the new age of trade. However, they viewed with great apprehension what had befallen China, the so-called 'sick man of Asia'—a nation then beset with controlling foreign influences. They required a hedge against the Western powers then pouring across the globe and demanding concessions from weaker states.

Initially, China had been greatly enriched by Western trade policy, amassing great quantities of silver through their silk, tea, and porcelain exports. The British classified this as mercantilism. In order to reverse the flow of silver, the opium trade was established, and tons of that narcotic was trafficked by clipper ships into the Cantonese ports. Horrendous, wide-scale addiction took hold, evidenced

1983 AERO-MIYATA: K955434

K: YEAR CODE FOR 1982 [1983 MODEL YEAR]

955434: BUILD NUMBER

by the nefarious opium dens; the Qing dynasty was overwhelmed with the severity of the situation. Prohibiting importation, they confiscated 20,000 chests of the contraband. Great Britain retaliated, destroyed Chinese junks, extracted huge concessions (called unequal treaties) and acquired Hong Kong in addition to the control of multiple port cities. This was the first of two such 'Opium Wars.'

Miyata was a master gun-maker, highly respected, working under the shogunate through the ancient patronage systems. Under the Meiji Restoration program, such arrangements were disbanded. Eisuke Miyata headed to Tokyo in 1881 and made his services available to all. It was an age of change—of wars abroad and trade exhibitions at home, new relationships between makers and merchants, of imports from America and Great Britain, of reformed tradition and anxious innovation. Japan would emulate the Western powers' imperialistic ambitions. In 1895 war with China was prosecuted and, after a string of victories, China lost their suzerainty over the Korean peninsula as well as their tributes from that state. Japan was increasingly seen as the principal power of the East, a perception that later became a certainty after the Russo-Japanese war. Russia also had imperialistic ambitions for the Korean peninsula. Japan wanted to preserve their sphere of influence and attacked the Russian ships in Port Arthur (now Port Lüshun). Aided by British intelligence, Japan secured victory in 1905. The war was an indication of the type of carnage industrialization could wreak: both sides suffered tremendous casualties in what is sometimes referred to as the first 'modern war,' armaments-wise. This was the first modern conflict where an Asian state bested a Western power, and the result was the greatly fortified imperial standing of Japan: their influence would long be unchallenged in Taiwan Region and the Korean Peninsula.

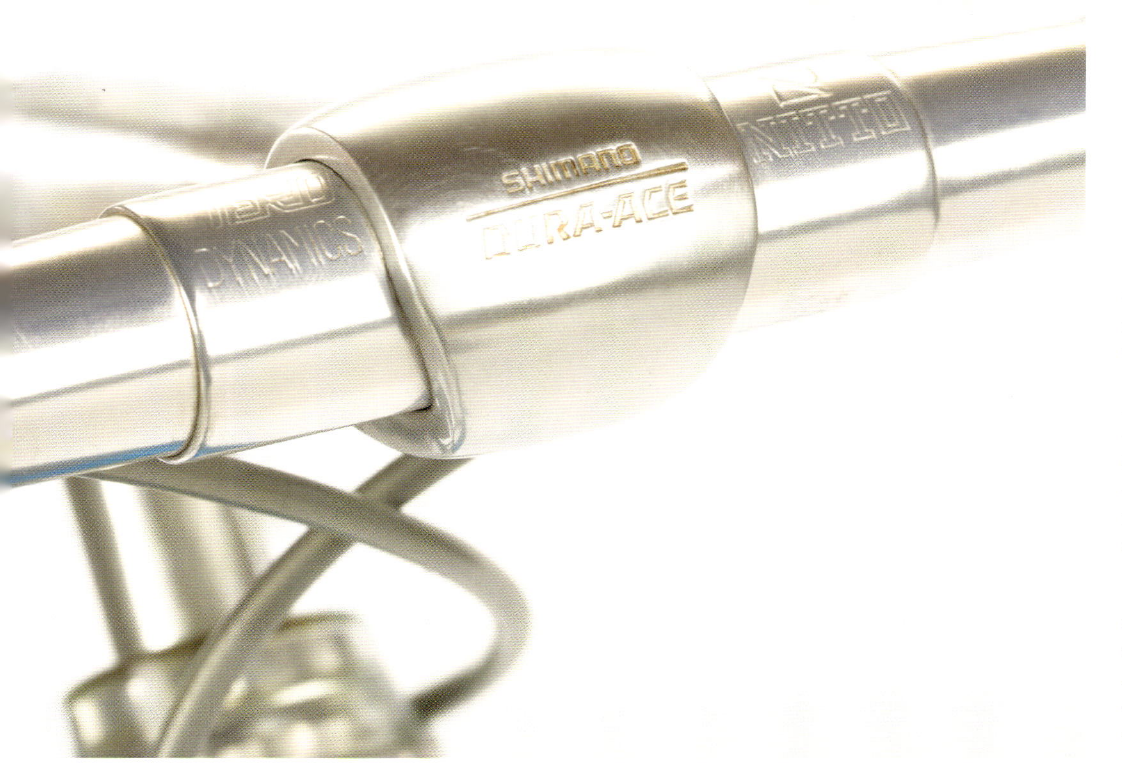

Tsunoda produced the greatest quantity of aerodynamic bicycles. Miyata was the second highest producer during the exciting, albeit short-lived, aero era. The Team Aero also wore the inimitable Miyata blue livery, but without a secondary color. The lugless headtube construction did not provide a distinctive area for another color; the bicycle might have appeared less streamlined with the gold accent.

The Aero Miyata was offered in 1982 and 1983. As with all of the Japanese aeros, they were high-, or highest-specification offerings equipped with Shimano's post EX Dura-Ace line, the exquisite AX aerodynamic groupset.

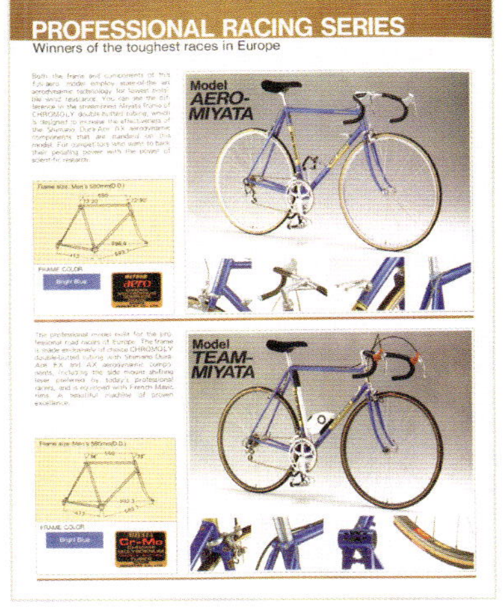

PROFESSIONAL RACING SERIES

Winners of the toughest races in Europe

Model AERO-MIYATA

FRAME COLOR

Bright Blue

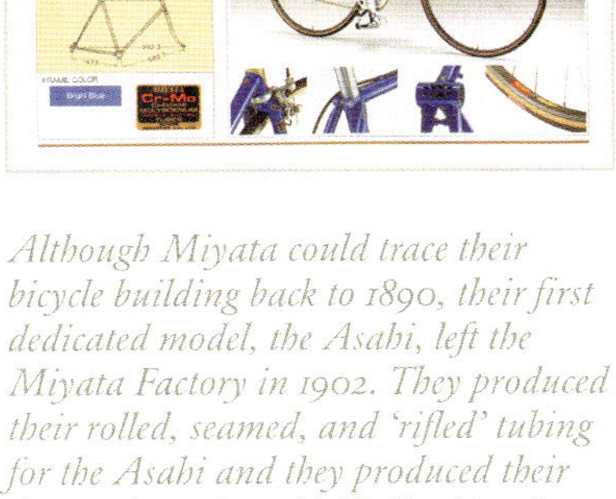

Model TEAM-MIYATA

FRAME COLOR

Bright Blue

Although Miyata could trace their bicycle building back to 1890, their first dedicated model, the Asahi, left the Miyata Factory in 1902. They produced their rolled, seamed, and 'rifled' tubing for the Asahi and they produced their drawn, butted, and 'rifled' tubing for the Aero, eighty years later.

Miyata would produce more Asahis in an average month then they would Aeros in their entirety. Another significant difference from that time until 1982 was the percentage of in-house components being manufactured. The Asahi was squarely based on an American import, the Cleveland model, from H. A. Lozier & Co. Most of the parts for those first bicycles were American-made as well. Over the first decade of building the Asahi, Miyata would begin to make most parts in-house.

It would not be long before the Asahi models were fitted with Japanese parts; Miyata could concentrate on frame-building and assembly. Miyata retained the capability of milling and drawing their own steel, a distinction that provided a valuable competitive advantage.

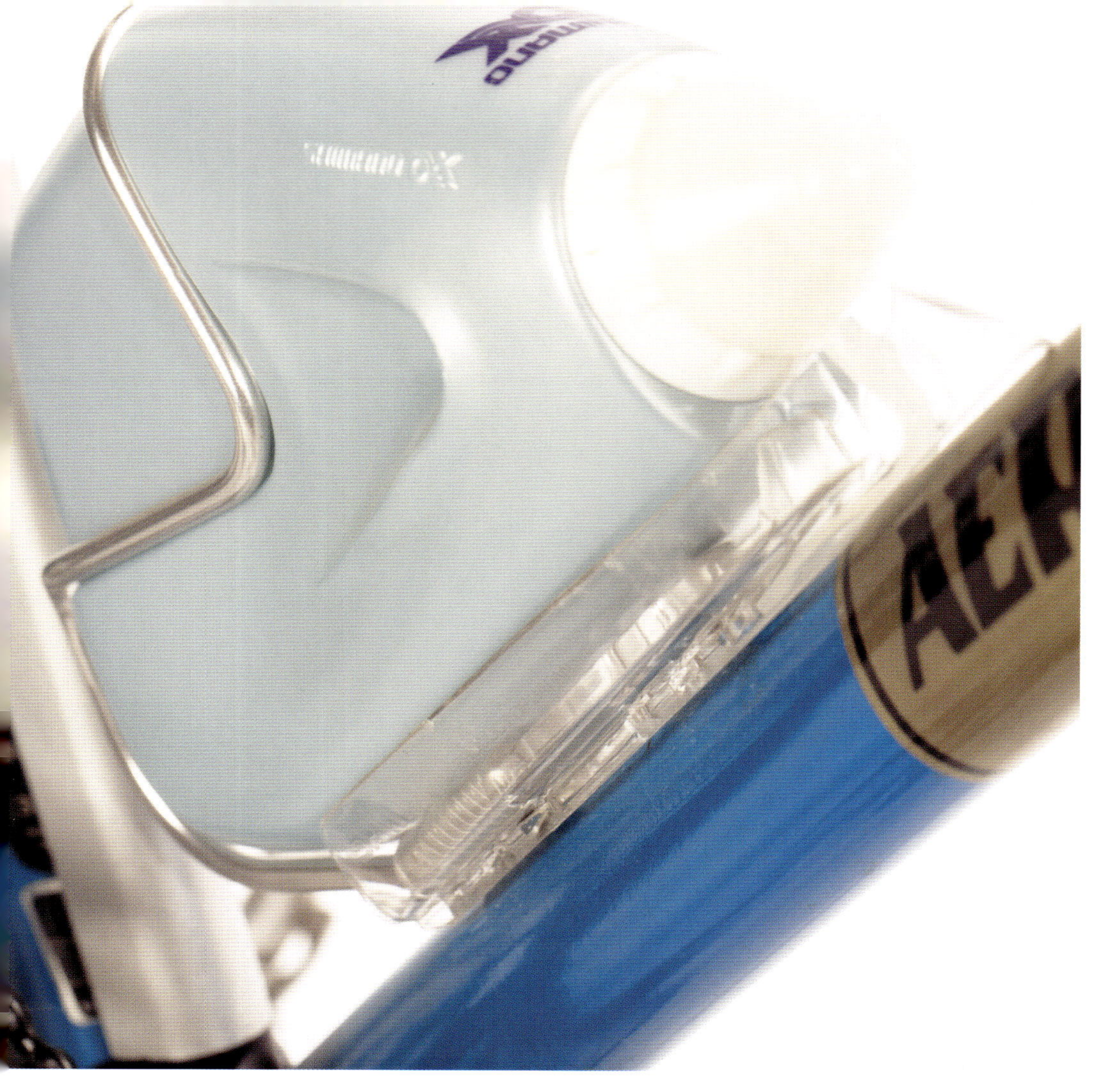

The Aero-Miyata was a fully lugless build sporting a sloping fork crown and internally routed brake cable housing and gear shifting cables—it was a masterpiece of the bicycle arts.

Either Miyata were not entirely forthcoming, or they were running extremely thin sidewalls in a tube profile that would be weaker than round tubes, because they cataloged their aero bicycles at 21.5 pounds. The tubes were not butted, but had a sharper tear-drop shape to add the requisite strength to the lightest of all production aerodynamic bicycles.

They specified Wolber tubular tires and the aero-profile 32-hole Araya ADX-2 *rims, along with the entire Shimano aero groupset (the Dura-Ace* AX*). One quirk of Miyata was their use of Italian thread specification for their headsets. The entire Japanese industry specified English thread for both headset and bottom bracket; Miyata mixed Italian and English standards, even on this aero model.*

UP
OUTSIDE

Although racing machines monopolized the first pages of the catalogs (until road bicycles lost that perch as the 1980s progressed) touring bicycles were the stars of the boardroom; they sold in higher quantities and provided a more ergonomic 'package' for consumers. The immensely respected Sheldon Brown said that the "mid-80s Miyata 1000 was possibly the finest off-the-shelf touring bike available at the time."

The 1984 model utilized Shimano Deore derailleurs known as the 'Deerhead' because of the endearing little pictograph. They were endowed with Shimano's 'Centeron' feature, which detected lateral chain tension and centered the cage on the nearest cog.

1984 MIYATA 1000: M 272921

M: YEAR CODE FOR 1984

27291: BUILD NUMBER

In 1890, Miyata formalized his operations in Sumida (Tokyo Prefecture) by establishing Miyata Gun Works. One day, shortly after opening this shop, a foreigner entered and asked if they had the capabilities to repair a bicycle. They did so, and then, as an experiment, embarked on building a complete machine. It was a fabulous project that took six workers about a month to complete. This event, and the 19th Century American bicycle industry, would have a cogent impact on Eitaro Miyata, Eisuke's second-oldest son.

In the late 1890s, American bicycle exports would excel and then ebb rapidly. Domestically, American manufacturing would peak in 1899 with nearly two million bicycles manufactured. Five years later, the number would fall to about one-eighth this total as the automobile age arrived and American bicycle manufacturing receded. Conversely, Japan would see a robust and steady increase until World War II. In terms of dollars and percentages, Japan received

DIA-COMPE

about 11% of USA exports between 1897 and 1899. At the peak, about one hundred thousand dollars in export value arrived in Japan. In today's currency, this would be about three million in wholesale value.

In that early period, domestic workshops could build two or three bicycles per month. Buyers would sometimes gang up on the fabricators, extracting the best price by approaching the establishments in groups of three or four and talking down the price. Advantageously, the entirety of the month's production would be accounted for, but profits were slim. It was a different story for importers. With a sizable mark-up they touted exclusivity and quality of the imported products; a single sale could net a month's salary for some agents. This was usually the result of renting bicycles (the only way the uninitiated learned to ride) and building this relationship toward a sale. Despite this, both fabricators and importers routinely went out of business.

The year 1900 was a watershed for Miyata. The great Eisuke Miyata, patriarch of the family, would pass away at the age of 60. In 1902, a bold stroke was taken: Miyata Gun Factory would be renamed, the company would shift its focus and 'beat their rifles into bicycles.' The new company no longer made a reference to gun production; it was simplifeid to: Miyata Factory (Miyata Seisakusho).

Every distinguished family had their sporting rifle, their camera, and had, or would have, their bicycle. Bicycles were no longer novelties upon the streets of Sumida and the rest of Tokyo's environs. The Miyata family would fulfil this demand under the direction of Eitaro Miyata, who had graduated from the prestigious Kyoto University with a degree in Mechanical Engineering. In an act of deference and honor to his father, the younger Miyata assumed his father's given name (a Japanese practice of craftsmen at that time) and now this 'second-generation

1985 TEAM-MIYATA: NS63594

N: YEAR CODE FOR 1985

S: FORTNIGHT CODE [19th FORTNIGHT]: LATE SEPTEMBER

63594: BUILD NUMBER

Eisuke' would unveil the 'all-Japanese Miyata.' It was to be their Asahi model (the name references morning's first light, or the earliest moments of the rising sun). The Asahi was *not quite* all Japanese: the exemplar for the machine was the Cleveland, an import from America's H. A. Lozier & Co. Similarities included the general frame angles and construction style.

Multiple components for the Asahi were sourced from American companies, such as spokes from Torrington and tires from Goodrich. Precision ball bearings were also of American manufacture, but the heart of the Asahi was Miyata's proprietary steel tubing. Each main tube possessed the hidden hallmark of the firm. They were rifled, the legacy of gunmaking. On the inner wall ran five grooves, each a helix—a lateral, parallel slice, spiraling from end to end. Rifling served to impart spin to a bullet, improving both its trajectory and accuracy as it exited

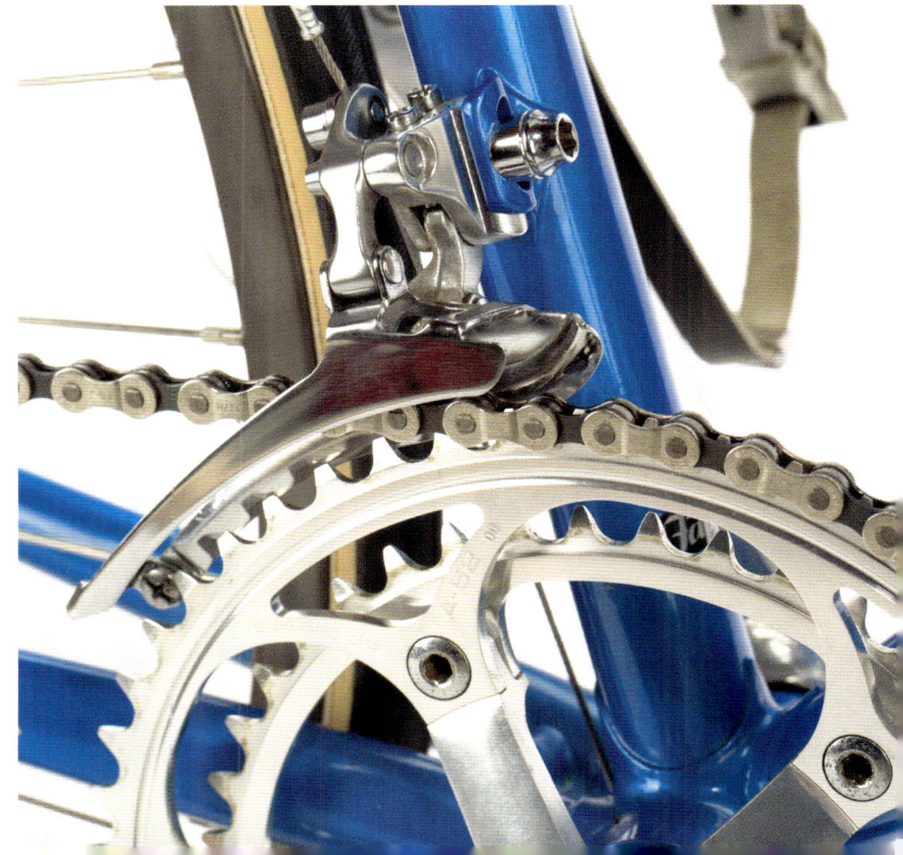

As Miyata approached their 100th birthday, they were the only bicycle manufacturer in the world manufacturing their own tubing for premium bicycles. Steel was at its zenith, even though titanium and aluminum, as well as carbon frames, had made their inroads.

In an uncanny and oddly prescient way, Miyata had predestined the duration of their export journey. For their serial number designation, a simple alphabased system had been instituted way back in the year 1972. Their 'Racer,' a smart and captivating 10-speed with a baby-blue and chrome livery had serial numbers beginning with 'A' followed by a numerical build sequence.

One year later, in year 'B' (1973), the Japanese bicycle market was still expanding rapidly—the nation produced nearly ten million finished bicycles—but the first oil crisis hit. An economy that had grown by ten percent a year for two full decades suddenly contracted. The yen, which had been pegged at 360 to the dollar, was allowed to float.

Years 'C,' 'D,' and 'E' were each subsequently more challenging than the former. The second oil crisis, in the year 'H' (1979), tripled the cost of oil for the second time within a decade. Miyata weathered the storm because they had a sizable domestic market. However, even the Japanese market was reaching saturation. As for year 'M,' the headline in Japan Cycle Press (May 1984) sadly proclaimed: "Gloomy Tone for Exports to the U.S." This was also a peak domestic year—the bicycle market was being hit from both sides.

It is something of a marvel, then, that for years 'N' and 'O' magic was still emanating from Miyata Industry. The Team model (that had now acquired the black and blue livery) was met with extremely favorable reviews. It was simply a jewel of integrated production. If this were not enough, the Team Miyata Pista (in bright blue and gold) was offered in the same year. It was painfully beautiful, but less than a hundred were manufactured. There were still many great years ahead but the beautiful years of 'Legacy Blue' were coming to a close.

the barrel. But these tubes of the Asahi would never know the smell of gunpowder; the advantage of rifling would be some strength through increased surface area and some deducted weight through the cutting away of material—a win-win.

The Asahi model garnered a critically important accolade on its very first birthday, winning a meritorious 3rd prize at the *National Industrial Promotion Fair*. Industrial exhibitions and World's Fairs were the rage of the day. *The Great Exhibition of the Works of Industry of All Nations* (aka *The Great Exhibition*) had been held in London in 1851 at the Crystal Palace. The French introduced these technical exhibitions as far back as the French revolution, but the 'Great Exhibition' was the premier International example. Chicago hosted the wildly popular *World's Fair: Columbian Exposition* of 1893. The Japanese pavilion, built for this last event, was an exquisite recreation of Hō-ō-den (Phoenix Hall), a sacred Buddhist temple. The pavilion was filled with significant historical treasures. It is noteworthy that the premier fairground location was given for its construction, underscoring (and advertising) the significance of the excellent international relationship that the United States and Japan enjoyed at that time.

According to a 70th-anniversary account of Miyata's history (published by the company in 1959), the firm set quality standards through team inspections and the use of limit gauges in 1907. These principles were introduced by Hikonosuke Miyata, 'the younger Eisuke,' who kept abreast of technical advancements in America. This was an impressive development. A limit gauge is a two-stage measuring device that permits a (properly dimensioned) component to pass through the first stage, but not through the next. There are many possible configurations for such a tool—the simplest are U-shaped limit gauges. Say, for example, one wants to check the external dimension of a tube: if the tube cannot pass through the mouth of the U, this would be indicative of excessive diameter. Conversely if the tube reaches the base of the U it would

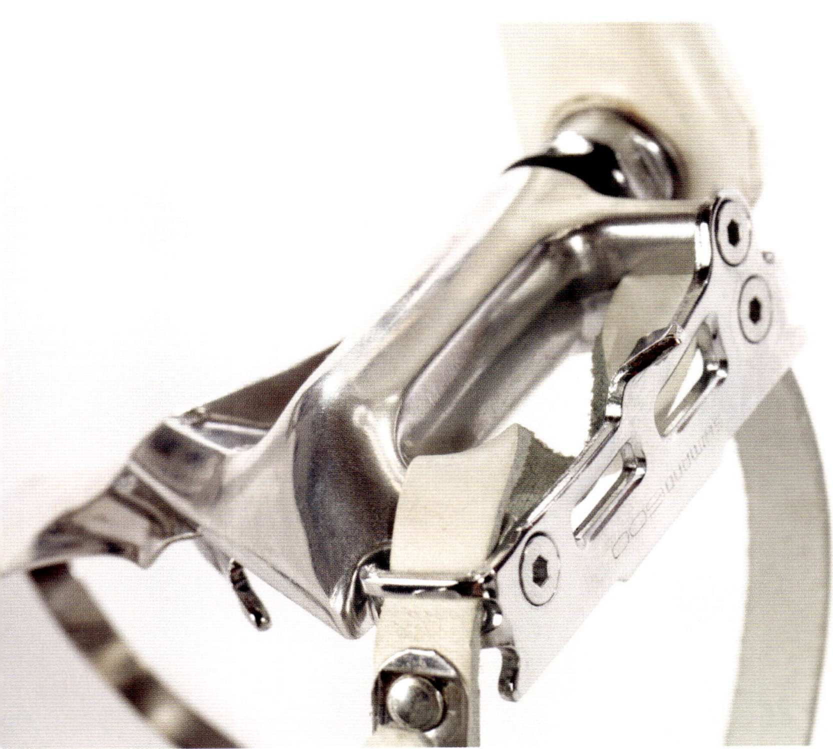

prove that the component was of too small a diameter. Ideally the tube will 'go' into the U, but 'not-go' to the base. Hence the terms 'go, no-go,' or 'pass, not-pass.'

A limit gauge has to be made to tolerances ten times those of the manufactured component. If Miyata was fabricating a tube with a dimension of 1 inch, then the limit gauge would have needed an opening of 1.005 at the first stage, and a 'limit' of .995 at the second stage. Today, uniformity is a given; then, the capability of uniformity was the gateway to interchangeability, a leap in industrialization. Instead of three workers building a bicycle as an integrated device of codependent measurements parts could be accurately, rapidly, and economically made. These standardized parts could then be interchanged with all the others: the larger the scale of the company, the more valuable the ease of interchangeability.

1988 MIYATA 1200: PS15299

P: YEAR CODE FOR 1987 [1988 MODEL YEAR]

S: FORTNIGHT CODE [19th FORTNIGHT]: LATE SEPTEMBER

15299: BUILD NUMBER

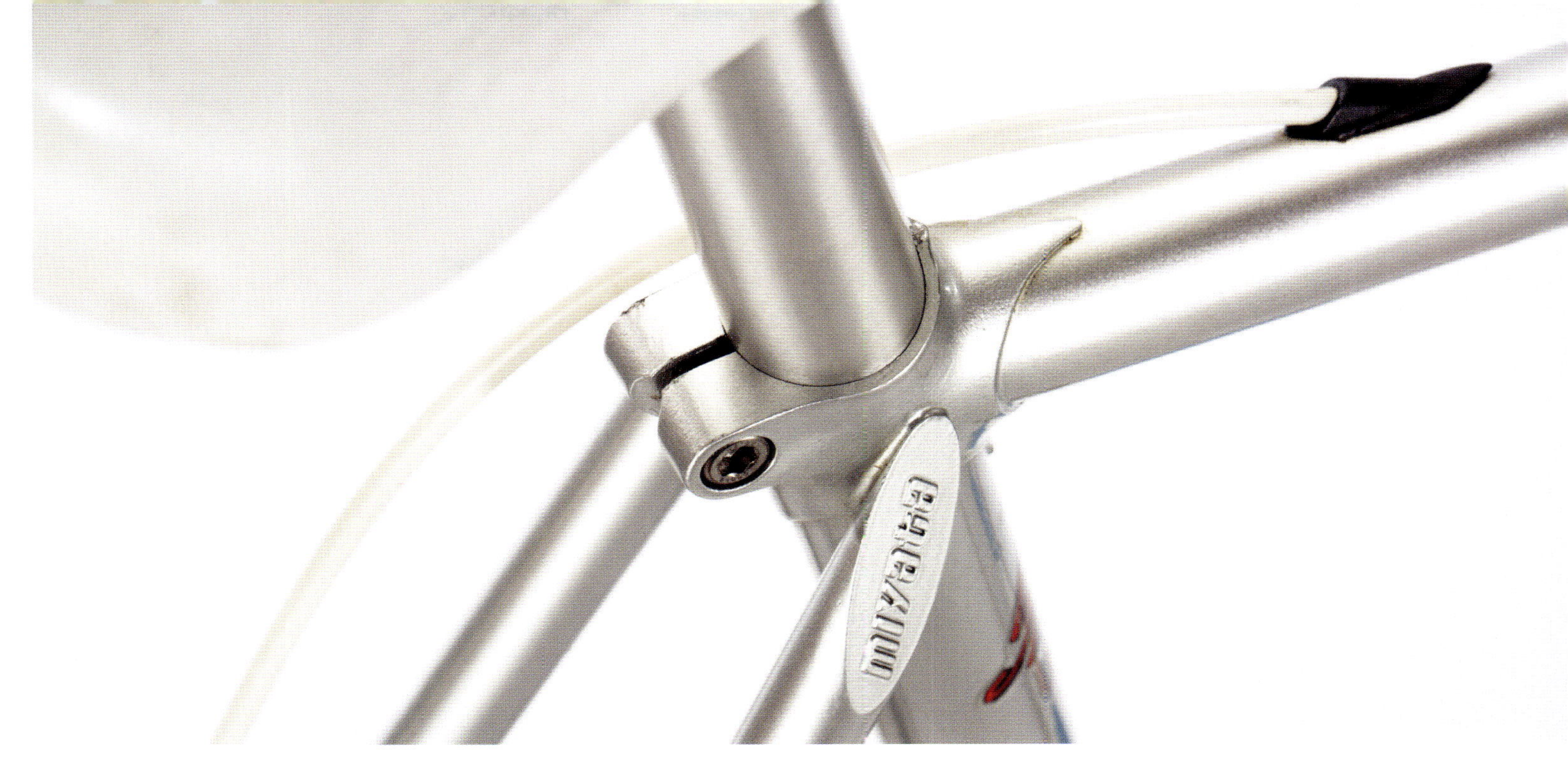

Bicycles with the 'P' designation at the beginning of their serial numbers were from the year 1987, a watershed year for Miyata. The steel–bicycle–making process was very highly automated and this was now supplemented by their Carbon Tech 1000, 3000, and 5000 models; as well as an entire line of Alumitech machines (the 6000 series).

The top steel model would still be the Team Miyata and a new Aero model, now configured as a time trial 'funny bike,' would cut through air resistance by lowering and tucking-in the rider—this instead of teardrop shaped tubes.

Miyata finaliy began to brag about their tubing in a significant way. They referred to the rifling as 'splined.' This made sense, as it was the opposite of a series of cut grooves; most of the spiral was now cut away. This left strips of material running along the length of the tube, which were called splines. Miyata catalogs explained just what was happening in those inner chambers.

For 1988 (alpha year 'Q'), most of the models would be identified purely through numbers. The 1200 was introduced as a triathlon machine. At its heart a splined-triple-butted Miyata thoroughbred, it was now spec'd for a new kind of beauty; buyers with disposable income—distinction that was a trifle more tasteful, if superficial.

Miyata became a centenarian in the year 1990. In that year they created the Century model: a black carbon-fiber showpiece with 14K-gold lugwork and a Brooks Pro saddle. It was also the last year for the steel-framed Team model. It was equipped with the same highest-specification Dura-Ace groupset as the Century, so it went out on a high note.

Serial numbers beginning with 'V' would signify bicycles for the 1992 model year; the top steel machine would be the Nine 16. The Nine 16 would continue into 1995, Miyata's alpha-year 'X.' The very last year of Miyata (USA) exports would be in 1997, year 'Z.' It's as if they planned it that way. Koga-Miyata would continue for three additional years, until 2000, the final year Miyata made their very own steel tubing.

Miyata was also a pioneer in their treatment of employees. They gave all employees Sundays off and never had employees working late into the evenings. On a bimonthly basis they invited a Protestant pastor to give talks on self-improvement, and they regularly sent employees to vocational schools in order to gain additional training. By the end of 1907, they were producing over one thousand bicycles per month. They would set up an extensive dealer network for domestic production that was only rivaled by Nichibei Shoten (who were mostly distributing imported machines, now from Great Britain). They would branch out into motorcycles, and even two-cylinder automobiles before, once again, their manufacturing capabilities would be swallowed up by war.

In 2012, one hundred and ten years after Miyata unveiled their Asahi, they produced the Miyata Japon. Finished in Legacy Blue, it features the highly proprietary 4130 S.S.T.B. chromoly tubes. The 4130 refers to the SAE steel specification of chromium and molybdenum, alloyed with other elements such as manganese and silicon. The last letters, 'TB,' refer to the triple-butted composition. The first two letters, 'SS,' convey a truly special designation: Spiral Spline. The main tubes are rifled; five grooves, each a helix running in parallel, spiraling from end to end.

4130 S.S.T.B. is fabricated by Kaisei using steel that Miyata still held in stock from their export heyday. Holding the frame, the consistent diameter of the main tubes provide no indication of the complex internal network of splines and butts—an interplay that honors the company's past, yet celebrates today's metallurgical possibilities. Is it truly necessary to put those splines in there? Of course it is; that's the fingerprint of Miyata's patriarch, Eisuke Miyata, gunmaker to the shogunate, spiraling down the center of every tube of steel.

Miyata's logo, a circle with a series of square cut teeth running along the outer perimeter, appears to be a gear. (A perfectly acceptable visual device to represent a bicycle company, a pictograph conveying mechanical rotation.) In actuality, it reflects the cut-away within a cross section of a tube. One could argue that the symbol conveys what a Miyata is on the outside, as well as the inside. The last in the line of Miyata's classic steel machines was their Nine 16. The model made it to the end of the 20th Century. After fifteen years their spiral splined triple butted tubing, from original stocks, came back to life through Kaisei, deservedly so…

FUJI

NICHIBEI FUJI CYCLE COMPANY, LTD., TOKYO/OSAKA

1899

Note: some documents of the Nichiebei Shoten, Ltd., cite 1897 as the founding year of the company.

At the age of 27, Kyujiro Okazaki leaves his employment at Mitsui Bussan, marries, and establishes Nichibei Shoten Company. He then sails to America and secures import arrangements with Leroy Bicycles. Soon after Kyujiro imports the Crescent, and the 'Built like a Watch' Sterling (the bicycle brand Annie Oakley, American sharpshooter, rode).

1917

By 1915, Nichibei Shoten imports the Rudge-Whitworth line from Great Britain. These are prestige bicycles with greater profits to the company. WWI disrupts supply lines when a German craft sinks the British ship carrying Rudge-Whitworths to Nichibei. In 1917, Nichibei commences the construction of a factory based on blueprints supplied by Rudge.

1928

Rudge-Whitworth ends license with Nichibei in 1928; Nichibei begins manufacturing Fuji models. The Rudge Monarch model becomes the Fuji Monarch.

1935

In 1933, Mitsubishi Trading Company supports Nichibei trial export efforts to China and the West.

In 1935 Senri Moriya becomes managing director of Nichibei Shoten.

1951

In 1951 Nichibei Shoten becomes the Nichibei Fuji Cycle Company, Ltd.

1957

Toshuku Japan and Fuji establish an export agreement, constructing bicycles under contract for third parties.

1964

Fuji's Dr. Shoichiro Sugihara both designs the bicycles for the 1964 Olympic team and serves as cycling team's coach.

1971

Toshuku establishes Fuji America and private-label models are discontinued. Fuji presents its line of bicycles at the Hilton Hotel in New York, officially launching the Fuji brand as an export model.

1998

After mergers and reorganizations, Nichibei Fuji declares bankruptcy. Advanced Sports Inc. (ASI) assumes the Fuji name and distribution rights. In 2004, Ideal Bicycle Corp., a Taiwanese manufacturer, invests in ASI.

2005

Fuji continues as major brand under ASI, reestablishing ties to Japan with the storied importer/exporter Akibo corporation (formerly the Asia Machinery Trading Company, Ltd.). Akibo designs bicycles for the domestic Japanese market. Fuji releases the 111th anniversary model (2011) with Japanese-built frame.

201

The Fuji Newest was debuted in 1971, at the 12th International Cycle Show. From the outset, Fuji would convey distinction through exclusiveness and a rarified lifestyle, as with this 'Silver Cloud' poster from 1973.

According to Consumer Guide (1973), it took two builders four days to completely prepare and construct a Fuji Newest frame. The Newest was built with Fuji's proprietary 331 tubing. Based on micrometer readings of the tubes and the weight of the completed frame, the model used Ishiwata's 022 'Speed Galant' tubing set. However, Fuji could use different suppliers under the umbrella '331' tubing identification for the Newest, Finest, Ace, Professional, and other top-tier models.

The year was 1971. On a rainy, late winter's morning in New York City, Nichibei Fuji initiated their third historical phase. In the distant past they imported American, then British bicycles. Later, they became domestic manufacturers under license; later still, domestic builders under their own badge. Recently, as a contract (private-label) exporter, they had tasted what it was like to be a ghost-builder, constructing machines for Sears, Roebuck, and Co., or Montgomery Ward. Something in this was lacking. Nichibei Fuji was ready to export under their own name; their time had come.

This debut would occur on March 7, at ten o'clock in the morning. The venue was the 12th International Bicycle Show, in the *lobby* of the Hotel Hilton on 59th Street. Within several years, Nichibei Fuji would become the leading Japanese bicycle exporter *as a percentage* of manufacturing and the most recognized Japanese brand.

Fuji was late in the process of registering for the event; by the time their application was received no more booths were available. Ironically, in what turned out to be ridiculously good fortune, the Fuji display was relegated to the lobby of the hotel. This assignment might have been a significant drawback, had it not been for Fuji's early marketing penchant. Whereas other manufacturers got their feet wet with moderately priced bicycles and then moved upmarket, Fuji came in strongly with top-tier models. They pitched to a retail clientele with disposable income, people who tended toward being first adopters. And these were precisely the people walking through the lobby of the hotel (and not so much those belonging to the wholesale crowd, meandering through the actual venue).

From this auspicious beginning Fuji would establish their niche for quality bicycles priced just above most competitors. Their advertising would reflect this. The Fuji Newest

1971 FUJI RACER "THE NEWEST": F6G08185

F: FACTORY AREA / BUILDER ID / FUJI BUILD
6: YEAR CODE FOR SHOWA ERA, 46 = 1971
G: MONTH CODE FOR JULY
08185: BUILD NUMBER

Fuji derived considerable pride from their frame-building prowess; a capability they actively promoted. To demonstrate the quality of frame construction, as well as reward important dealerships, they presented cut-away frames of the Fuji Newest to ten of their top sales performers.

These close-ups show the similarity to the Cinelli sc livery of slightly earlier vintage. The seat cluster area, however, was unique to Fuji. The filled wrap-around seatstay ending (cut laterally in the presentation frame) is impressive. This was Fuji's most time-intensive lug-work until the Design Series frames were released nearly fifteen years later.

A Nichibei Shoten division was maintained for export purposes after the Nichibei Fuji Cycle Company name was established in 1951. Exporting to America had been tried in the 1930s with little success due to very high import tariffs, the financial depression, and the general lack of desire for certain foreign goods during those years.

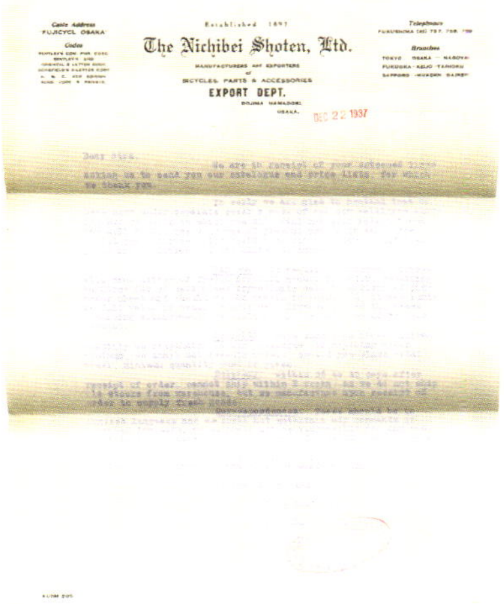

The Nichibei Shoten, Ltd.
EXPORT DEPT.

By the 1960s there were still pejorative perceptions of Japanese quality and provenance, but that challenge was soon overcome. Fuji grew to be a well recognized and well favored brand. The Fuji Newest remained unchanged for its second outing at the 13th International Cycling Show, still held at the Hilton Hotel in Manhattan.

model would be seen juxtaposed with a Rolls Royce or a Ferrari. The Fuji liveries were also very sophisticated, taking cues from the best Italian bicycles as well as from the color charts of luxury automotive lines, such as Mercedes Benz and Jaguar.

Fuji shared its historical character with another major Japanese bicycle firm, Maruishi Cycles. Both companies had their origins in the late 19th century as *Shoten* (or *Shokai*). These were Japanese stores or trading companies that imported lucrative foreign goods for the domestic market. In the 1890s, such lucrative foreign goods included American-made bicycles that were being manufactured at a break-neck pace in Chicago, Detroit, Milwaukee, Cleveland, Dayton, New York, and other cities of industry. The name Nichibei Shoten, Fuji's founding identity, was coined in direct response to this import arrangement—the words translate as *Japanese-American store*.

The parallels between the still-unfolding bicycle boom in 1960s and 1970s, and the bicycle craze of the late 1890s, were manifold. A major factor was a demand fueled by an untapped demographic that was purchasing for the first time (in the 1890s boom due to the appeal of the *safety bicycle* with its equally-sized tires; in the 1960s and 1970s, due to the ten-speed adult bicycle). In addition were technical and competitive shifts that made bicycles within the financial reach of more individuals. And, perhaps most importantly, a shift in social behavior that the bicycle purveyors first instigated and then fulfilled.

One factor, however, was decidedly inverted—in the 1960s and 1970s, American entrepreneurs looked eastward, toward Japan; in the 1890s Japanese entrepreneurs, looked westward, toward America. Travel and international merchandising was clearly fraught with risk in the late 19th century. Yet, for enterprising young men

1973 FUJI SPECIAL ROAD RACER "S-10S": K8G01299

K: FACTORY AREA / BUILDER ID / USA EXPORT DESIGNATION
8: YEAR CODE FOR SHOWA ERA, 48 = 1973
G: MONTH CODE FOR JULY
01299: BUILD NUMBER

BELT
FUJITA SADDLE MFG CO LTD
TOKYO

of Tokyo the potential for prosperity would appear commensurate with the risks taken. Kyujiro Okazaki, Fuji's intrepid founder, decided to take that risk.

Before setting off on his own, Okazaki worked for Mitsui Bussan, a trading company that was established under Japanese ownership in 1876. Many trading firms in the late 19th century were foreign concerns; Mitsui Bussan aimed to rectify that imbalance (it was the root company of several major Japanese corporations today, even though the original firm was dissolved by General McArthur's General Headquarters after WWII). Such independence was imbued within the spirit of Okazaki. People who knew him said that he would willingly "start from nothing." His life does appear to be a Horatio Algers 'rags to riches' adventure. When he arrived in America, it was noted that his clothes were shabby, but he commanded, and received, a good degree of respect. Later, these two trips to America would also build respect for his accomplishments back in Tokyo and Osaka.

The import arrangements that he contrived in America were good ones. Okazaki first contracted with a brand named *Leroy,* and some two years later with the well-recognized American manufacturer, *Sterling.* By the time he was thirty he had set up a successful store in Tokyo and was about to open up another facility in Osaka. However, as the 19th century closed, so too ended the American bicycle craze. The Nichibei name stuck, but Kyujiro turned his attention to Great Britain.

In 1905, Nichibei Shoten initiated arrangements with the Rudge-Whitworth factory. The story of Dan Rudge traces back to 1870. It was Rudge who developed early patents for ball-bearing wheels and pedals. Joseph Whitworth had developed the first system for thread dimension standards decades earlier. These thread standards would set

The Fuji Special Road Racer model s10-s succeeded on a level few might have foreseen or imagined. Everything about this bicycle was right from the first iteration. It was tough and reliable. It was a smooth, responsive riding machine that was perfectly suited to international roads and readily suitable to a non-Japanese (read: heavier) physique.

Consumer Reports magazine, through their style of objective praise, could not have been better advocates for the s10-s. In their January 1974 issue, they noted that the shifting ease was "far above average." The handling was recognized for being "nimble and precise." Pedal response was cited for being "well above average," and the overall ride was "more stable than most at low speeds." In 1976, they again praised the this backbone and breadwinner of the Fuji lineup.

The model, with continued improvements, remained cataloged until 1983. It may arguably be the most produced single model from the 10-speed age (the final model was an 18-speed variant). To this day, these bicycles are regularly found chained to poles throughout urban streets, many still bearing their original wheels and sundry parts. A quick tune-up and their "nimble and precise" handling proves comparatively undiminished after forty years.

the basis for English, and thereby future Japanese, norms. All ISO thread standards for bicycles are evolved from the work of Joseph Whitworth.

The open-palm emblem as used on the Rudge-Whitworth originated from the Whitworth side of the combination. Branding was an important part of modern Japanese culture, and the hand placed inside a spoked circle was an appealing graphical device. Kyujiro set pricing standards for any distributors or downstream sales facilities that sold the Rudge-Whitworth. These sales outlets were forming as the result of repair shops offering new or used bicycles for sale. Through sound management practice, Nichibei Shoten would establish a sterling relationship with Rudge; a relationship that set the tone for the future of Fuji, and influenced the Japanese bicycle industry in general.

One concern for Kyujiro was that the Rudge, as with most of the better British models, cost about twice the

1974 FUJI RACER "THE ACE": K9B10021

K: FACTORY AREA / BUILDER ID / USA EXPORT DESIGNATION
9: YEAR CODE FOR SHOWA ERA, 49 = 1974
B: MONTH CODE FOR FEBRUARY
10021: BUILD NUMBER

price of near-equivalent American bicycles. However, their image and prestige value, among the growing number of would-be Japanese purchasers, could justify such an outlay: the Rudge-Whitworth cost 250 yen in 1905. The value of the yen then being about one-thousand times its value today.

Bicycle-wise, industry-wise, Japan-wise, and world-wise, the first decades of the 20th century were to become increasingly tumultuous ones for Kyujiro and Nichibei Shoten. Before deeper challenges set in, there were numerable successes: before 1910 Kyujiro had sold over 3,000 Rudge-Whitworths, including taking an order for 157 bicycles for the Tokyo post-office authorities. He'd set his sites on creating better parts supply procedures and building complete bicycles. In order to create a more stable marketing and selling environment, a mutually beneficial arrangement would be devised with Rudge.

Fuji had a close relationship with the Fujita brothers, owners of Fujita Saddle and makers of 'Y.F.C. Seamless' racing saddles. Fuji specified the exotic 'Nu-Buck' variant for their 1974 Ace model, complimenting the equally exotic Pearl Orange paint. The big story was that the Fuji Ace was the first production bicycle equipped with full Shimano Dura-Ace components. Shimano had begun a new line under the 'Crane' name. When the front derailleur proved dimensionally inadequate for tight wheel-to-frame clearances, they moved to create a new competition-level groupset. The Dura-Ace name, already used for individual components, would now become the paramount brand under Shimano. The level of technical and marketing support would set new standards for bicycle components; and the stories surrounding the evolution of the Dura-Ace line would become as exciting as the components themselves. The most brilliant of these took place in the fall of 1983 at the second Interbike show in Las Vegas; on day one, all of Shimano's displays were draped in black cloth. At midnight that evening SunTour's slant parallelogram patent expired. Boom—the New Dura-Ace 7400 SIS groupset, the world's new leader in shifting precision, was dramatically unveiled the next day.

The plan would be for Nichibei to build, under license, the British marque for domestic sale in Japan (as well as export to other Asian nations).

The relationship was initially so strong that a new factory was planned and blueprints from Great Britain were sent to Nichibei Shoten, providing for the construction of a state-of-the art bicycle-making factory. However, as the industrial relationship strengthened, world politics continued to deteriorate. WWI forced disruption of world trade. As the war between Germany and Great Britain intensified, Rudge-Whitworth turned their efforts to manufacture of munitions. The Japanese Navy allied itself to England, partially as a result of the Anglo-Japanese alliance (an agreement signed between the two nations in 1905), partially in effort to project Japanese power internationally, and partially to secure or expand into territories that were held by Germany. Japan's most

critical role, from the British perspective, was the Japanese securement of the vital sea lanes, permitting (though still precariously) maritime movement through areas of both the Pacific and Indian oceans.

As the conflict advanced, the Nichibei-Rudge relationship became increasingly unsupported from the British side. Two disasters befell the alignment: in 1915, a large supply of bicycles to Japan from Rudge-Whitworth was lost at sea when the trade ship carrying the cargo was sunk by a German war vessel. Then, when the promising new Nichibei factory was complete and awaiting the arrival of British engineers for its start-up and implementation, no personnel arrived. The war effort completely engulfed British manufacturing, as well as the engineering departments; no staff were spared for previous arrangements. This had a disastrous ramification: the company pushed ahead without vital consultation and a massive fire broke out at the new factory. By this time, a confluence of challenges led to a simple new mission for Okazaki Kyujiro—to build a fully domestic, premium bicycle.

Kyujiro always envisioned a stronger parts-making environment for the industry, so he helped to form a consortium to do so. *Dainippon* was formed, a company that would be well-poised decades later when the bicycle boom was underway to supply a wide range of parts. They went by the three-letter code *DNB*—some readers may recall that the first three Japanese manufacturers of derailleurs would be Shimano, SunTour, and DNB. Nichibei Shoten joined in by initiating the manufacture of Fuji-branded chains.

By 1922, Nichibei was able to begin reimporting the Rudge line. By this time, the supply of quality bicycles was sufficient to foster price-cutting competition; Nichiebei could no longer hold such stringent price controls.

1976 FUJI PROFESSIONAL: 75K50034

75: BUILD YEAR 1975 [1976 MODEL YEAR]
K: MONTH CODE FOR NOVEMBER
5: BUILD LEVEL CODE: PROFESSIONAL LEVEL
0034: BUILD NUMBER

Professional

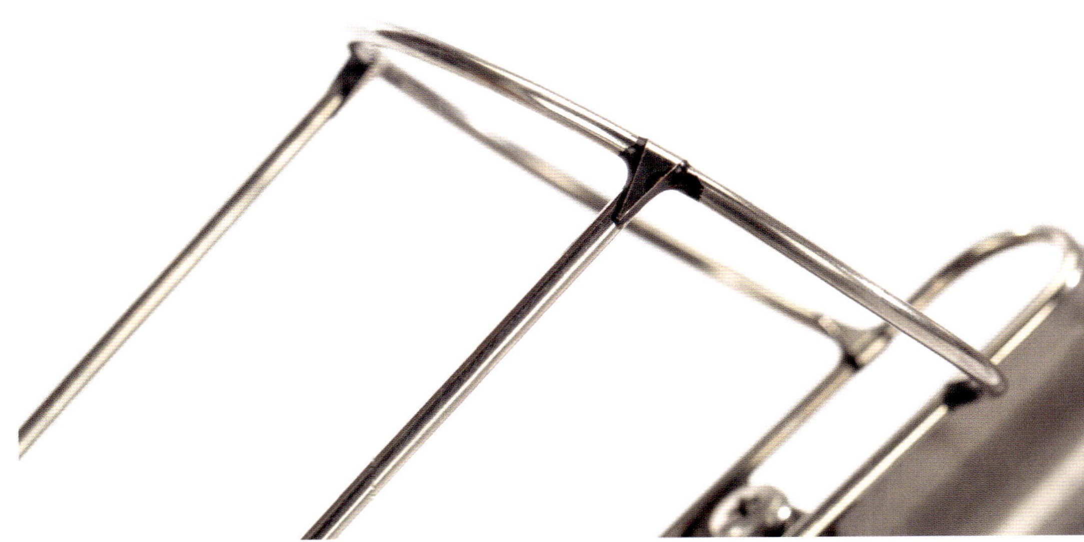

ROAD RACER MODEL PROFESSIONAL

SPECIFICATION

FRAME: Hand-made.

GEAR & CRANKS: "SUGINO" model MIGHTY VICTORY 1/2" x 3/32" x 47 and 52 T. double chainwheels. With 6-3/4" light alloy forged cotterless cranks.

WHEELS: Tyre & Tubes – "SOYO" model #70, 27" x 1-1/8" Tubular racing tyre with French pattern valves.

Rims – "UKAI", 27" x 1-1/8" Racing model light alloy tubing rims 36 x 36 holes.

Hubs – "SUNSHINE" Road Racing, light alloy small flanged quick release hubs, 9 x 10 mm spindle.

Front derailleur – "SUN TOUR" model CYCLONE.

Rear derailleur – "SUN TOUR" model CYCLONE.

Freewheel – "SUN TOUR" model WINNER 1/2" x 3/32" x 14, 15, 16, 18 and 22 teeth light alloy multiple freewheels.

HANDLEBAR: "NITTO" model UNIVERSIADE.

BRAKES: "GRAN COMPE" model #500.

CHAINS: "HOKOKU" Road Racing, 1/2" x 3/32".

PEDALS: "MIKASHIMA" model UNIQUE ROAD.

SADDLE: "FUJITA" model PROFESSIONAL.

ACCESSORIES: Frame pump – "KARASAWA" model PRIMUS DX, light alloy pump.

Water bottle – "SUGINO" white vinyl water bottle with cage.

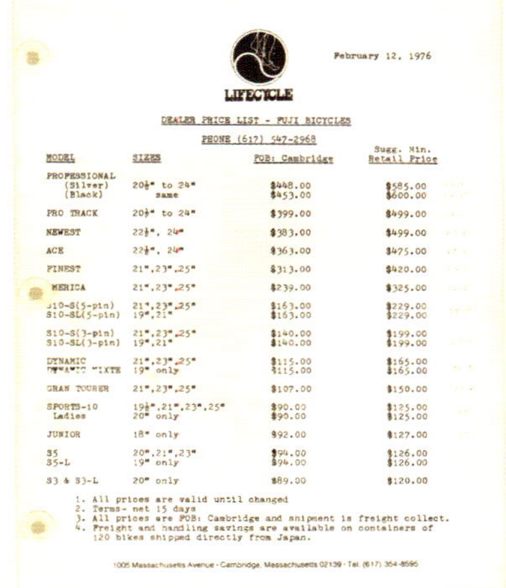

LIFECYCLE

February 12, 1976

DEALER PRICE LIST - FUJI BICYCLES

PHONE (617) 547-2968

MODEL	SIZES	FOB: Cambridge	Sugg. Min. Retail Price
PROFESSIONAL (Silver)	20½" to 24"	$448.00	$585.00
(Black)	same	$453.00	$600.00
PRO TRACK	20½" to 24"	$399.00	$499.00
NEWEST	22½", 24"	$383.00	$499.00
ACE	22½", 24"	$363.00	$475.00
FINEST	21",23",25"	$313.00	$420.00
MERICA	21",23",25"	$239.00	$325.00
S10-S(5-pin)	21",23",25"	$163.00	$229.00
S10-SL(5-pin)	19",21"	$163.00	$229.00
S10-S(3-pin)	21",23",25"	$140.00	$199.00
S10-SL(3-pin)	19",21"	$140.00	$199.00
DYNAMIC	21",23",25"	$115.00	$165.00
DYNAMIC MIXTE	19" only	$115.00	$165.00
GRAN TOURER	21",23",25"	$107.00	$150.00
SPORTS-10	19½",21",23",25"	$90.00	$125.00
Ladies	20" only	$90.00	$125.00
JUNIOR	18" only	$92.00	$127.00
S5	20",21",23"	$94.00	$126.00
S5-L	19" only	$94.00	$126.00
S3 & S3-L	20" only	$89.00	$120.00

1. All prices are valid until changed
2. Terms- net 15 days
3. All prices are FOB: Cambridge and shipment is freight collect.
4. Freight and handling savings are available on containers of 120 bikes shipped directly from Japan.

1005 Massachusetts Avenue · Cambridge, Massachusetts 02139 · Tel. (617) 354-8595

In 1975 Fuji produced a mid-year catalog with the newly introduced Professional, but it's generally regarded as a 1976 release. These first two years were pre-groupset builds, produced in silver-mink with subtle chrome-plated details on the fork crown and dropouts. A gorgeous prototype Nitto water-bottle cage was presented with the first examples.

The tubing used would continue to be Fuji's premium 331. (9658 would take over in 1983.) This was a semi-custom bicycle available in one-half inch increments (later one centimeter increments).

The Cyclone rear derailleur, controlled by ratcheting shifters, in conjunction with the beautifully crafted, light-weight rear SunTour Winner five-speed free-wheel, provided uncanny shifting speed and (pre-indexed shifting) precision.

Dr. Shoichiro Sugihara designed this bicycle for responsive road racing. The frame had a 74-degree headtube angle and an aggressive 75-degree seat tube angle. Uncanny shifting was matched to exceptional ride responsiveness.

Lifecycle's February 1976 pricesheet indicates the availability of a black variant, but only one black Professional is known to exist—the one that Gene Ritvo, the owner of Lifecycle, ordered for himself. It was Gene who championed the development of this new, high-specification flagship model.

FUJITA
SUPER

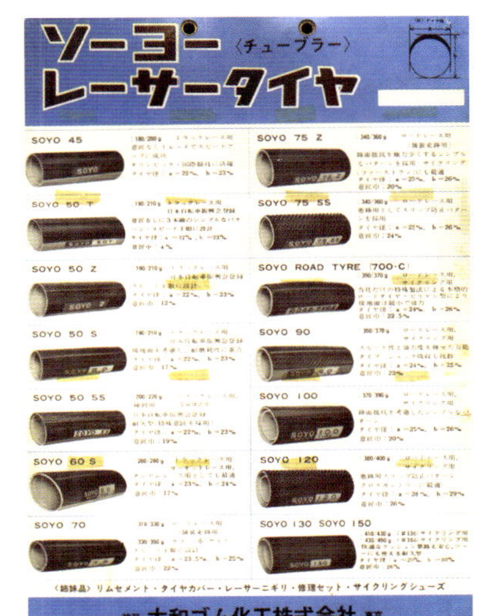

Daiwa Rubber and Chemical produced a range of tubular tires that were unlike anything coming from Europe. The compound was hard, nearly plastic-like. Soyo tubulars were well formed, durable, and quite puncture-resistant.

But they were brutal to stretch upon the rims. We'd leave them on hot tarmac for hours to make them more pliable, yet they'd still break the tiny capillaries in your palm as you struggled to stretch them over the rims. They fit so tightly you could almost forgo rim cement. Soyo still produces exquisite racing tires today under the parent company of Daiwabo—now easy to stretch on the rims, and necessitating quality rim cement.

As Tokyo advanced a more integrated bicycle manufacturing base, the city was struck by the Great Kanto earthquake of 1923. The devastation was of brobdingnagian proportions; nearly 150,000 souls were lost. What did not collapse or was structurally weakened was destroyed by fires that raged uncontrolled throughout the city. Nichibei's Tokyo facilities were, again, destroyed. Employees retreated to Kyujiro's residence.

In Osaka (and after rebuilding in Tokyo), Nichibei Shoten continued to construct the Rudge-Whitworth bicycle under license. The agreement had been signed back in 1915 (about the same time Rudge had turned to munitions production) and lasted thirteen years. As these years lapsed and the merchandising relationship ended, Nichibei's Fuji's chain sales surpassed the 100,000 mark. It was then, in 1928, that Nichebei Shoten began to roll out a fully constructed bicycle under the Fuji brand.

1977 FUJI PURSUIT: FG77320

F: FACTORY AREA / BUILDER ID / FUJI BUILD
G: MONTH CODE FOR JULY
77: BUILD YEAR 1977
320: BUILD NUMBER

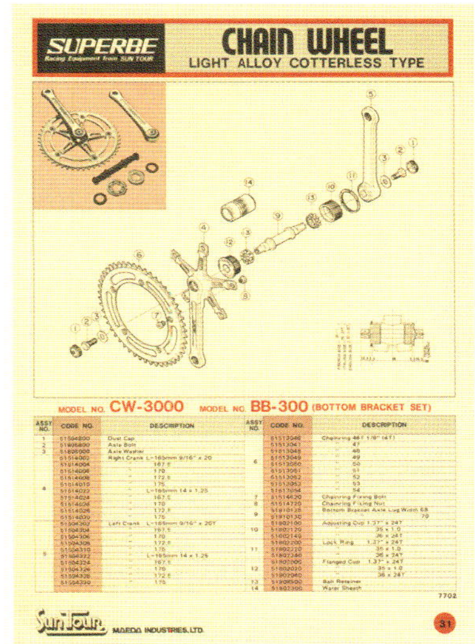

SUPERBE Racing Equipment from SUN TOUR

CHAIN WHEEL
LIGHT ALLOY COTTERLESS TYPE

MODEL NO. CW-3000 MODEL NO. BB-300 (BOTTOM BRACKET SET)

ASSY NO.	CODE NO.	DESCRIPTION	ASSY NO.	CODE NO.	DESCRIPTION
1	51504800	Dust Cap	6	51513046	Chainring 46T 1/8" (4T)
2	51906400	Axle Bolt		51513047	〃 47
3	51805000	Axle Washer		51513048	〃 48
4	51514002	Right Crank L=165mm 9/16" x 20		51513049	〃 49
	51514004	〃 167.5		51513050	〃 50
	51514006	〃 170		51513051	〃 51
	51514008	〃 172.5		51513052	〃 52
	51514010	〃 175		51513053	〃 53
	51514022	〃 L=165mm 14 x 1.25		51513054	〃 54
	51514024	〃 167.5	7	51514620	Chainring Fixing Bolt
	51514026	〃 170	8	51514720	Chainring Fixing Nut
	51514028	〃 172.5	9	51810128	Bottom Bracket Axle Lug Width 68
	51514030	〃 175		51810130	〃 70
5	51504302	Left Crank L=165mm 9/16" x 20T	10	51802100	Adjusting Cup 1.37" x 24T
	51504304	〃 167.5		51802120	〃 35 x 1.0
	51504306	〃 170		51802140	〃 36 x 24T
	51504308	〃 172.5	11	51802200	Lock Ring 1.37" x 24T
	51504310	〃 175		51802220	〃 35 x 1.0
	51504322	〃 L=165mm 14 x 1.25		51802240	〃 36 x 24T
	51504324	〃 167.5	12	51802000	Flanged Cup 1.37" x 24T
	51504326	〃 170		51802020	〃 35 x 1.0
	51504328	〃 172.5		51802040	〃 36 x 24T
	51504330	〃 175	13	51909500	Ball Retainer
			14	51907300	Water Sheath

7702

SunTour MAEDA INDUSTRIES, LTD.

31

In the summer of 1977 a very special prototype issued from the Nichibei Fuji works. This bicycle was called the Pursuit, and, like the thinly disguised sports cars of the 1950s, it was equally at home on road or track.

In the mid-1975 catalog tear sheets, Fuji listed the TF Sprint. Bicycling Magazine noted (July issue) that only twelve a month were to be exported, they are "definitely in the class of the custom frame builders' products." This is a road-enabled version of that rare TF Sprint. The appeal of the bicycle included Fuji's 331 tubing, sweet lugwork, flawless deep-black finish and chrome details, as well as the component set.

The first generation SunTour Superbe track group is specified for the bicycle. The low flange bolt-on hub is as pure as mechanical things can get—the aluminum alloy, the chrome, the black paint—resulting in composition that is visibly edible.

The Fuji Pursuit predates the urban 'fixie' by at least twenty-five years, although there are a number of bicycle messengers who claim an older provenance for multi-cum-fixed-gear machines. Fascinating details include the round fork blades and water-bottle cage fittings. The Pursuit is not a compromised fixie, but a truly modified track machine, as pure and clean as it gets—the very ideal of a fixie.

The 1977 Fuji Pursuit is not only one of a kind, it is unchanged from the original. Note how the Fujita black leather bar tape has shrunken and receded back from the lovely Nitto Crystem, an inch away from the ferrule of the Nitto 55 bars.

It is the semi-track version of two black Fuji pros, ex-Ritvo collection, sourced through Warren Koebler of Belmont Wheelworks. Although the original Soyo 300s were well aged, they withstood about 100 pounds of pressure.

I had the joy of riding through Central Park, across 57th street, and down 2nd Avenue. Easily passing the taxis once up to speed, the bicycle rode as a matt knife slicing through paper. In deference to those period Soyo 300 Special tubulars (plus fear), I took caution on turns. As I returned to my studio, I thought: "How can there be just one of these–such a crime of omission!"

GRAN-COMPE
JAPAN

With the turn of a pedal the Rudge Monarch, surely the most prestigious of the stately bicycles produced during the interwar years, became the Fuji Monarch. In the exquisite novel by Wu Ming-Yi, *The Stolen Bicycle*, a Fuji Monarch figures prominently. Wu notes that the Monarch was Emperor Hirohito's machine of record. The Monarch was such a stalwart machine that it was assuredly deserving of an emperor, and yet British Bobbys used home-grown versions faithfully into the late 1980s. The bicycle was truly a paradigm of elegance and practicality.

By 1930, two years after the introduction of the Fuji-named Monarch, combined Japanese domestic bicycle production would achieve manufacturing quantities of well over half a million machines. This was nearly equal, in one year, to all the bicycles domestically produced in all former years (1919 onward). It would be the first year that domestic manufacturing exceeded importation. Still, about 94,000 bicycles were imported, down from half a million the year before. One can see, therefore, that the import/export numbers had precisely reversed between 1929 and 1930. Imports would continually decline (with a spike or two) until well after the Second World War. As a portent of things to come, about 5,000 of the 1930 bicycles would be exported (primarily to Taiwan Region and Korea). This number would grow.

The early 1930s would see some important shifts for Nichibei Shoten. Their relationship with Mitsubishi Trading Company, Ltd. would begin in 1933. By this time Kyujiro Okazaki, having previously served in Japan's House of Representatives under the Imperial Diet in 1912 and again in 1916, took a break from politics and became the first president of Sagami Railroad Co., Ltd. (a line that runs within Kanagawa Prefecture to this day). Okazaki then returned to politics for another four terms as a

1977 "BLACK RITVO" FUJI PROFESSIONAL: 77B50003

77: BUILD YEAR 1977
B: MONTH CODE FOR FEBRUARY
5: SERIES CODE, PROFESSIONAL LEVEL
003: BUILD NUMBER

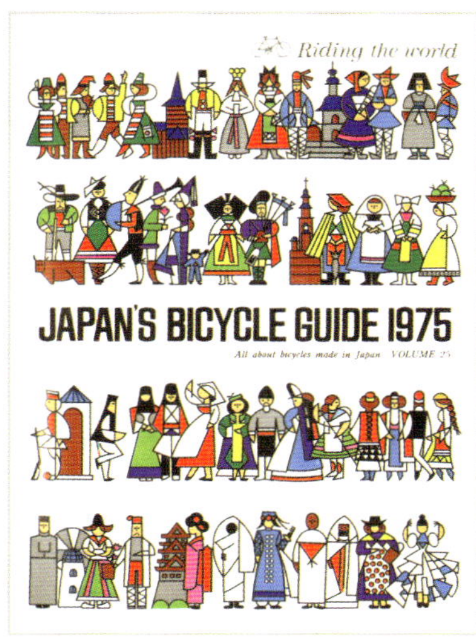

The Japan's Bicycle Guides began to feature increased information about the manufacturing capabilities of the domestic bicycle industry. The editorial committee shifted slightly year by year but always featured the 'movers and shakers' of the industry—those who deserved the most respect for industrial innovation and marketing perseverance. Individuals such as Kunio Shiraki (Chairman) of Miyata, Kiyoshi Tano (Deputy Chairman) of H. Tano & Company, Shozo Usui were members. In these years, Nichibei Fuji Cycle Company was represented by Toshio Kawasaki, head Auditor. The Executive Editor and Art Director was Yoshiya Kakita.

legislator. Meanwhile, Senri Moriya would be promoted to managing director after having served as president of Japan's National Bicycle Trade Association. One of Moriya's goals was to expand the Asian export market for Fuji bicycles and simultaneously endeavor to create viable sales inroads throughout the United States.

Both Asian and Western buyers were initially discouraged by the cost of the Fuji brand. In Asia, it was the raw cost of these now-superior bicycles; as for the United States, there were political costs as well. The American economic landscape of that time was challenging to any Japanese bicycle importer. The country was still deep in the decade of the great depression; consumers with the financial wherewithal to purchase a bicycle were not easily swayed to part with their money. Worse was this: import tariffs ranged from 30% upward, even reaching 50%. This meant that any shipment of arriving bicycles would immediately require a sizable payment to customs in order to secure the shipment. Finally, the same prejudice that would meet Japanese imports in the late 1960s was yet more keenly felt in the 1930s. There was an uptick in bicycle sales through that decade, but Japanese exports would not be a part of it.

As nations, once again, slipped into war and the Japanese theater of conflict expanded into China in 1937, opportunities dwindled further. With the signing of the Tripartite Pact (the alignment of Japan, Germany, and Italy in 1940), the door was slammed shut. A year later came the attack on Pearl Harbor in the Hawaiian territories.

Fifteen years would elapse before the Japanese bicycle industry would recover to the level it had achieved in 1940; the road to exporting would have to be paved anew. After the devastation of war, markets shifted and the world's currencies revolved around the US dollar.

SUPERBE

Professional

Fuji introduced the Dura-Ace groupset in 1974 on their Fuji Ace model. Three years later they equipped their new Fuji Professional with the SunTour Superbe groupset. The Superbe groupset was a collaborative effort of the members within the JBX group.

Dia-compe created a caliper and brake lever similar to their Gran Compe 400 series. It was a big jump in form and finish from anything that had come before; the design was reflective of the iconic Campagnolo Record brakeset, the undisputed exemplar.

Sanshin had reworked their lovely Pro-Am hubs with extra-milky anodizing and beautifully finished hardware. The bearing surfaces were extra polished and hardened, which resulted in the smoothest-spinning hubs ever to grace a Fuji.

Sugino's redesign, or update, for the crankset and chainrings was significant. Although the new parts were still interchangeable with the 'Mighty' line (that had served on all of Fuji's top-tier models), the newly redesigned Superbe variation appeared more streamlined and yet simultaneously classic in appearance.

Tange produced the headset, which was a technically robust and visually substantial design.

In addition to coordinating the entire manufacturing effort, SunTour modified their Cyclone components for the groupset. The Superbe was an easier derailleur to set up than the Cyclone but still benefited by the flawless, quick shifts. Precision and lightness were the hallmarks of their 'miracle' Cyclone derailleur of two years earlier. The Superbe derailleur was more robust, with stainless-steel contact points, and therefore heavier than the Cyclone. For some, the first-generation Superbe series is the finest, non-indexing road racing or light touring derailleur ever made.

One shortcoming was in the friction shifters, which displaced the superior ratcheting models of the earlier Professional. The lovely cut-away levers of the Superbe groupset were lithe and far lighter. The design was a necessary marketing compromise, but a step down in functional performance.

The goal of every country, and businesses within that country, was to acquire dollars in order to execute trade to other nations. Not surprisingly, it was the rice exporters who were the first Japanese entities that could acquire capital through trade. Once these began to establish pools of dollars, their capabilities to leverage such capital into commodity, and general trading, grew exponentially.

Although some accounts claim an earlier date, it was not until 1951 (Showa year 26) that Nichibei Shoten became Nichibei Fuji. The Fuji brand, a name that was first used to identify chains, now identified the company itself. (Nichibei Shoten was still maintained as a sales division for some time.) It was Nichibei Fuji that began arrangements with the Tokyo Food Products Company as their exclusive exporter. Tokyo Foods morphed into Toshoku Japan, thence to Toshoku Ltd. The American division was then formed as Toshuku America, under which was established Fuji America in 1971. And this takes us back to that cool, rainy, late winter's morning of March 7th, in the lobby of the Hotel Hilton. Fuji had come to America under its own banner, and this time, unlike their attempts for export in the 1930s, it was going to be a very successful endeavor.

Takeshi 'Ken' Moriya was the first individual to set up an exclusive Fuji bicycle shop in the United States. He'd approached Toshuku America and they had agreed to his proposal as an agent under the condition that a Fuji-only retail facility be established. In a whirlwind of activity he secured a bank loan, rented a location, undertook months of training, and opened Fuji Cycle Center in Rochelle Park, New Jersey.

Ken had arrived in the United States a decade earlier under the employ of a Japanese ceramics and pottery firm. When the company called him back to Japan he was faced with a dilemma. He had fallen in love and married

1981 FUJI PROFESSIONAL: FD156052

F: FACTORY AREA / BUILDER ID / FUJI BUILD
D: MONTH CODE FOR APRIL
1: YEAR CODE FOR 1981
5: SERIES CODE, PROFESSIONAL
6052: BUILD NUMBER

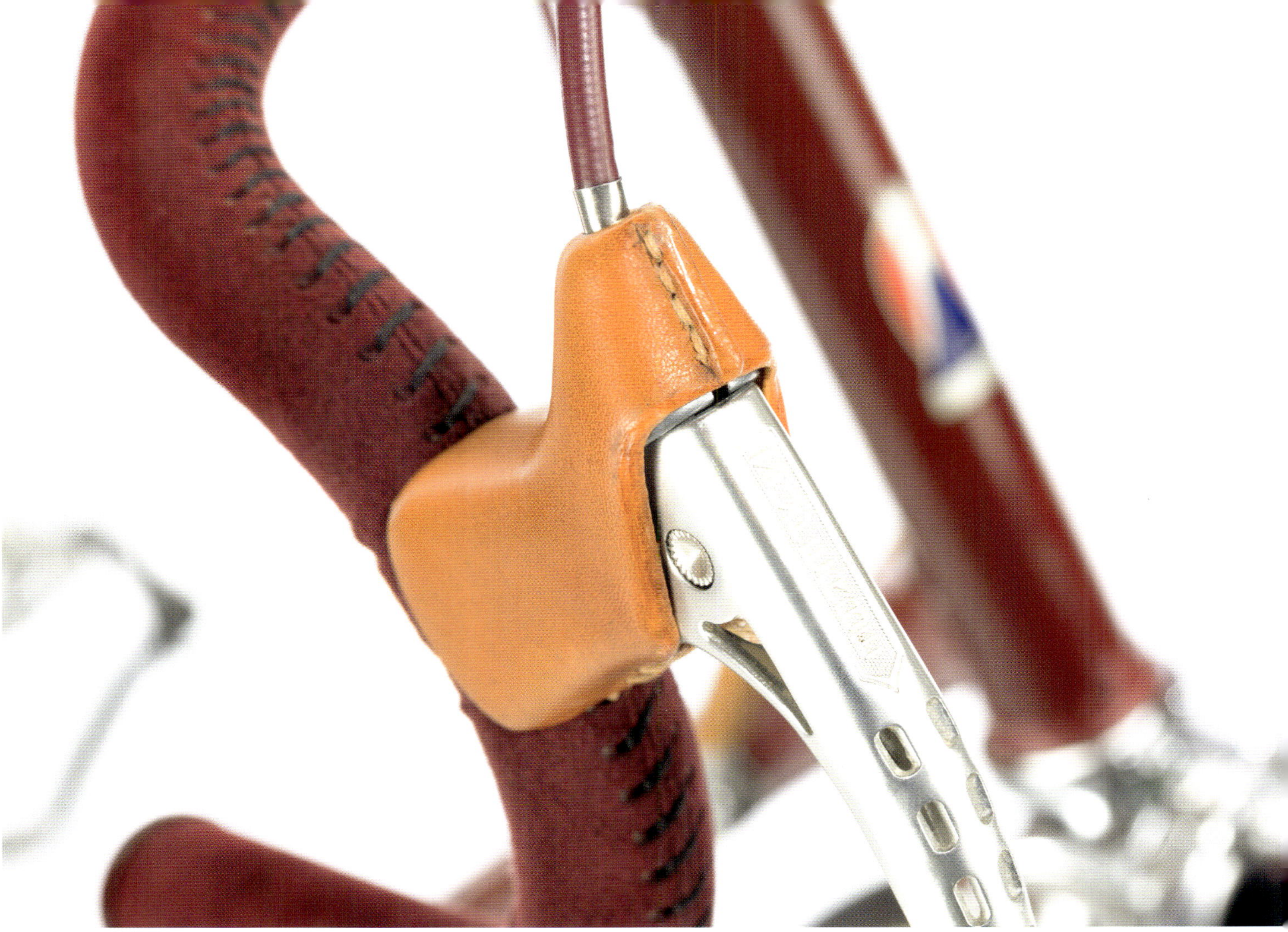

In 1977, Fuji offered ten different models under their export catalog. In comparison, their Japanese domestic catalog offered nearly a hundred variations.

By 1981, the export line had doubled to twenty offerings (which included the introduction of a racing tandem machine and the expansion of their BMX line). This was also the year when Fuji introduced their exquisite ruby-red color scheme. This red, and several variations of it, would identify the Professional until the model's discontinuance after 1985. A similar color would then be used on the Design Series framesets.

The full livery was wonderfully coordinated with a matching medium-burgundy suede saddle and bar-wrap material, matching brake-cable housing, and matching or complementary toe straps—the whole affair being strikingly pretty yet undeniably purposeful.

The first generation SunTour Superbe rear derailleur was a little marvel. About a third of the cost of the contemporary Campagnolo Super Record, it tracked the rear freewheel with close tolerance for fast, clean shifts. The pivot and gear spring bolts on the Super Record were titanium, so the Campagnolo component beat out SunTour's by thirteen grams. (182 versus 195).

Whether equipped with the Super Record or the Superbe, Fuji specified the SunTour Winner Ultra freewheels and the matching silver Ultra-6 chain to round out the drivetrain.

Perhaps the earth shifted upon her axis in 1981, or Italian bicycle forces breached the walls of Fort Fuji. The top line offering for the 1981 model lineup was not SunTour equipped, nor Shimano equipped. Instead, the Campagnolo Super Record groupset graced one of the two Fuji Professional bicycles shown above. The tubing for both was still Fuji's venerable 331 specification. But the Professional Super Record was built with Campagnolo Record drop-out fittings, while the Professional utilized the SunTour Superbe fork ends.

At first, Nichibei Fuji was hesitant to take on the logistical burden of stocking and importing Campagnolo dropout castings. It would require that twenty-six different frame configurations would be necessitated. (Frames were available at each centimeter size from 52 up to 64.) In the end, LifeCycle argued that the shifting of the Campagnolo Super Record derailleur would be compromised if not matched to Campagnolo dropouts.

Fuji got the last laugh. After testing the Super Record against the SunTour Superbe, they decided to use the six-speed SunTour New Winner with the Campagnolo-equipped model. For the Superbe-equipped Professional, the seven-speed cluster was used. The smallest cog on the Superbe model was a 12-tooth unit; on the Campagnolo bicycle it was 13-tooth. So, in hushed undertones, the argument was made that the SunTour-equipped bicycle was faster!

There were a couple of quirks on both models. Fuji learned that a Campagnolo Super Record front derailleur, with perforated front changer fork (the cage the chain runs through), had once broken in a Tour de France event. So the Super Record Professional was always specified with the solid Record variant.

As for the Superbe-equipped model, Gran Compe 400 brakes were used, which (from a purist's perspective) diminished the groupset. In both cases, buyers often corrected these component deficiencies.

For the 1981 through 1985 model years the lovely ruby red duotone livery would grace both the Professional and Professional Super Record offerings.

Under the skin, however, a major change would take place in 1983. Fuji would then use Ishiwata's 019E tubing under their 9658 identifier. This was a heat-treated, quad-butted tube that was remarkably stiff, light, and responsive. Another more subtle change was the final adoption of the full SunTour Superbe groupset, the sidepull Superbe brakes finally being seen for the 1983 release.

By this time, owners of the prior two years' Superbe-equipped bicycles had generally made the upgrade. In the image to the left, a 1981 Fuji Professional has been retrofitted with the SunTour Superbe calipers (replacing the original Gran Compe 400 series).

during those years, and he and his bride had a daughter. Returning to Japan was not a viable option. Fortunately, his tenure had provided good experience in export marketing. Although he pursued other options, Fuji bicycles were in his bloodlines, he was inspired by his grandfather's managing directorship at Nichiebei Shoten.

Ken did return to Japan, for training, while his young wife was left with the considerable task regarding the logistics and preparation of setting up the shop. Upon his return he assembled a veritable fleet of bicycles, mostly S10-S models, and opened Fuji Cycle Center in November 1971. In that commencement month, Ken sold precisely one bicycle. This was alarming; the risk of taking out a loan and foregoing a salary to set up a bicycle shop suddenly appeared financially precarious.

Fuji's reputation would build fairly rapidly, however, and by the spring of 1972 sales were trickling in at a break-even rate. By this time the 13th International Cycle show had transpired and retailers around the country were placing ever-increasing orders from Fuji Cycle Center and five other distributors.

Nichibei Fuji was thrust into a challenging middle-market. Fuji needed to make headway against the well entrenched Italian brands (and other continentals) at the luxury level, and the massive American manufacturers at the commodity level. Other Japanese exporters would become major competitors, but not quite so much in 1972. Still, bicycles that seemed similar, but were mechanically inferior, cost 30% less. And there was the natural suspicion among cycling enthusiasts, which was to be reactive to anything new. Japanese road bicycles were not openly welcomed into the European and European/American fold. Many of us recall being spat upon and assaulted with bicycle pumps during supposedly non-competitive rides simply

1983 FUJI OPUS III: K207

K: MONTH CODE FOR NOVEMBER
2: YEAR CODE FOR 1982 [1983 MODEL YEAR]
07: BUILD NUMBER [LIKELY, A CHERUBIM BUILD]

FUJI OPUS II

for not being a part of the Campagnolo/Huret/Simplex fraternity. (A bicycle frame pump was about the only weapon one had against an approaching, ravenous dog in those days, so being smacked with one by an adjacent rider was doubly insulting).

Fuji lauded their quality, and Ken undeniably contributed to enforcing these standards. If a bicycle came in with below-par lug work (say an area where the brazing did not properly flow into the joints, evidence of solder splatter, or even poor pinstriping) Ken would take a hacksaw, cut out the flawed section, and ship it back to the factory. Several episodes like that were all it took to get the requisite attention. The flaw would be rectified, banished; never to be seen, nor ever discussed, again.

This pursuit of quality would be well rewarded. When *Consumer Reports Magazine* would specifically recognize the merits of the S10-S in both 1974 and 1976 (and yet

The Opus III is both a superbike and a sleeper disguised as a Fuji. From 1983 until 1985, Ishiwata's 019E tubing would be specified for many of the top models emanating from Japan. This was a tubing that one needed to take particular care with; it was not, by any means, a typical factory specification. For this reason either special training or depth of experience was a requirement to assure successful outcomes.

Manufacturers had several options: train their builders on the new material, seek out and hire qualified personnel, or subcontract. Fuji took all three approaches. They purportedly subcontracted to Cherubim, one of the earliest and most prestigious custom builders in Japan (established 1965).

The Opus III is one of Fuji's 'stop press!' bicycles. The short serial number gives away the provenance of the ex-factory build. Although a second-tier road model, it is a revelation to ride: sweet and sublimely responsive.

Fuji used Ishiwata's 019E tubesets for their 1984 and 1985 Touring Series v. This would seem a highly counter-intuitive framebuilding approach for a touring bicycle; yet it was their culminating edition of the Fuji America (a touring model that had been introduced a decade earlier).

The model was available in five sizes (in 3-cm increments). Unless one was looking for particularly unusual frame dimensions, the Touring Series v was, in essence, a fully custom-built touring machine. Like the Miyata 1000, the Series v was an all-day cruising bicycle, most happy when weighted down toward some purposeful, long-distance mission.

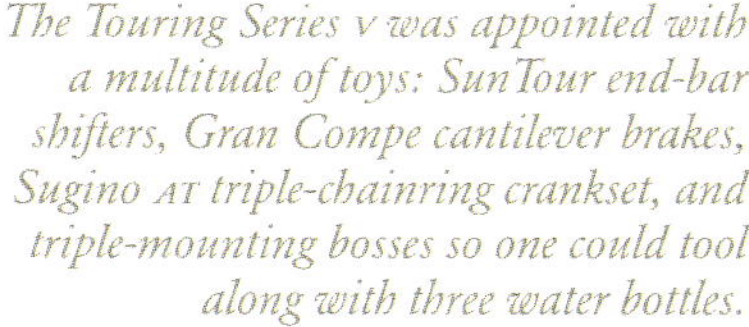

The Touring Series v was appointed with a multitude of toys: SunTour end-bar shifters, Gran Compe cantilever brakes, Sugino AT triple-chainring crankset, and triple-mounting bosses so one could tool along with three water bottles.

But the crowning jewel was the double spoke holder that was brazed onto the off-side chainstay. In the event that a brutal descent or some rough terrain took out one of the straight-gauge #14 spokes, you'd be back on the road in a jiffy.

The wheels on the Touring Series v were 40-spoke affairs and well suited to taking considerable road punishment (so broken spokes would be an absolute indication of overloading).

1985 FUJI "AMERICA" TOURING SERIES V: FB50004

F: FACTORY AREA / OR BUILT BY SUBCONTRACT FOR FUJI
B: MONTH CODE FOR FEBRUARY
5: YEAR CODE FOR 1985
00048: BUILD NUMBER

SUGINO AT

The American and Japanese approaches to bicycle touring were quite different during the boom years. (Even today, there are still strong stylistic distinctions.) Here's a story from that earlier time:

He does not venture out for the views. The distance and destination are the siren call; "No gain without pain," he states. Yes, sightseeing has its place, but for him it is a quest for storied adventure. Smiling earnestly, he says, "I need to find that elusive something outside of myself." The American cycle-tourist is an independent, persevering, self-reliant breed.

There he is, filling panniers made of ripstop nylon and waterproof duck with prodigious loads. Tent, sleeping bag, cookstove, poncho, paper maps in moisture-proof pouches, lots of water, essential tools… He has secured these things with Velcro closures and spring-loaded tie-downs. Small tarps provide extra weatherproofing. Stuff is everywhere.

Occasionally, he cheats by catching a bus to bypass some urban (or unappealing) stretch. Look as he places his thickly mud-encrusted Touring Series V into the vast underloader, and then seeks some conversation among the passengers before drifting off to sleep. The bus strains back to highway speed and heads into a long stretch of darkness.

6,700 miles away, it's morning. A Japanese touring cyclist is ceremonially disassembling her gorgeously maintained Fuji CE-10-A. Her older sister acquired the bicycle in 1978, it still looks new. She craftily fits all the components into a Rinko bag: all's taut and tidy. "No conductor will allow a dirtied, disorganized bicycle upon the train," she says to herself. She's prepared everything to the regulation travel size.

Her saddlebags are of traditional materials, leather and canvas, tied up with woven cords. Soon she'll board the Shinkansen and rapidly distance herself from the dense, urban areas, toward nature's sounds and serene views. She's en route to a location that already possesses stories: a temple and an ancient garden that her mother told her about long ago. She's not going to bring a story back, but rather, to leave something of herself, wandering within those sacred places.

again in 1980) these efforts would be well rewarded… The S10-S was Fuji's superstar (introduced as a 10-speed, then becoming the world's first production 12-speed). But let us now return to the winter of 1972—and allow me to roam briefly into the autobiographical.

My father, a product control manger for Bendix Corporation at the time (one of the many companies that worked in avionics in the 1970s), was inspecting my 10-speed bicycle one morning. It was a *Paris-Sport,* the brand that Mike Fraysse (the famed bicycle racer, importer, and coach) designed and sold from his Ridgefield Park, New Jersey location. As my father ran two fingers across the base of the toptube, he noted the evidence of a seam along the underside. From here the discussion turned to the process of making seamed versus drawn tubes. I enquired, "Who makes the best steel?" My father explained: "Us, the British, and now the Japanese, they have the newest mills, all of them built since the war." As for the British or American, I could not afford a Raleigh Professional, nor a Schwinn Paramount, not on a paperboy's salary. I referenced the yellow pages and discovered that there was a Fuji Cycle shop several towns away.

Upon entering the shop on a blustery, cold morning, my eyes came into contact with the silver and orange Fuji Newest. It had such an alluring and purposeful aura. Upon closer inspection I noted the all-important decal: Double Butted Chrome Molybdenum Steel Tubing. I ran my hand, as my father had, along the base of the toptube to see if I could detect a seam. No, no seam.

Hearing someone approach, I turned about and saw Ken Moriya looking at me with empathetic, yet judgemental eyes. In several brief sentences he summarized the quality and build dimensions of the frame. Then he spoke about the SunTour derailleur. I was shy and nervous, fourteen

1985 FUJI PROFESSIONAL SUPER RECORD "CHERUBIM": FF501

F: BUILT BY SUBCONTRACT FOR FUJI
F: MONTH CODE FOR MAY
5: YEAR CODE FOR 1985
01: BUILD NUMBER [LIKELY, A CHERUBIM BUILD]

The 1985 Professional Super Record is probably the most rare of all Fuji production models. Oddly, the 1983 through 1985 (Super Record) models were not even photographed for the catalog. The Professional with the SunTour Superbe groupset was shown, but the Professional Super Record was only identified via text.

In textual reference to the Super Record the copy read, "Or, for those that insist that each component be recognized as the very best of its kind in the world, the race-proven, quad-butted CrMo frame is complemented by the Campagnolo Super Record Group, Mavic Rims, Clement tires, Fujita suede saddle, Nitto bars and stem, and SunTour Winner Ultra-6 freewheel."

Instead of the duotone ruby red on all previous models, the 1985 Professionals had a ruby-red and black livery. The Super Record variant appears to have gone even farther: as these photographs indicate the model has black suede Fujita bar wrap, black suede toe straps (the MKS reenforced type with the sandwiched nylon centers), and the fastback– style Fujita professional seamless suede saddle.

The black and red livery is rounded out nicely with the black, hard-anodized Mavic GP4 rims (which were used on both the SunTour and the Campagnolo-equipped models). It is likely that Fuji was still using the Campagnolo groupsets they'd acquired back in 1981, when the Super Record was introduced

It would be six more years before Campagnolo equipment would again be specified for a Fuji. Much would occur by that time: most Fujis would be made in Taiwan Region; road bicycles (even the Campagnolo-equipped model) would be in the back of the catalog; steel would not be the tubing material of that premium model, titanium would be. Campagnolo would have introduced their futuristic C-Record groupset, and Fuji would specify this in the dark-silver anodized Century finish.

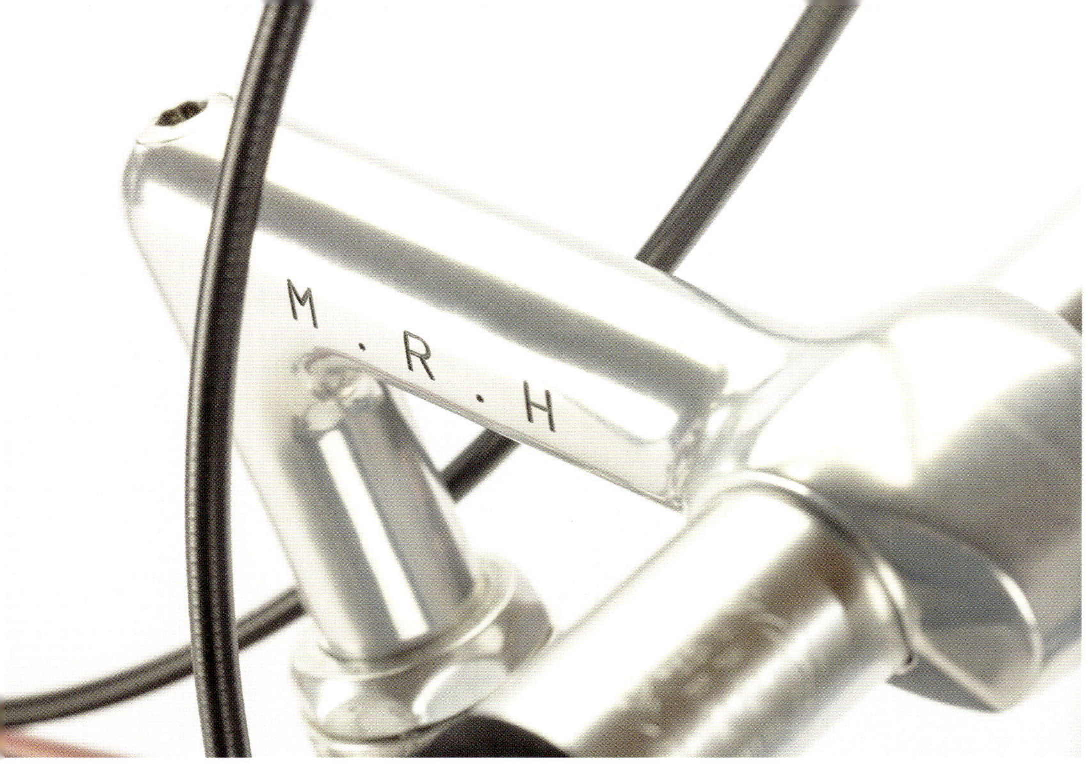

1985 would be the last year of the Fuji Professional, the closing of a ten-year run for the model. It had gone through three color series and two tubing profiles. The color series included the understated silver mink single or duotone liveries up until 1980. Then the victory red and gold was offered (one year), and the ruby-red sequence followed. Any model could have the owner's initials engraved upon the Nitto Crystem (the stem specified for every post-1979 model).

Even though the 1981 and 1982 bicycles had the new look of the ruby red, they were still 331 machines with lugwork and framebuilding aspects that reached back to 1975 (1974 for the first known builds). The ride was stiff, crisp, highly responsive, glorious over smooth roads, forgiving over rough surfaces, and replete with intense yet unimposing, near-instantaneous feedback.

The post-1982 models are entirely different bicycles. From ten paces away they appear as twins. But Ishiwata's 019E tubing (Fuji's 9658) and the Cherubim build make them radically different within a narrow range of higher-speed feedback. At slower speeds the difference is minimal, but as one increases the pace the 9658 machines seem to disappear—one's input is immediately transferred to motion. The best features of the 331 tubing were maintained, yet exemplified into a kind of flawless 'singleness.' Before you were joyfully aware of what the bicycle was doing; now it seemed only you were there, the bicycle disappeared.

years old at the time (going on fifteen). Still, I mustered up the courage to ask for a catalog.

That evening I read and reread the specifications—the Newest, the Finest, the S10-S, the Newest, the Finest, and the S10-S—until I was too tired to keep my eyes open. As everyone knows, studying a catalog is halfway to ownership. By the next morning the Fuji Newest, the Fuji Finest (in rainbow blue) and the S10-S (in white) were therefore, conceptually, mine. I rode back to the shop that day, the next, and the one after that.

During the winter months, potential customers would arrive infrequently. I would come to the shop, inflate tires, align the bicycles precisely on the floor (35-degree angle from the walls). If Ken was not involved in correspondence, on the telephone, or otherwise engaged, we'd play backgammon.

One day, two groups of potential customers arrived nearly simultaneously. As Ken approached the sales floor, he gave me a nod that seemed to indicate that I was to engage with the first-entered pair, a father and daughter. I was petrified. I had zero sales training (except for valuable insights picked up as a paperboy and during the backgammon sessions). Ken gave me my only direct advice as we approached the sales floor, whispering, "Tell them, when they buy Fuji, they never have to buy another bike."

His customer remained for several minutes, then departed. I sighed a bit in relief—I knew he would come to my rescue. Instead, he walked back to the office. I was alone, the most vulnerable boy on earth. The father was something of a techy; the daughter was extremely attractive. I was flustered and outwardly hyperactive. Fortunately, she was very inquisitive (a trait obviously imparted by her father). The rapidly-sequenced questions saved me from

Purchasing a frame only, not a complete bicycle, from any manufacturer was certainly an option. This might be due to seeking a replacement for damage, or someone who wanting to build up a model with their own selection of parts (a costly undertaking). Unlike Miyata, Fuji had never listed frames within their catalogs as stand-alone purchasing options. For 1986 they did so.

The Professionals were discontinued as the Opus III took the top-tier "page 1" position. Many changes occurred with the updated Opus. There was a dramatic shift in colors for the new bicycles, far less old-world luxury in feel, but still deploying tasteful, bright combinations.

Many bicycles became single, not duo-colored. Decaling shifted as well. One other change was the phasing out of tubular tiers. Fuji had faced a lawsuit earlier when a tire rolled off a rim and this might have contributed, along with other general trends, to no longer offering bicycles with tubular tire. This was a soft blow for traditionalists.

Yet there was hope. Ruby red became "rosata" and the former Professional took refuge in a "frame-only" offering from Fuji. This was called the Design Series and it everything a street-steel purist, or true professional, could ask for. The Fuji Design Series was offered from 1986–'88 in both track and road versions. Many were fitted with tubular-tired wheelsets.

self-consciousness. Over an hour had transpired as I presented a 21" Fuji Finest (rainbow blue) to the father-daughter and described the machine part-by-part. They purchased it. To Ken's utter yet well-hidden astonishment, I had sold the top-tier Fuji Finest with a swapped-out wheelset (clinchers for the stock tubulars). Unbeknownst to me, I was hired (and, as my first professional bonus, I would come into possession of that tubular wheelset).

At that time Fuji supplied bicycles to the newly formed United States Military Academy's West Point Racing team. One day a brace of cartons arrived with impact damage. They contained white Fuji Finest frames for the team. Upon close inspection the rear drop-out adjustment screws were bent, yet the dropouts themselves looked entirely serviceable. As I walked into the stockroom to procure new adjustment screws, Ken walked outside and tossed the frames into the dumpster behind the shop. That night I rode home with two frames draped across my joyously-shuddering shoulders. The next day Ken, smiling, handed me the tubular-tired swap-out wheels, and I had my first Fuji. I was the happiest young man on the planet.

As soon as I had enough money I purchased the very first secondnd-generation Fuji Newest model that arrived in America. This was the bicycle spec'd with the next-generation SunTour v derailleur (the v-luxe), the high-tech titanium alloy rear cluster (the SunTour Winner), and the delightfully effective ratcheting 'power-shifters.' Dia-Compe contributed their 'luxurified' centerpull called the Gran Compe (they were working on a premium sidepull brakeset at the time, but it was not ready for release). Sugino supplied their cut-away, drilled crankset, and chainrings (giving the bicycle a very distinguished look along with a modicum of weight reduction). Mikashima created the alloy-caged Unique Custom Pro pedals.

Another improvement was that the Fujita suede saddle, was at last, padded.

As mine was the first 1973 Fuji Newest to reach American shores, it was the very bicycle used in the Rolls Royce ad (an example of which is shown on page 136). So I had a glossy poster of the *very* bicycle that *I* owned hanging in my room—a bicycle that would change my life.

I rode for three reasons: to get somewhere, to race at amateur level, and, later, to attempt 'double-century' rides laden with panniers and 40 pounds of gear (upon a re-purposed, heavily-laden Fuji Finest or Newest). I decided to add a new task to my cycling itinerary: I set a goal to visit every bicycle shop within a hundred miles. I wished to learn what I could about the industry. My objective was to hone my skills as mechanic and salesman while learning of all the brands and models consumers could choose from; to understand the competition.

During one of these visitation runs (through Nyack, New York) I arrived at a bicycle shop with a Bianchi Super Corsa in the window. That celeste green, wonderful, but that logotype, transcendent! The letters *B-i-a-n-c-h-i* stretched across the downtube in their bold, extended, sans serif glory—graphics so confident, so articulate, so modern, so identifiable. The next day I cycled there again and looked at that Bianchi logo for a generous hour and made some sketches in a tiny day-planner I carried.

When I was next at the shop I mustered-up the courage to address Ken. "Moriya-san," I said with a slight bow, "Fuji needs a new logo, something bolder, more modern. The one we use on the water bottle is not strong enough—I think." He looked at me and softly replied, "In Japan we do not criticize, we offer solutions, we show a comparison between what is and what may be."

1986 FUJI MARK GORSKI SIGNATURE DESIGN SERIES: B5210

B: MONTH CODE FOR FEBRUARY

5: YEAR CODE FOR 1985 [DISCREPANCY FROM CATALOG]

210: BUILD NUMBER [LIKELY, A CHERUBIM BUILD]

1986 was a year of extremes. As all the entry- and mid-level Fuji bicycles were being churned out in the new world of Taiwanese factories, something quite different was occurring across the East China Sea. The highest levels of old-world craftsmanship and meticulous construction were being lavished on Fuji's Design Series frames. This would be the last year when steel was at the vanguard across Fuji's lineup.

Purportedly built by Cherubim under the watchful eyes of, or by Hitoshi Konno himself, the Design Series have short serial numbers. Sometimes ex-factory frames begin with an additional prefix code—F, for Fuji. Without that additional letter reference the latter ones could possibly be built in-house. The Fuji catalog specifically states, "Our Fuji craftsmen hand braze, miter, and file each and every frame with uncompromising attention to detail."

Design Series

Fuji's flawlessly handcrafted framesets are available in either the competition-proven Road-Racing Series or the Mark Gorski Signature Series Track Model. The Design Series Framesets are constructed with Ishiwata's prestigious 019E Quadruple Butted Chrome Molybdenum tubing, Suntour Superbe dropouts and an Investment Cast fork crown and bottom bracket shell.

Our Fuji craftsmen hand-braze, miter and file each and every frame with uncompromising attention to detail. Each frameset goes through a five-coat paint process including a clear final coat, for a unique two-tone color scheme. Experience the ultimate Fuji class today, enjoy the feeling forever.

Ishiwata's 019E tubing was the steel Fuji went with (or stayed with) for this premium offering. The E in 019E stands for 'Exactus,' which was a proprietary tempering process that distributed stress across the tube's length. The base (non-Exactus) 019 tubes went all the way back to Ishiwata's Glories Victory tubes from the early 1970s. This was a fairly light set, but the Exactus process increased the carrying capacity of the completed frameset, if properly executed.

In the mid-1980s, the Ishiwata factory was turning out over 150,000 framesets a month. By 1993, they would no longer be in business; however, Kaisei would inherit the company and continue to produce all the highest-quality products that Ishiwata Seisakusho had formerly offered. 019E is still manufactured by Kaisei and still well regarded by experienced, custom builders.

Except for the smallest-sized road frame, the 75/74-degree frame angles remained from the Professional line but tolerances were tighter on most of the tube lengths. This gave an even greater tautness to the build—as expected, Design Series frames afford about the finest riding experience that Fuji ever provided within the world of steel.

That evening I rode to a Brentano's bookstore at the Garden State Plaza and asked if they had any books about creating logos. The salesperson did not even know what a logo was, but kindly brought me to a 'commercial arts' section. There was book upon the shelves entitled *Graphic Designers USA*. Interestingly, it was a Japanese imprint, by Universe Books, published two years prior. I slid the book out, opened it, and looked down upon a spread of pages that showcased the work of Rudolf deHarak. I was mesmerized: three thoughts overtook me simultaneously. The work was purely graphic and intensely compelling; there existed a profession 'out there,' wherein one could make things like this for a living; and, with further study, I could design a logo for Nichibei Fuji.

Over the next two weeks I studied graphic design and typefaces. ("Oh my, they each have a name!") I purchased two more volumes within Universe Book's *Graphic Designers* series and I made sketches. The jots over the 'i' and the 'j' rendered an obvious reference to a pair of bicycle wheels. I wanted something a bit more, and then I recalled Ken's advice on the sales floor: "Tell them, when they buy Fuji, they never have to buy another bike." So I sketched a period after the logo—it gave me the chance to use a third circular element, and it declared to the viewer: Fuji. Period. Your last bicycle.

Next to the cycle shop was an art-supply dealer. Under the influence of my new passion, I'd spent hours ogling the beautiful Kern (Swiss) *Hartchrom* (hard-chromed) drafting equipment there. The owner kindly let me borrow a ruling pen and inking compass. After hours of practicing, I made a master of the logo and presented it to Ken.

He looked at it for nearly a full minute and said nothing. Apparently he shared it within the relevant Fuji America and Nichibei circles. About a month later, he said,

FUJI
SUNTOUR
CUSTOM MADE
CUSTOM MADE

The Design Series embodied the tradition and history of craft framebuilding, yielding a most glorious ride. Two other factors added a propensity of pleasure to these core attributes. One was the sheer presentation of the unadorned frame. The other equal yet opposite thrill was the process of adorning the Design Series with components of one's choosing.

Campagnolo's c-Record equipment had become available by 1986. To build up a Design Series with this groupset was akin to draping the future upon the past in a glorious commingling of aluminum alloy and rosata red. For a technical kick, the remarkable Dura-Ace 7400 SIS was also on the market and gorgeously suited to the task. For those who knew the most about Fuji's historical propensities, nothing would suffice but SunTour's Superbe Pro equipment (in its third and last iteration). The choices were enough to require three frames in order to play dress-up most fittingly.

The steel itself was fully chromed underneath. Upon this substrate, four coats of polished paint plus a clearcoat were applied. The only word for what resulted is 'resplendent.' Finally came that Fuji twist: the rear stays were finished with a translucent, high metallic paint over the chrome. The resulting color was humorously referred to as 'Dentyne' because of its resemblance to that ubiquitous chewing gum color.

"We like the logo." He presented me with a check for $500—it was the most money I had ever seen. I was now the happiest and wealthiest young man in America. Over the next weeks I discovered that Rudy DeHarak taught at the Cooper Union, a prestigious full-scholarship art and engineering school in the East Village, New York. I applied there two years later and was accepted. I'll always accredit that professional Fuji '3-dot' logo for tipping the acceptance scales to my favor. As a senior there I did indeed have Rudy deHarak as an instructor, later interning for his studio, *deHarak and Associates*. All this because my father ran two informed fingers across the base of a bicycle tube and instructed me to "look closer."

When *Consumer Reports Magazine* singled out the S10-S in their January, 1974 issue, it was a huge boost for Fuji. Fuji America violated the strict decrees of *Consumer Reports*' policies by stating that they were so recognized.

Fuji was always invested in style. Not a superficial style, but the kind that comes from long hours and hard work, but to the outsider looks so right and easy. Parts makers, led perhaps by Shimano in this respect, had mostly caught each other in the functionality race. It was time to have fun and show off–the Santé mini-groupset may have been the first example of this fad.

Bicycle fine art had its ups and downs, but the undisputed master was Hajime Kato. His work graced the first decade of Fuji's export catalogs. The flawless balance between a dynamics of motion and tight composition of objects within a fluid space informed his work.

I recall Ken saying that a letter was received specifically chastising the company, even to the point of legal action. It was, perhaps, a calculated risk, but it brought many customers to the door. Twice later *Consumer Reports* would again give accolades to Fuji; by this time they were truly hitting their pace. Fuji's export sales would reach a thousand bicycles a month by the late 1970s. All the other major brands—Bridgestone, Miyata, Maruishi, and Panasonic—were following (or would soon follow) with their own self-branded models.

Fuji's image as a (justifiably) slightly more expensive Japanese import had taken hold. The 'Fuji Class' slogan was enforced with styling cues from Gene Ritvo of *LifeCycle* in Cambridge, Massachusetts (a major distributor and retailer for Fuji). Gene was a sports-car *affectionato* with a discerning eye for things of good taste. Although others put in suggestions and observations, Gene is credited with the

1987 FUJI TEAM SANTÈ: FA709695

F: FACTORY AREA / BUILDER ID / FUJI BUILD
A: MONTH CODE FOR JANUARY
7: YEAR CODE FOR 1987
09695: BUILD NUMBER

Mere manufacturing can attain the greatness of art—touching both the physical and the mental attributes within us. The exceptional companies of today make things that build our memories for the future, but the greatest of these manufacturers have left behind a history of culturally rich milestones. Fuji had such a deep product line that one is nearly overpowered with delightful choices.

Does one go back to the root exports of 1971? or push forward to the initial Professionals of the mid 1970s? cross the boundary into the ealy '80s? or march forward to the timeless builds from Ishiwata 019E tubing? Perhaps it is best to move to the end-game (considering some of the more exotic offerings) such as the 1987 Team, replete with cow-horn handlebars, sweet Santé components, and an outrageous crackle-paint finish?

Maybe you are drawn to the magical catalogs that Fuji graced with the work of Hajime Kato? There all the machines are laid out before you and you can dream of hunting them down, or merely capturing the specific knowledge of their existence.

introduction of those great color combinations from the 1970s into the mid-1980s. Fujis were beautiful, desirable, and selling well.

Ken and Fuji America were fans of both the JBX group (the SunTour family of components) and of road bicycles. These assertions are borne out by the fact that the 1986 catalog listed sixteen full-bore road bicycles, each specified with SunTour equipment. That year also saw the introduction of the sublime *Design Series* frames, handmade with Ishiwata 019E tubing. These were fabricated in road- or track-frame variations; the track frame was an 'endorsed' model. For the first time in nearly twenty years, someone else's name was on a Fuji—not as a private label, but as an endorsement by Mark Gorski, the 1984 Olympic Gold medalist in the 1000-meter match sprint race.

Although Fuji America's affiliation to SunTour was an ardent one, at least for their export bicycles, they had specified Shimano's Dura-Ace ensemble way back in 1974 for their Ace. The Ace was the very first production bicycle to be offered with the Dura-Ace groupset. At that time, most mechanics still recognized the SunTour *V*-series as a superior derailleur, but the Dura-Ace hubs and brakes leapfrogged the competition. When the first packages of Dura-Ace parts arrived in their gorgeous, cream-toned, thick-walled, red-felt-flocked-lined boxes, it was clear that Shimano knew that bicycle parts were more than interchangeable commodities. Shimano collateral became more compelling and brand-conscious by the year; the Shimano voice was growing. It would take longer to gestate, but by the 1980s had most decidedly had done so.

The epochal years had arrived. In 1987 Fuji introduced a titanium road bicycle with Dura-Ace as their top specification machine. Next in line was the Fuji Team 'funny bike,' of lugless construction and built with Osi45 tubing. By

Clément
LOW PROFILE
SHIMANO

By 1987, the term 'lugless construction' had found its way into the Fuji lexicon; classic colors had succumbed to a newfound hippness; and, at least for this Fuji Team, top tubes were no longer straight. This was the only 'funny bike' that Fuji ever offered. The window for doing so was a small one—by 1989, the Union Cycliste Internationale no longer sanctioned dual wheel sizes for official record-keeping. They are a blast to ride (in the short term) and certainly a joy to collect.

1987 would also be the first year that steel would be knocked from the premium perch; the Team would follow the Titanium model in the catalog.

this time the classic Fuji color selections were memories. The Taiwanese builds had eclipsed the Japanese. Fuji had dispatched engineers to establish controlled specifications and model lines fourteen years earlier; by 1991 the entire line was of Taiwanese manufacture. All Terrain Bicycles (ATBs) preceded road machines in the catalogs. Twenty years after the steel-framed Professional Super Record had been introduced, a Campagnolo C-Record-equipped *Titanium Record* model was offered. The *Team, Roubaix, Club,* and *Saratoga* would represent the remnants of all the former road models, each Shimano equipped.

In 1997, a week prior to Christmas, Nichibei Fuji applied for corporate reorganization. Advanced Sport International became the new owner of Fuji America. Ken Moriya—'Mr. Fuji,' as he was then affectionately known—stayed on to insure an effective transition. ASI has been a loyal caretaker, advancing the brand while remaining both sympathetic and proudly enthused by their acquired history. In 2011 a steel-framed anniversary model was built and designed in Japan to celebrate Fuji's then 111-year history. Many past model names are preserved within the line. In a particularly elegant stroke they released a retro-inspired 'Nichibei' collection several years ago. More importantly, ASI has forged ahead in an extremely significant, technology-proving way. More Fujis have been ridden to notable victories in the past ten years than in their past one hundred.

Today, free of the hype and prejudices of the past, we can ride Fuji's classic road bicycles with a newfound appreciation. This book's photographer recalls long lusting for, and finally obtaining, a coveted European bicycle of the highest pedigree and, after two days of riding, realizing that his 1971 Fuji Newest had been faithfully delivering a much more satisfying ride for decades.

The European catalogs were of larger format, contained more pages, and even had a slightly different model lineup. The format was an excellent proportion for Kato's work. One can distinguish the earlier paintings by softer backgrounds; the harder edges were yet to come.

YOSHI KONNO: BUILDER & ENTREPRENEUR, CHIBA

3RENSHO

1942

Yoshi Konno, second eldest of six brothers, is born in Koga, Ibaraki Prefecture.

In his youth he engages in competitive cycling and continues to do so in college. Yoshi tries out for the 1964 Olympics; he later serves as a racing coach for Hosei University and the Japanese Amateur Cycling Federation.

1965

The Konno bicycle building dynasty begins with Hitoshi Konno's Cherubim.

Hitoshi's younger brothers create the Cyclone, 3Rensho (Yoshi), and the Miyuki brand (Shin). The Konno brothers establish a lasting foundation for both tradition and innovation in Japanese framebuilding.

1973

Yoshi establishes a Cherubim branch in Tokyo. His 3Rensho Cyclone receives certification for Keirin racing in 1975. As Yoshi continues to develop the 3Rensho line, he begins exporting in 1978, and also constructs private-label models.

1980s

In the 1980s Yoshi develops proprietary reinforced lugs, fitted dropouts, and offset fork crowns for 3Rensho frames.

1995

A grievous automobile accident claims the lives of five souls and leaves Yoshi in a paralyzed state; the cause of the crash is linked to his intoxication. He conveys the shop to his foreman, Makino Masahiko, who continues 3Rensho for several years.

201

Cherubim continues to build super premium bicycles in steel (Kaisei) and stainless steel (Reynolds 953) under the direction of Shinichi Konno, the son of Hitoshi Konno.

Through the experience of the engineer and metallurgist, and under the practiced hand and eye of the craftsman, the bicycle frame becomes the epitome of form conjoined to strength. We make steel our ally. But uncontrolled, or wielded with malicious intent, steel is a deadly adversary. Every cyclist knows this: the properties of velocity and inertia are not to be trifled with. Accompanying our wings of speed is the ever-hovering danger of unforeseen *deceleration.* Crashing into another cyclist, being hit by a car, contacting pavement after unsuccessfully traversing layers of wet leaves are all very undesirable ways to come to a stop. Together, machine and rider are a marvel when upright and in motion, but when they fall out of balance one can only pray for the best of all possible outcomes.

During an interview about Cherubim (the first bicycles built under the Konno brothers' adept hands), Shinichi Konno referred to steel as "mankind's oldest companion."

Shinichi is the heir and president of Cherubim. He is also a master builder and the son of Hitoshi Konno, the honored founder of the firm. Cherubim is Japan's most award-winning bicycle-building establishment. Although many Cherubims have found their way out of Japan in the last fifty years, it was never a focus of the company to export; the premium Cherubim jewels that did leave for distant shores often did so under the livery of other brands.

In addition to Shinichi's father, two of his uncles—Yoshi Konno and Shin Konno—were also renowned framebuilders, but their companies no longer exist (only Cherubim, the original marque, continues). Shin constructed the sublime Miyuki frames. Yoshi was the builder/entrepreneur who created the celebrated 3Rensho brand. Here, we shall follow Yoshi's story, because, for over twenty years, it was the 3Rensho frames (and the full 'Cyclone' models) that held both domestic *and* export significance.

c.1982 SAN RENSHO 10-PITCH TRACK TIME TRIAL: No Serial Number

The 3Rensho bicycles featured in this section are all exhibition models that were acquired by Ralph Carnevale. When Yoshi Konno built these bicycles, Ralph owned a shop in Huntington Beach, Southern California. Carnevale's Bike Shop always featured a superbike (or several) hanging in the window.

This was Ralph's advertising strategy. The hanging bait was ex-showbikes that Ralph could bargain for at the conclusion of exhibition events (saving the presenter the effort of repacking and shipping materials back home). That is the story of how the examples showcased here were acquired from Yoshi Konno's 3Rensho booth at the Bicycle Dealer's Shows in Long Beach, California.

These bicycles are exceptions to the others featured in this volume. First, they can be attributed to a specific builder—Mr. Yoshi Konno; second, they are prototypes, and not production bicycles. Their purpose was to bring attention to 3Rensho's production offerings. The 3Rensho shop was both a bespoke house, with a central focus on domestically produced Keirin racing machines, and a semi-custom export builder, with a focus on high-specification road, track, and tandem bicycles.

All custom builders who wish to directly support their craft through commerce must be entrepreneurs. The success of many framebuilders can often be attributed to their marketing, as well as their framebuilding, skills. Yoshi Konno was adept at marketing, but there was a more essential purpose for his need to produce frames in quantity.

Yoshi was not trained as an engineer, so his learning curve was directly linked to executing his ideas in steel. Every frame he made was a testbed from an engineering perspective, and a springboard from an artistic perspective. This may also be why he would readily sell the show bicycles at the close of an event. They had served their purpose; he had gleaned the requisite knowledge from the build. His mind was always ahead of his hands, and the next build would bring him closer to structural perfection.

Competition machines are all about the transfer of power. A good frame must 'oscillate' between input and output states with exceptional harmony. High levels of stiffness are required on the input side in order to capture and channel the greatest possible energy from the rider. Conversely, the bicycle must possess an ideal amount of 'stickiness' (the machine cannot just bounce stiffly over the road surface). Specific, 'targeted' flex is critical to achieve this elusive quality of stickiness at the output level.

Energy flows across fixed and rotating points within the machine's composition. The material between these points is crucial, yet surprisingly choiceworthy and adaptable. Steel, aluminum, carbon fiber, ceramics, bamboo, titanium—any of these or other materials may be used toward this balancing goal.

Yoshi Konno, above all else, was an inventor. He deconstructed frames, made observations, and rebuilt them. He was self-taught in 'the way of steel.' Every build was an exploration of the fixed versus floating points. Mostly the tubes were straight; sometimes they were curved, lengthening the distance between two points—this would allow power to be stored for just a moment prior to transfer, modifying the output.

Yoshi would also use a shorter-than-expected distance between two points (such as in seatstay length) and then add reinforcement in some unexpected manner (perhaps through extra braces). This increased stiffness and decreased flex (though it did add weight).

All these structural decisions—and all the brazing, filing, sanding, and prepping—would be gently blanketed in protective layers of paint. The livery for the bicycle was such a natural extension of the 3Rensho experience, it was the 'breathing out' phase. Although Yoshi did not paint his frames, he was passionate about their graphic representation. When he took his exhibition bicycles out on the marketing road he was well aware they would probably not be ridden, only seen. On the show circuit, at rest, they were peacocks; but he knew that if unleashed, at speed, they'd be peregrine falcons.

Yoshi Konno's genius with steel combined a foundational artistry derived from a thorough analysis of traditional framebuilding and a singular creativity built upon innovation. Through continuous observation and experimentation in constructing frames, along with feedback from the competitors who rode them, Yoshi's genius evolved rapidly. His bicycles surprise us with rebellious beauty. They are paradoxically gaudy and discreet, flamboyant and restrained. He was a proud perfectionist whose work followed the maxim of the great French (Italian-born) automobile engineer and designer, Ettore Bugatti, who said: "If it looks right, it is right." Yoshi Konno made steel "look right"—he persuaded it to do what he wanted it to do.

For two decades Yoshi would work marvels with steel, until that tragic night in the late summer of 1995—a night when a lifetime's success succumbed to a ruinous, ill-fated decision. On that night, while driving under the influence of alcohol, steel became the uncontrolled enemy. The crash resulted in the deaths of five others and left the gifted artisan devoid of his former capabilities. Severely paralysed from the neck down, he would never again construct a bicycle. In one terrible stroke a story that had begun not with the building of bicycle frames, but with the *unbuilding* of them, was largely concluded.

When foreign competitive cyclists descended upon Japan's 1964 Olympiad they came equipped with Italian craftsmanship. The situation demanded analysis. Yoshi would not only ride these bicycles—he would begin a self-imposed training program by studying them. Initially, his curiosity would be sated by deconstructing Cinellis; but the bulk of his education would be acquired in the construction of prototypes. The talents of the youthful Yoshi were forged in the crucible of his competitive nature, his self-analysis, and his fervent quest always to find better

1985 SAN RENSHO TRACK TIME TRIAL: D522

D: MONTH CODE FOR APRIL
5: YEAR CODE FOR 1985
22: BUILD NUMBER

In 1985 Sugino introduced their comprehensive groupset, aptly named "75" in commemoration of their 75th year. By this time the groupset mentality was well entrenched for both manufacturers and buyers. Unfortunately (for Sugino), the "default" hierarchy of Campagnolo, Shimano, and SunTour meant that they faced a hard-to-penetrate marketplace for their "gruppo" to be incorporated into any manufacturer's line up. One brand exception was Lotus Bicycles.

Lotus released the "Elan 75" for 1987. It was equipped with the full range of Sugino 75 components and it also featured Tange Prestige tubing. It was a premium-bicycle, the third from the top in their lineup. The dealer wholesale cost was just under one thousand dollars for the model—the recommended retail cost was unspecified.

The Sugino 75 groupset utilized carbon composite materials, aluminum alloys, and black finishes to convey an aggressive, next-generation look. Further panache was achieved through a range of twelve color coordinated bar tapes and toe straps. But the most desirable elements in the collection were the carbon skinned honeycomb composite aero disc wheels and cranksets. These components were sensationally forward-thinking—ideal compliments to Konno's 3Rensho time trial fixed gear marvels with their low slung, reinforced seat stays.

ways to do things. Notwithstanding the absence of a traditional apprenticeship, Yoshi would become known for his craft. When Keirin racers began to use his frames in competition Yoshi achieved a significant milestone: professional recognition. Such acknowledgment was also an invitation to continue to experiment and move beyond the highly restrictive modes of the classic Keirin track frame.

Yoshi was as involved in marketing and racing bicycles as he was in building them. While working for Maruishi, he both sold and raced bicycles. He coached new riders sponsored by the firm. This led to coaching positions for both his alma mater, Hosei University, and later, for the Japanese Amateur Cycling Federation. He poured this experience into the brand that he created. The new brand, 3Rensho, would become known for detailed craftsmanship as well as outbursts of design innovation. One may say *Three*-Rensho or *San*-Rensho ('San' is the Japanese word for 'three'). Those in the know use the latter. 3Rensho refers to the exemplary feat of achieving three consecutive victories, the 'triple crown,' in Keirin racing. First in qualifying, then in the semi-finals, and ultimately in the finals. Although there is some confusion between Cyclone and 3Rensho, generally, 3Rensho is the *brand name* and Cyclone can be considered as the *model* under the brand. Mr. Yoshi Konno marketed his efforts under Cyclone, Ltd.

For Cyclone, the 1970s were heady years—a decade of great achievement. This period set the stage for expansion into the 1980s, when 3Rensho would become something of a powerhouse among the boutique builders. Yoshi's collective grew to have six builders, two Chiba-based workshops, and a retail store as well. At the height of their production, nearly four premium frames were being crafted *every day*. This output of super-premium frames would compare favorably to a similar quantity of

Yoshi had a great relationship with the Ishiwata firm and they supplied the steel that Konno used to build his 3Renshos. Ishiwata assembled kits from their range of tubing and numbered these based on the total weight within that collection. Yoshi drew mostly from their light, 019 series. However, he went for the ultralight (.7mm–.4mm–.7mm) top-tube from the super light 017 series and selected chainstays from the 022 series. Heavier chainstays added stiffness across the drive train and minimized flex for powerful riders.

A nifty decal combining the 3Rensho name with Ishiwata was created to promulgate this relationship. It featured the words "super strong" and to underscore this notion it depicted a highly stylized graphic of an elephant with an uplifted trunk, a symbol of good fortune.

Another decal used on many of his builds was a panel with his signature. This underscored the custom aspect of the frame, and in addition to the functional details, brought a heightened satisfaction of ownership. One 3Rensho graphic element borrowed heavily from Cinelli. This was the 3Rensho insignia composed of three outline circles with the numeral "1" enclosed. The device had two wings (one in yellow, one in blue) projecting form the one of the circular elements. The resemblance to Cinelli's "flying-C" logotype (with three such wings) is undeniable.

top-of-the-line models built by major Japanese manufacturers as a fraction of their model line.

Yoshi's productive outreach covered multiple fronts: supporting the domestic Keirin racing scene through framebuilding; designing and casting fork crowns, lugs, and dropouts; cultivating a prestigious export market; constructing top-tier models for third-party entities; and enticing the cycling fraternity with experimental and sometimes outrageous concept bicycles (which brought attention to all the former efforts). Of all these activities the most prestigious was the first—building for recognized Keirin riders. In 1983, Yoshi estimated that roughly 10% of Keirin racers were riding his frames—a fairly stunning percentage (at the time that it would have represented about 400 riders). Even the legendary Koichi Nakano rode some of his frames (although the near-undisputed maestro, Nagasawa, was his principal supplier). Nakono achieved a mind-boggling *ten consecutive* gold medals (from 1977 until 1986) at the Union Cycliste Internationale (UCI) Men's Track Cycling World Championships. However, many Keirin superstars only rode on Konno's frames. These defacto endorsements were significant in Japan, but they did not readily bring fame from audiences outside of the country.

The importance of Keirin racing to Japan's steel framebuilding culture cannot be overstated. Steel frames are not a mere romantic nod to the past; they are *the* contemporary standard requirement. Parts makers also thrive under the empowering endorsement of 'NJS' (Nihon Jitensha Shinkokai). The equipment must be absolutely consistent in design and quality. Today, Keirin racing is held under the authority JKA (Japan Keirin Association). As the sport involves gambling it is closely monitored. No commercial sponsorship is permitted; riders must purchase

One of the most elegant bicycle configurations is the Track Time Trial machine. The 3Rensho showbike collection presented here is composed of three such examples (joined by a fourth, the Cyclone Super Record Aero Export, Time Trial bicycle for the road).

The design combines the purity of a track bicycle with the low slung nature of the time trial. The rider needs to "disappear" within their lithe, aero-inspired framework. Because the rider needs to accelerate and maintain the highest speed possible over the prescribed distance, a tad more weight, than might be found in a pure track bicycle, is permissible. Solid disc wheels, time trial bars for the "superman position," some experimentation in the frame, heavier aero profile tubes, a smaller diameter front wheel are all par for the course. In short, an ideal configuration for the creations of Yoshi Konno.*

Most of a rider's energy is consumed in overcoming air resistance; after a rider achieves the speed of 15 kph (approximately 9.3 mph) their energy is mostly dedicated to pushing air out of the way. The adversary, air resistance, consumes energy at a square of the rider's speed. So for each doubling of speed, eight times the energy is required to overcome that increase in air resistance.

Obviously, if riders traveled within aerodynamic enclosures the absurdity of fully exposed non-aerodynamic humans fighting off hundreds of pounds of air would be addressed. But what's the fun in that? We want to see our competitive heros in all their non-aerodynamic glory! In early tests, Shimano estimated that the bicycle presented about 12 percent (average) of air resistance and the rider the balance of 88 percent. As aero tubes and equipment added weight, the small advantage gained on level ground and descents would be lost on the uphill sections. However, for time trials on ovals this is not a concern: significantly improved aerodynamics is essential for reasonably improved performance.

** non-uniform wheel diameters are no longer sanctioned by UCI regulations, 1980s TT bikes, or "funnybikes," are therefore readily identifiable.*

their own equipment. Their classic frames are equipped with traditional (NJS-certified) parts, wheels have 36 spokes, and tubular tires are the only game in town. (Providentially, ex-tubulars from the Keirin racing fraternity are the world's greatest source of discounted, high-quality sew-ups, because they may only be used for one race).

Justifiably, the build requirements for Keirin machines are highly controlled; within these guidelines Yoshi experimented with the design of lugs, fork crowns, and dropouts. This led to a line of frame-building elements that Yoshi felt advanced performance—particularly in aspects of stiffness, control, and feedback. 3Rensho builds incorporated these components. Additionally, through Cyclone, they were made available to any builder. Of particular interest were Yoshi's fork-crown designs. The first of these was created in 1981 and four other designs were developed and released through the next several years.

1984 SAN RENSHO TRACK TIME TRIAL: C 98

C: YEAR CODE FOR 1983; CODE FOR "CUSTOM" OR CODE FOR EXPORT MODEL

98: BUILD NUMBER

Design by
JAPAN
GUARANTEED BUILT WITH DOUBLE 
Cr-Mo
SUPER
STRONG

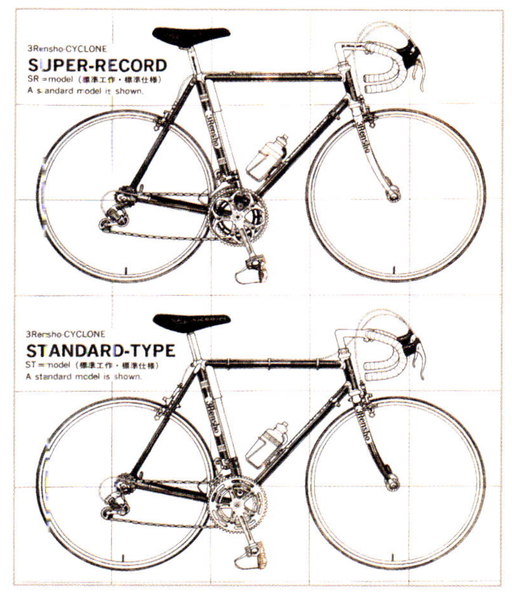

The very earliest Cyclone models were constructed under the Cherubim brand. When Yoshi introduced 3Rensho the Cyclone model name was retained. In addition to the 3Rensho and Cyclone identifiers on the main tubes, the livery included a sub-model name as well, such as 'Super Record Export' on the chainstay. 3Renshos were replete with decals. After the decals were applied the frame received a final clear coat. In this manner the decals could not peel off as they were effectively sealed below the final coat of finish. The reference 'export' was used on all his premier work as the term added cachet—the allusion to export quality carried the notion of 'the very best' in Japanese markets. The drama of this graphic ornamentation was further heightened by rich base colors. A classic among these is 'Murasaki'—deep violet. The export models were made available from 1981 until 1995 through Ariel Trading Company, Ltd. (Madison, Wisconsin). For several years after 1995, through the efforts of Makino Masahiko (shop foreman and framebuilder), the 3Rensho brand continued—the 'Atlanta 96' being one of the last export models.

Each had a unique function specific to track or road use. One of the four was an aerodynamic design (used for the Super Record Export 'Aero'). Some of the frame components, such as the socketed rear drop-out, were considered a bit clunky design-wise, but Yoshi would always pursue 'functional aesthetics.'

Yoshi was an individual who could not look at anything without formulating a vision toward its improvement. For him, the process of designing was a scientific and controlled one—yet this did not curtail the unexpected. One of the most beautiful lugs he produced incorporated a delicate gusset, which yielded an aerodynamic and 'Jules Vernesque' quality. Beyond the frames and frame components themselves, the same art and design process was applied to clothing, gloves, tools, and even a custom transit case for the safe transportation of precious 3Rensho frames.

Cyclone Ltd. was also a 'ghostbuilder' for other companies. The most storied of these are the early 1980s 'Allez' (and very earliest Sequoia) models constructed for Specialized—now a prominent American-Taiwanese owned firm founded in 1974 by Mike Sinyard. Sinyard initiated his company importing premium Italian parts, then began manufacturing tires and other accessories. In 1981, Specialized offered mail-order framesets: many of these were contracted to Cyclone. At the time Yoshi was considering semi-custom frame building to expand his line, so the Specialized offer was serendipitous. For collectors, tracking down a 'YK' Specialized Allez is a worthy quest. The Allez model is immortalized in the 1985 Warner Bros. film *American Flyers* (Kevin Costner and David Marshall Grant are the protagonist riders). Much footage depicts the Specialized team van traveling across open landscapes adorned with four red Allez machines,

1983 3RENSHO SUPER RECORD AERO EXPORT ROAD TIME TRIAL: G312

G: MONTH CODE FOR JULY
3: YEAR CODE FOR 1983
12: BUILD NUMBER

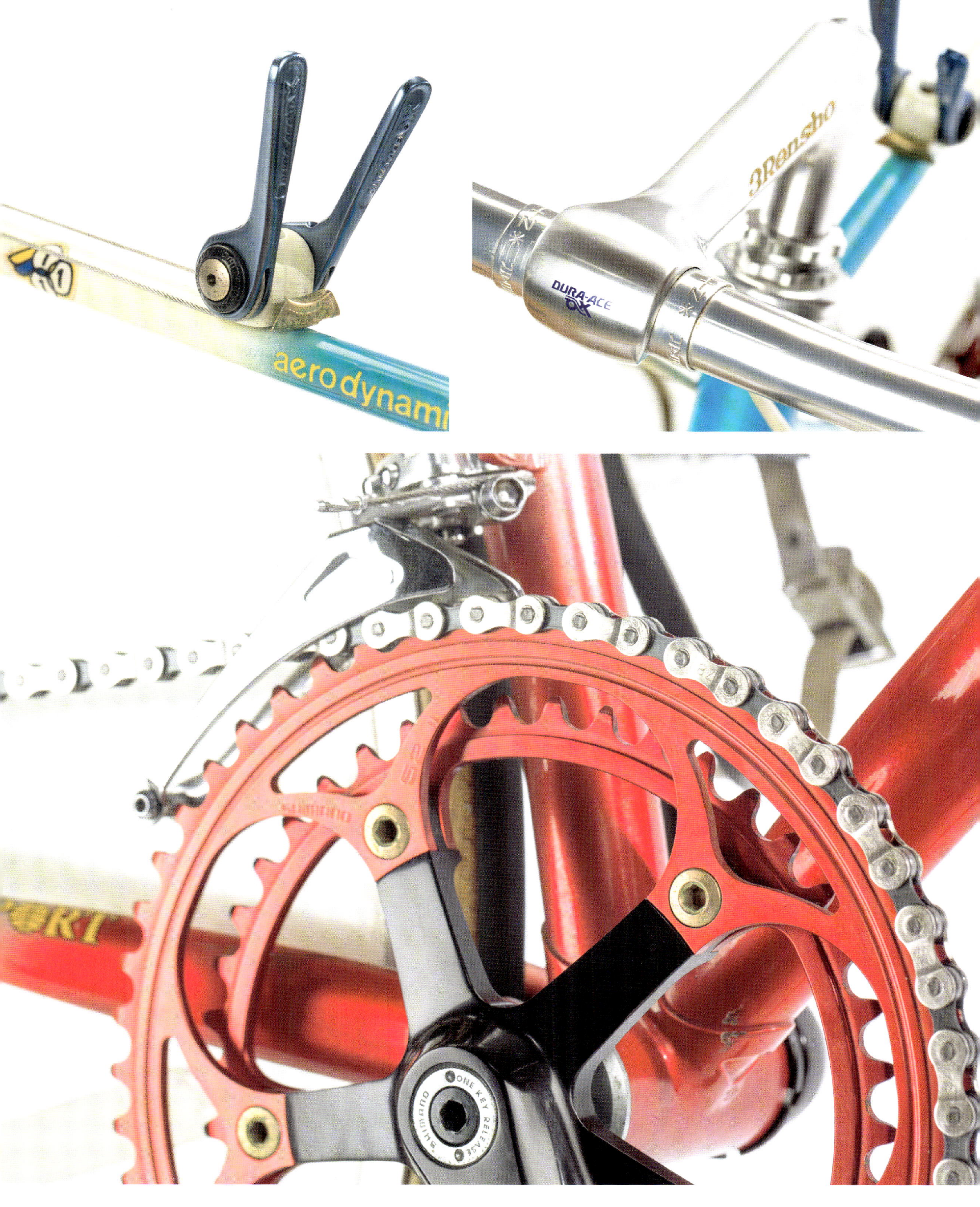
aerodynami
3Rensho
DURA-ACE
AX
shimano
52
SHIMANO
ONE KEY RELEASE

Framebuiders of Yoshi's era often remained behind the scenes when they produced high specification products for export manufacturers (as Cherubim did for Fuji). However, most of the 3Rensho export machines would proudly bear their own name, and often, his signature.

His catalogs cited the heritage and provenance of 3Rensho with a particular emphasis on Keirin and World Champion victories. This information was supplemented by thorough technical specifications. The printed material did not possess high typographic or photographic finesse, nor polished and persuasive marketing language. Instead, potential buyers were given the sense of being insiders into what made a custom bicycle particularly desirable.

Every export story involves a partnership. For the United States the export effort was handled through Andrew Muzi and his Ariel Trading Company, Ltd. Ariel was located in Madison, Wisconsin, and linked to the famous, and once extensive, Yellow Jersey shops. In 1973, Andrew Muzi arrived at Yellow Jersey and, over the years, he assumed ownership and built a bicycle sales, repair, and restoration empire.

Andrew forged a friendship with Yoshi and was a significant advocate, promoter, and distributor of the 3Rensho brand. He even served as a stylist. The magnificent metallic colors (Rose, Lilac, and Aquamarine) of the later Super Record Aero models (with their aero fork crowns, fastback seat stays, and bottom bracket aero plate, etc.) can be attributed to Andrew's input on a "dreary November afternoon at Maruishi." All of Yoshi's frames were painted at the Maruishi facilities, his former employer, and the fourth largest manufacturer in Japan.

Andrew had come prepared with some advanced intel from the fashion industry on next year's hot colors. They were perfect, and Yoshi's machines took on more color drama thenceforth. Now, highly collectible, the 3Rensho Super Record Exports are functional artifacts commemorating that friendship and entrepreneurial achievement.

conspicuously riding on the roof. The film revolves around tense family dynamics and a defining bicycle race (the Tour of the Moon, a.k.a. 'Hell of the West,' which takes place in majestic Grand Junction, Colorado). The real stars of the movie are the bicycles. Unfortunately, only a small percentage of Allez models are Konno-built. These all sport thinned lugwork, a forward-offset fork crown, and lovely detailing on the rear brake bridge.

Konno's brilliance reflected the kind of genius that undermines itself; a destructive genius that moves through phases. First gifted, yet innocent: all energy striving simply to know and to create. Next, doubt: a long period of relentless work to prove to others (and oneself) that the genius is real. Last, a world so rarefied that it excludes—few can comprehend. There is no time for the simplest of human ceremonies—being with a loved one for no reason at all, reading a book to no apparent purpose—there is *always* a more essential, elusive, pursuit to attend to. Genius cannot gauge itself.

Revealingly, in one of the 3Rensho Cyclone catalogs, this statement is to be found under a section entitled 'An Artist from Akibo:' "Each time a new design is tried and tested he learns something new about his product and this improvement is then built into the next model. Often he becomes so involved in what he is doing that he seems to be in a world of his own. Sometimes even his own family members seem unable to reach him. He has the mark of a true artist." The artistry of curved tubes, thin-diameter tubes transecting large diameter tubes, flying buttresses, semicircular reinforcements, and those wonderful gusseted lugs make one stop, stare, and admire. Escaping from the mundane was Yoshi's full-time occupation. He succeeded: nothing mundane ever issued out from his mind, nor from his workshops.

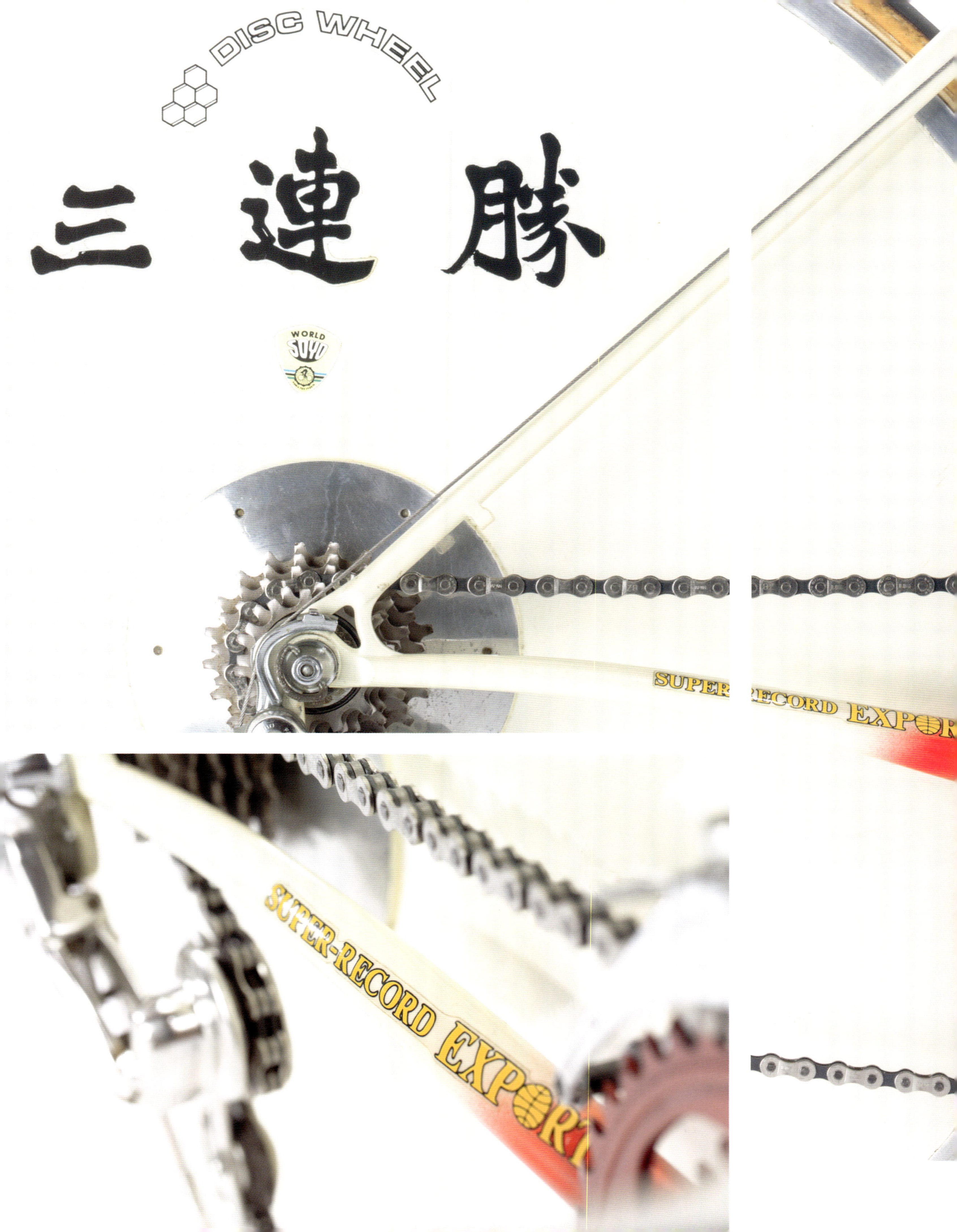

DISC WHEEL

三連勝

WORLD SOYO

SUPER-RECORD EXPORT

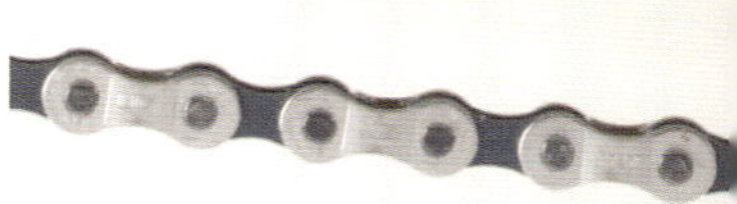

Nothing says "aerodynamic" like a spokeless, disc wheel. In the mid-1980s Araya introduced their impressive version with either a carbon skin or an alloy sheath over an aluminum honeycomb interior. (These were far tougher than competitor's foam-filled offerings). Araya's "aluminum discs" gave the bicycle uncanny stiffness between the rear stays. At speed, it felt like you were riding upon a monorail.

Rear discs provide a marketing bonus. With all that flat expanse the bicycle becomes a billboard in motion. Konno used this real estate to great effect, depicting a lovely calligraphic rendering of "San Rensho" in Kanji (Chinese) characters upon the surface. Most touchingly, the exquisite calligraphy work was that of Yoshi's mother.

In the East, the arts of writing and painting are closely aligned–the brush is the gateway to both literal and figurative expression. Some scholars argue that Chinese characters have evolved into purely phonetic forms, still, there are pictographic and ideographic roots that can be assigned to the radicals (base components) from which the characters are composed. The 3Rensho characters represent: three (pretty obvious); sequence (two carts being pulled in line, or an object following a course); and victory (a very heavy object being lifted by strong arms). Ideographic interpretations vary, but the meaning of the combined characters is certain: three victories in succession!

Tsunoda invests heavily into aerodynamic bicycle design and becomes the world's major producer of aero bikes, creating two models, the premium Saturn Aero Road, and the Aero Grand Prix. These models never achieve production goals, remaining a mere fraction of their 3,000 monthly exports achieved by 1983, when the aero craze faded and production lines ceased.

Tsunoda exports cease by 1990. Nagoya land values rise and by 1997 Tsunoda transitions to become a real-estate holding and management company; bicycle building ends.

TSUNODA CYCLE INDUSTRIES CO., LTD., NAGOYA / LOTUS

TSUNODA

Lotus International Corp., Syosset, New York, is formed by Sidney and Ernst Star; Tsunoda is the initial supplier of Lotus bicycles, formerly under Alpha Cycle & Supply Corp

1979 **1990**

1925 **1950s** **1970s** **1980** **1997**

Tsunoda Cycle Industries is established in Komaki City (Aichi Prefecture) by Shimataro Tsunoda; by 1927 they begin selling branded bicycles under the 'TU' name. Some years later they will begin to use the Saturn brand.

Tsunoda develops rust-proof plating processes and initiates the manufacturing of complete bicycles. Tsunoda also deploys radio advertising, highly innovative at the time.

Tsunodo exports bicycles under third party labels. Domestically they introduce their Gran Lotus, a model purpose - built for camping, fully equipped with panniers and lighting.

In recognition of their 55th anniversary, Shigenobu Tsunoda, the founder's son, announces a major initiative to significantly increase their export market share; he modernizes their extensive factory, purchases land, and receives government Quality Achievement award. Tsunoda ramps up to produce 40,000 units per month, their target being to achieve a monthly output of 120,000 units by 1985, however, sales fall as the market rapidly declines.

We cyclists must daily tip our caps to the horde of inventors, both the recognized and the unknown, who have made our cycling experience sweet through their toil. Bicycle design history is brief, containing periods of change-adverse 'fits' and momentous 'starts,' but it is primarily a tale of evolving refinement. The bicycle is an equal-opportunity wonder, providing practical transportation to the breadth of humanity. In consideration of age or sex, financial means, nationality or political bias, the bicycle makes no preferences. Instead, it is the fairest form of transportation, rendering such egalitarian attributes as economy, efficiency, and durability, to all. Thank you, inventors, for helping to make it thus.

Next, we praise the craftsmen, the manufacturers, the assemblers—all those who have invested life and labor into setting up a workshop, or building a factory where bicycles can be made in the tens, the hundreds, or the thousands. David Pye, craftsman and professor who taught at the Royal College of Art, wrote the seminal treatise *The Nature and Art of Workmanship*. In this essay he introduces a comparison between *design of risk* and *design of certainty* for industrial and product designers. So it is that the hand-builder goes through a kind of design risk for each bicycle created, while the industrialist seeks design certainty; each bicycle a reflection of the one preceding it.

One need not be a bike snob to appreciate the work of gifted hands and the experienced eye; but what can be said of an assembly-line machine—say, a Lotus Unique? Fly down the avenues upon this commoner, in her brazen, look-at-me, Pearlescent Rose finish. Do you then care if there is one or 10,000 of these? This model, like all her stablemates, tracks beautifully, while swallowing the rough edges of Brooklyn's urban streets. Hours later, after crossing the George Washington Bridge and

1981 LOTUS AERO SUPER PRO: MD01776

M: CODE FOR 1981
D: FACTORY PRODUCTION RUN
01776: BUILD NUMBER

The crafted shape, and heavier weight, of aero tubing made all the difference regarding performance. Tsunoda used Tange Aero 30 for their premium bicycle. The wall thickness varied from .9 mm for the top and base of the tube, to 1.2 mm for the sides. This compensated for the ovalized profile which would otherwise be less stiff than a round tube. In their February 1982 issue Bicycling praised the frame construction, stating, "It's as solid as any roundtube bike you're likely to ride.... The bike aced every test." This praise followed their forewarning, "Aerodynamics. Anyone in the bicycle business has grown weary of the word in the last few months."

No bicycle manufacturer placed as much emphasis on their aerodynamic models as did Tsunoda. Their factory included a section designed in cooperation with Tange specifically for the manufacturing of aero bicycles. This involved customized jigs and purpose-built assembly lines for two models: the Aero Grand Prix Road and their premier Aero Saturn Road. This streamlined production facility could generate an annual run of 2000 Aero Grand Prix Roads. The Aero Saturn Road, however, was predominantly hand-built, about 500 a year could be made.

As other Japanese manufacturers had done before them, Tsunoda wanted to discontinue ghostbuilding for third party labels. The post-1980 goal was to self-brand their bicycles, or at the least, to always indicate that they were "made by Tsunoda for…" As quality was now a hallmark of Japanese production, third party buyers had no issues with revealing the provenance of the maker.

Tsunoda's top-tier Saturn was the model that Alpha Cycles sold under their Lotus Aero Super Pro model. It was an incredibly imposing bicycle, even the metallic pink option—like an 1980's "power-tie," radiating a kind of snarling, intimidating attitude.

The period of the aerodynamic bicycle may have been short-lived (under one thousand days of glory) but the style's influence was to be long-lived. Shimano, along with other Japanese parts manufacturers, were no longer followers, they became the design-leaders. The European manufactures began to find themselves in the catch-up role.

Another factor was integration; suddenly a bicycle, even a great one, was no longer the sum of its parts. The frame and the component sets began, from aero bicycles on, to have closer design cross over. This meant that the easy interchangeability of parts was to soon to become a thing of the past.

heading north on Route 9W, the bicycle unwinds eagerly while cruising under a canyon of majestic trees—the color now nearly blending with nature's fantastic autumn foliage. The Lotus Unique may not be unique, but this moment is; as is this singular partnership of bike and rider.

David Pye comments on how ugly the design of certainty can be, how items churned out of a factory can be dull and uninspiring in their unyielding monotony. But there are exceptions (he notes), where design of certainty does have a beauty. A row of bicycles, all alike, achieves this beauty; a team of riders clustered within their ranks upon their similarly-liveried machines—gorgeous!

We are thankful to the custom framemakers for each and every bicycle that proceeds from their shop; but we must be thankful too, for Tsunoda, when they strived (not nearly achieving) to pump out more bicycles per month than any other manufacturer in the entire world.

Following those who invent, and those who make, there is yet a third accolade to bestow upon those men and women who place the goods into the hands of expectant owners. These are the entrepreneurs, the traders, and the merchants who take financial risks. These keep a failing marque alive, start up a new brand, or when gifted with rare and prescient insight, are able to create whole new markets (which, in turn, bestir anew the creative forces of the inventors and churn up the foundries and factories).

In Syosset, New York, when Sidney Star was setting up Alpha Cycle & Supply Corp.; a world away, Komaki City, Nagoya, Shigenobu Tsunoda was pacing the factory floor of his bicycle enterprise. Who could have then guessed that by 1980, when Ernst ("Sid's" son) joined Alpha Cycle, that Syosset and Nagoya would have teamed up to supply the most glamorous production 10-speed ever built for the cycling fraternity? A collective that was then

1986 LOTUS UNIQUE: 050800

05: CODE FOR YEAR AND MODEL

0800: BUILD NUMBER

From Nagoya, Japan, to Peoria, Illinois, Lotus and Tsunoda brought quality and charisma to the commoner. In 1925, Shimataro Tsunoda longed to even touch a bicycle. At that time in Japan, only the most affluent could purchase a bike. In today's pricing terms a single imported bicycle of that day would exceed 100,000 dollars in value!

Tsunoda's dream was to breach this exclusivity and make quality bicycles for all those who coveted such exotic machines. In order to achieve this goal he apprenticed himself to a bicycle shop, learned all he could, and years later, began selling bicycles that were manufactured under the "TU" name (TU is an abbreviation for Tsunoda).

By the 1980s the march toward affordability, as well as quality, was well behind the Japanese manufacturers. Bicycling ran the headline, "Italian Panache and Japanese Quality Control–Which one do You Want?" The question was really a rhetorical one. Shimano (et al), Tsunoda (et al), and individuals like Ernst Star made bicycles that clearly proclaimed, "You can have both." The having was at a competitive price, as well.

Lotus liveries evoked the color and style of grand touring machines, or flamboyant racing marques–Ernst's color sense was spot on, yet timeless. Lotus equipment was also pragmatic: precisely specified to hit an ideal price-point.

Sid and Ernst Star had a penchant for the dramatic, by 1981 they supplied over 200 dealerships with the Lotus model, so press attention was invaluable. At that time there was a heightened fascination with both record setting and aerodynamics (even Popular Mechanics featured aero bicycles in their July 1982 issue). Alpha Cycle decided to sponsor a cross-country record setting attempt that involved both elements.

The rider was to be Jim Black, and the time to beat was just under 12 days, 4 hours. Jim Black ran Black Star Bicycles in Ithaca, New York, worked for Alpha Cycles in the summer months, and was also a ski instructor (in winter). Even though he was fit for such an expedition the ride would be 2900 miles. He would need to average 300 miles per day with a stretch over the Rocky Mountains and some grueling desert work.

Alpha Cycle & Supply Corp., took out a full page advertisement in the June 1981 issue of Bicycling to promote the event and it was widely carried in many local newspapers. Black was unsuccessful, but the cross country event continues to fascinate. In 1982 the official "Race Across America" was organized by John Marino. The 2014 record is currently held by Christoph Strasser, from Australia, who completed the event in 8 days and 8 hours.

so very hungry for an injection into the arm of flagging bicycle sales? The planning and logistics for such a global enterprise represented a monumental task at the time: one which cannot be easily appreciated today. And yet, ten or fifteen such entrepreneurial partnerships were blossoming, or fading simultaneously between the east and west.

In a book replete with excepted accounts of the travels of Twells Brex *(Twells Brex, A Conqueror of Death)* written by Hamilton Fyfe (British writer and journalist), Brex offers this exultation: "I am one of those zealots who would have a special corner in Westminster Abbey for the honoured bones of the men who invented the 'push cycle,' the pneumatic tyre, the free wheel, and the little oil bath, and thus brought to perfection this slender, whippet thing of steel and rubber that carries a man far and fast, by his own glad effort, on the open road, and takes him away from his cares, back into his old world, as nothing else can." The technical descriptions are quaint, but the spirit of the message is enduring. This brings us to the final group that I must not neglect to thank.

It is you, the rider. Oh what a goodly thing that the creative minds of inventors, the toiling efforts of makers, the risked fortunes of entrepreneurs, and the patient energies of merchants are ransacked in order that we have bicycles. It is our aggregate influence, we, the millions of bicycle riders who push the breed forward, or find something of the past that must be maintained. Collectively, the riders adopt a new technology and give it life, or fail to adopt and cause it to quickly perish. This yields the grand, one-sided bargain within the bicycle world. The inventor, builder, trader, and merchant all receive their due, but those rewards are fleeting. For the owner, however, the reward is renewed with each and every ride. A bicycle rider is a very lucky fellow, indeed.

CASE STUDY: A RESTORATION

T.F. SPECIAL

In fine fettle was the cycle.
After ten years' service, thirty thousand miles on British roads, thousands of miles in railway vans, and many strange stables on many tours, he has been re-plated and re-enamelled, his brave old heart beats under a new skin, and he shines like the morning sun.
—*Twells Brex, 1917*

1973

Dr. Shoichiro Sugihara develops a set of ideal measurements for both a track and road frame for Tom Franges. These frames possess design features that will be found on the upcoming Fuji Professional model.

1998

David Allen purchases the road frame—by this time moisture has permeated the clear coating, causing surface rust. The clear coat is removed, and the frame is painted silver; years later the frame comes into the possession of the author.

201

The T.F. Special is restored to specifications as originally conceived by its first owner in a livery of black chrome, black leathers, and black anodized components.

The more fallen, dismembered, or unoriginal the state of the bicycle, the greater the pleasure and glory of its restoration. Restoring a classic bicycle requires a disciplined mind and an adventurous spirit. The devout restorer must be a dexterous polymath, adept as: a library scientist (archiving catalogs and spec sheets, collecting excerpts from blogs and posts), a keen-eyed huntsman (pursuing auction sites, going to jumbles, tracking down requisite parts), a craftsman (painting, polishing, preparing components), and a mechanic (adroit with tools and tolerances; feeling a machine back to wholeness). The restorer is something of a philosopher as well in their quest for functional purity, aesthetic integrity, and historic vitality.

Typically, it is one of these three area—function, aesthetics, or history—that ignites the restoration spark. It was the last of these, history, which triggered the investigation of a frame that had come into possession of the author.

The story begins in the autumn of 1973. Late that year, Tom Franges (a trade consultant) and Ken Moriya crisscrossed Japan on a two-week excursion, visiting bicycle parts and accessories manufacturers each day. The goal was to reliably supply the newly formed Brookdale Associates with high quality components (this group eventually became Fuji America's parts and accessories division).

During the trip Franges visited a keirin (track racing) training school near Tokyo and met with the famed Dr. Sugihara. Using the facility's ergonometer for optimizing angles and tube lengths, it was here that Dr. Sugihara designed both an optimal road frame and track frame to Tom's dimensions, hence the *T.F. Special* designation.

At that time smoked glass and smoke-chrome furniture were the go-to of the jet set (*see* James Bond movies c. *1973*). When Tom arrived at the Fuji factory with Dr. Sugihara's specifications he conveyed his eagerness for black

T.F. SPECIAL, FUJI PROFESSIONAL PROTOTYPE: FA97030

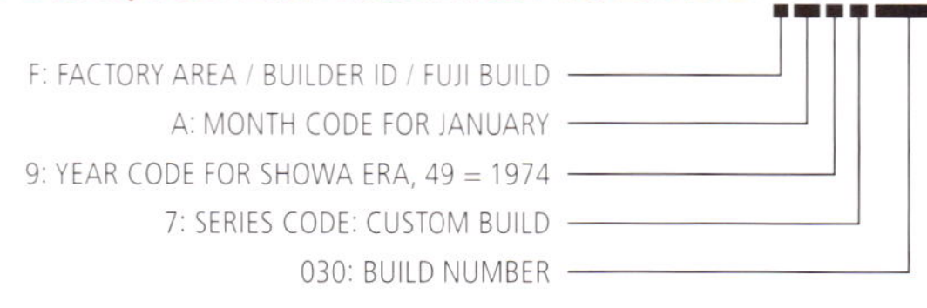

chrome. However (for unstated, but equally impassioned reasons) the desired finish was never applied. Instead, a polished clear coat was layered upon the meticulously finished frame, revealing the finely brazed build quality and the delicate file marks. Although based upon the current Fuji Newest, the frame was a precursor to the Fuji Professional model, with next-generation, Nervex-style lugwork. It was a transitional build with exacting construction.

Three months later, Tom received the frames. He fitted the road frame with components from the JBX (SunTour) group, and he fitted the track frame with Shimano's 10-pitch groupset. They were resplendent. Alas, the clear coating, which at the time was not completely impervious to moisture, allowed surface rust to steal the grandeur of the highly polished finish. As time passed, the surface further degenerated, and other projects, with newer bicycles, eclipsed their glory. The 'specials' went into storage.

Dave Allen, an enthusiast at the time who would go on to spend his entire life in the bicycle trade, admired the construction of the road frame and purchased the bicycle. He had it refinished in silver mink to match the Fuji Professionals. Later, through the generosity of Mr. Allen, the frame, scratched and forlorn (but under that paint still a thoroughbred) was most happily adopted by the author.

The *T.F. Special* languished until a conversation with Tom invoked the challenge for restoration; what if the initial desire for black chromium could be achieved, over forty years later? The process involved a scrupulous preparation of the base steel to absolute smoothness, then a meticulous chromium finish. This was then dipped into a nickel chromate bath and finished through high temperature baking via multiple steps. Intense care must be applied in the prepping of the frame or the nickel chromate can bubble out from vent holes spoiling the entire effort—

The T.F. *Special exhibits striking visual drama via the highly reflective black nickel plating and matte black anodizing. This is set off by satin aluminum, and bright, reflective chromium.*

The very rare, early Fujita unpadded black suede saddle and black leather bar wrap provide additional counterpoint to the livery. (These period saddles are particularly rare because, when replaced, they were generally discarded.)

The seat tube decal, gum rubber brake lever hoods, and natural-sidewall tires provide warm accents. On the road the bicycle is a breathtaking composition of taut handling, stiffness, precision, and classic-era beauty.

When undertaking the restoration of the T.F. Special, aesthetics were given equal weight to period correct parts. The typical restoration formula is to follow factory or catalog specifications. When there is more latitude (as in this case with a custom frame) then general principles can be applied. What is the essence of this period "correctness?"

Except for aero models, the classic bicycle does not have oversized tube members, nor does it have a sloping toptube. The whole is composed of clear, straight geometry. The silhouette of the frame is a telltale indication of the period it belongs to.

Wheels are next in importance. Again, with the exception of solid rear aero wheels, the classic models possess fine gauge, butted spokes, emanating from small or large flange hubs. Tires are about as thin as one can bear, with tubular tires for the most passionate and demanding.

There are no "weird" saddles, overpadded handlebars, or threadless stems. For the most part there is no significant plastic of any kind; natural leather is placed at each of the points where the buttocks, hands, and feet make contact with the machine. Pedals are adorned with toe clips and leather toe straps.

In fact, most everything is in contrast to the modern bicycle where greater thicknesses and increased points of curvature dominate. Where cables are buried, tires are chunky, spokes are few and uncrossed, and the collective of material attached to the handlebars makes a monolithic statement.

Good design possesses an inherent consistency which is a manifestation of a strong concept and excellence in execution—there are many paths to achieving this. The muscular road bicycles of today evolved from the lithe classics of yesterday. What looks so right on one would look absurd on the other; luckily almost no parts are interchangeable.

it's not a project for the faint of heart. Some bicycles, such as the Austro-Daimler Vent Noir, were available in a smoked-chrome livery, but it was a fairly rare finish for bicycles, despite the craze for it on furniture. The newly prepared fame was completed with a period alcohol-and-water Fuji decal (kept in a drawer for decades for this unforeseen mission). Now the frame was ready to be built up with new-old-stock components plucked from their stockpiles, storerooms, cabinets, and cubbies. Fujita black leather wrap with white stitching consummated the build.

Fortunately, the classic bicycle fraternity is not overly autocratic and fastidious, historically possible restorations are generally appreciated—not every bicycle need be returned to factory specification. Period machines are happy to have aspects of their owners infused within their character. Oh—and as for the track frame, Tom sold it years ago, it's out there somewhere. Happy hunting!

UNNO, TOKYO

TANGE STEELWORKING INDUSTRIES, LTD., OSAKA

UNNO TANGE

1955 **1964**

Unno Technical & Engineering Research established in Setagaya, Tokyo. D²xD²· Day by Day butted tubing #1 weighed in at 49% of the commonly used 1.2mm straight gauge tubing of the day. Unno tubing used to build Japanese competition bicycles for the 1964 Olympic Games.

1920

Tange Iron Works founded by Yosujirou Tange, initially for the exclusive production of bicycle forks.

1950

All manufacturing facilities are relocated to Sakai City, Osaka Prefecture. The following year manufacture of butted bicycle tubes is initiated.

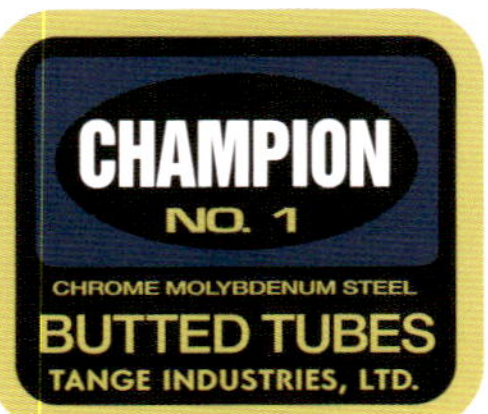

Average chemical values for type "A" D²xD² tubing:

C –.30
Si –.25
Mn –.63
Cr –.10
Mo –.20

.8mm	.5mm

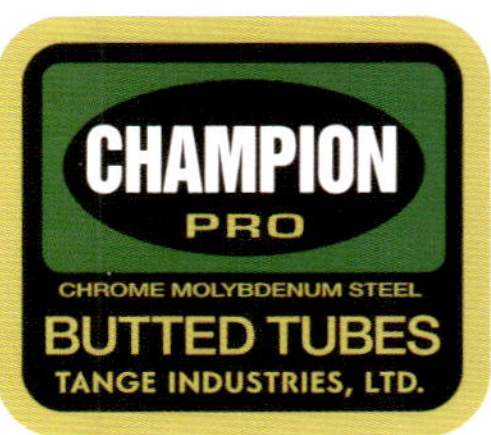

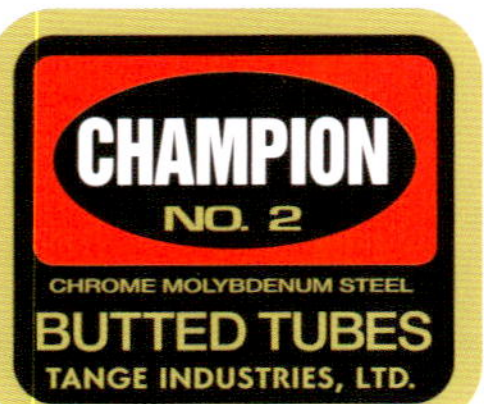

PRO	.6mm	.3mm
No. 1	.8mm	.5mm
No. 2	.9mm	.6mm
No. 3	1.0mm	.7mm

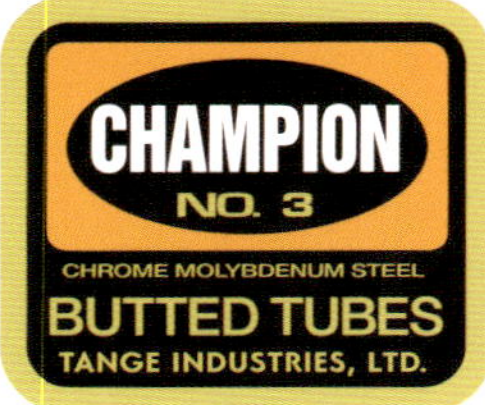

If, in the early 1960s, you were a good friend of Masashi Omiya, you could be assured of one thing—he'd have no time to meet with you. Day by day, for the two years leading up the 1964 Tokyo Olympics, he'd be out at the Nissan test track riding behind a pace car traveling at 50KPH. Masashi believed in the power of repetition, of going on-and-on, and the resolve to persevere through all obstacles.

As his determined brain spun his determined muscles, they created a cornucopia of rotations: pedals, crankset, chain, cogs, wheels… all to one aim. He strove to send this collective of man and machine toward ever more potent revolutions around the test track. Because the earth, too, was revolving: October 22nd, 1964 would soon be history. That was the scheduled road race date for the XVII Olympiad event. Ultimately, Masashi would not finish first, nor second; yet even after a crash on a bicycle with a frame of markedly light tubing, he'd manage to cross the finish line .13 seconds (with the rest of the chase peloton) behind Italy's Mario Zanin, the winner. His bicycle was of fascinating construction, built by Katakura (Silk) with a lugless construction (as recommended by Unno, the tube maker) prior to the application of bi-laminate finishing lugs. Having had the opportunity to observe the bicycle closely (it resides in Hasegawa's famed Tokyo bicycle shop, a worthy pilgrimage for classic cycling enthusiasts) it reminded me of what Bridgestone perfected by encasing tubes with cast lugs for precision and strength. The frame is simultaneously crude and refined, it is a pure, purpose-built racing ensemble. It looks like it longs to be racing again.

I wonder if Unno Technical & Engineering Research were similarly inspired by Omiya's philosophy of persevering "day by day." For Day by Day is the brand name under which they made their *Type 1* butted tubing. It was drawn with an extremely thin wall (particularly for the time)

1957 Tange becomes Tange Tekko Co., Ltd.

1958 The Japanese Industrial Standards Society grants JIS certification to Tange for the production of bicycle forks.

1965 Tange initiates their next-generation front tapered forks, with butted, oval blades.

c.1967 Cataloging of 11-piece numbered frame-sets begin, later named the "Champion series." The lightest, "Pro," weighed 1.45kg.; set number 3 weighed 2.3kg. 4 and 5, originally included, would be later discontinued.

1974 An integrated "complete frameset package" is initiated involving the production of lugs and dropouts along with full frame tube components.

1975, Tange introduces their Premium, fully hand-made Champion Cr-Mo front fork.

1979 Tange Seiki, Ltd., is established as an independent company for the manufacturing of high-quality headsets by Michiaki Tange.

1984 Super high-tensile strength, heat-treated "Prestige" tubing introduced: center areas drawn to .4mm. Three years later, 1987, a "Super-lite" version becomes available, matching Tange's earliest thin-wall racing tubing, "Champion Pro." Between the release of the premium grade "Prestige" tubing sets, "Infinity" is produced in 1985, a seamed, continuos-taper tubing.

1988 Tange establishes overseas facilities including: Tange USA Corporation in 1988, Tange Taiwan (China) in '89, and Shenzhen Tange (China) in '90. They introduce a fork combining Cr-Mo steel and heat-treated light alloys called "Fushion."

1991 "Ultimate" is produced, a super premium tubing that remains in production for both regular builds and NJS (keiren racing) specification.

1997 Ownership of Japan Tange Inc., is transferred, through sale, to Shenzhen Tange. In 2011 new facilities are constructed in Taiwan Region. Four years later the bicycle brand "Yasujiro" will be launched in honor of the company's founder, including the "Yasujiro Naked," a polished steel bicycle with a clear coating and the odacious speedback, or gavity bike, that descends mountain roadways at the highest speeds that riders are capable of travelling. One recorded example shows Serge Nuques (endoro driver and French Moto champion) descending at over 130KPH. (If Yasuji Tange could have seen the future of his company one wonders if he would have been bemused or bewildered).

Tange Inc., will continue to produce "Ultimate," "Prestige," and "Champion tubing," as well as major components and complete bicycles.

Aero 30	CrMo DB	1.2/.9mm
Aero 25	CrMo Double Gauge	
Aero 20	CrMo or Mangaloy	
Aero BMX	CrMo DB	1.2/.9mm

1.0mm .7mm

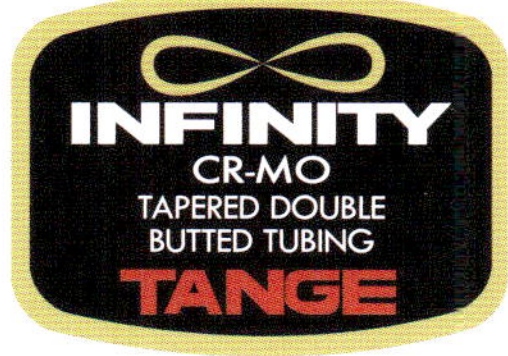

1.0mm~.6mm

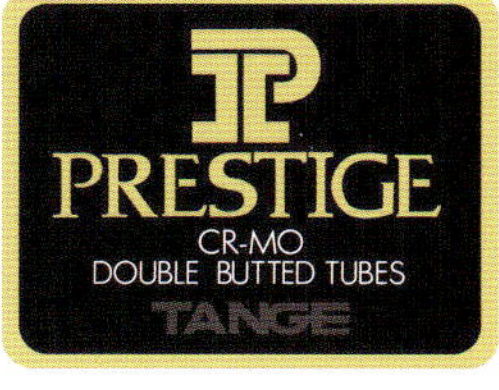

.7mm .4mm

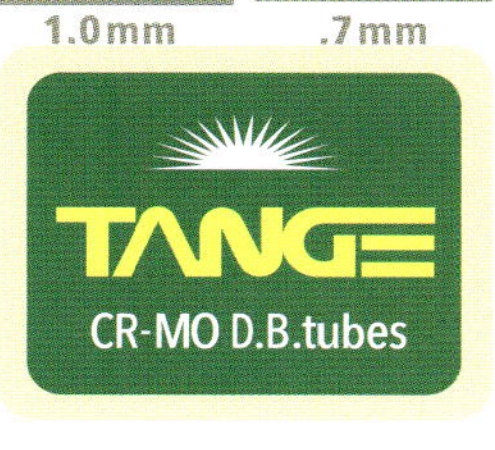

1.0mm .7mm

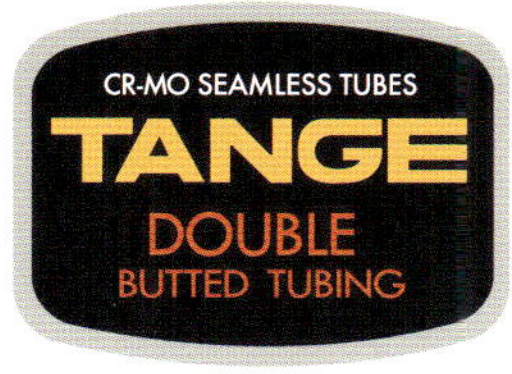

1.0mm .7mm

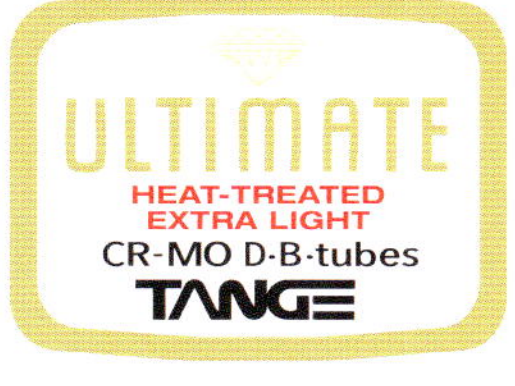

.65mm .45mm

of .8mm at edges and .5mm at center. Small diameter tubes (½") were available down to an incredible .3mm wall thickness. Day by Day (or D²xD²) published deflection stress tests with 20,000,000 repetitions yielding no damage. Returning to original form after deflection is mechanical memory; but steel has such a marvelous history one wonders if it might possess a sentient memory as well. Perhaps every steel bicycle, built with butted tubes, knows that Reynolds is their progenitor?

The *Patent Butted Tube Company* (later, Reynolds) began producing product in 1898. The bicycle fraternity's most recognized line of steel tubing, *Reynolds 531* ("five-three-one") was released in 1935. Varied thicknesses along the length of the tube solved fabrication problems while permitting far lighter frame construction. Builders were justifiably enthused to inform their customers of what great steel they were using. A celebratory final step in the framebuilding process was affixing the 531 decal. Unlike these European builders, who proudly placed the tube maker's decals on their finished products, the Japanese builders tended to hide their source material under their own names, or were otherwise more vague in labeling.

One reason for this was the advantage of procuring similar specification tubing from multiple sources (of particular importance during the headiest of the bicycle craze years). While decals from Reynolds, Columbus, Vitus (Ateliers de la Rive) directly identified what existed below the paint, the Japanese machines would use their own indirect nomenclature (such as *331* and *9658* for Fuji). As Ishiwata and Tange garnered more accolades, this practice of "badge engineering" decreased. By the late 1970s more and more Japanese exports carried the Tange or Ishiwata decal (or custom decals were made that identified Tange or Ishiwata origins in conjunction with the builder).

ISHIWATA SEISAKUSHO CO., LTD., KAWASAKI

ISHIWATA

1944

Ishiwata founded in Kawasaki (Kanagawa Prefecture) and began production of bicycle tubing.

Ishiwata developed a rider weight classification for each tube set.

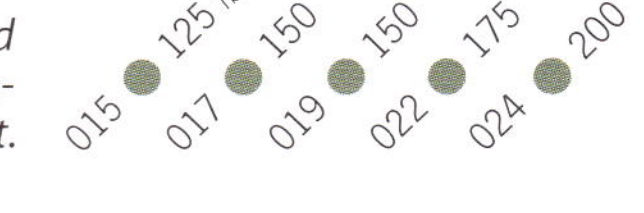

.6mm .4mm

Note on naming protocol: Ishiwata produced tube sets under collections that were both named and numbered. Their lightest frameset, "Alpha 015," weighed 1595 grams, or 15.95 hectograms, hence 015. Another example, "Ultra Strong 024," weighed 2360 grams (23.6 hectograms).

.6mm .35mm

.7mm .4mm

.7mm .4mm

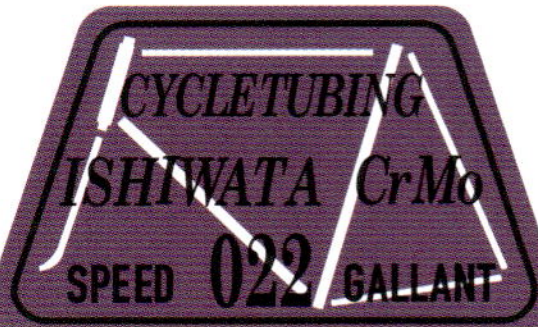

.9mm .6mm

.8mm

.8mm .5mm

1.0mm .7mm

SUPER CYCLIST 025

.9mm .6mm

LONG RUN 020

.9mm .6mm

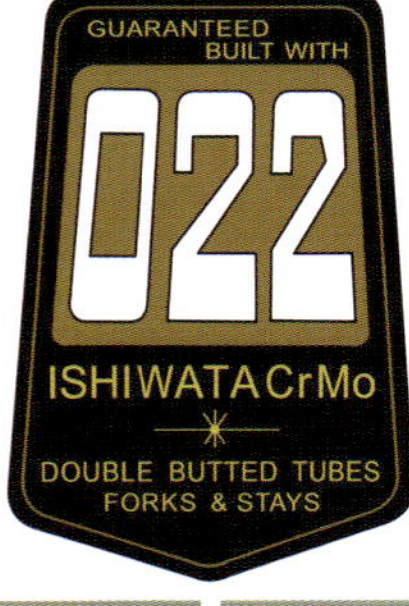

.9mm .6mm

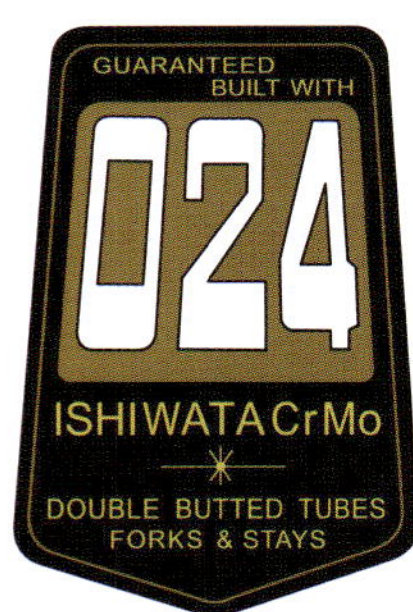

1.0mm .7mm

Of course a "bento box culture," would be enticed by the idea of sets. Tange and Ishiwata developed sets of tubing with a range of appropriate wall thicknesses matched to the to mission of the frame. The toptube is generally the lightest member with the thinnest walls. So this is the tube to brag about. However, the very lightest sets of tubing, despite their strength ratio, performance, and marketing potential, were not ideal choices for export manufacturers.

In addition to the cost (still far more competitive than European tubes) and the craft experience required to braze and assemble, there were serious concerns of potential liability. These concerns included possible litigation should a ultralight frame fail as well as the marketing fiasco that could result. But the greater concern was that the lightest sets from Tange and Ishiwata were intended for riders between one hundred and one hundred and twenty-five pounds. Japanese riders, and custom builders, could use the lightest sets, but export manufactures were beholden to respect the weight of their potential riders as well as the *character* of their riders. Today, looking back, It is notably impressive that the quantity exporters got it so right. They made bicycles that were just "heavier-enough" to thread the needle of all necessary requirements. Until more advanced heat treating methods were applied in the early 1980s (by both Tange and Ishiwata) the very lightest tubesets were used with circumspection.

Tange had their Champion line. (Initially the logo was highly reminiscent of the storied Everlast boxing brand.) The lightest road racing set was represented by the Champion *Pro series, No. 1,* and *No. 2.* These were designed for track or road. *No. 3* set was designed for touring and camping applications. Tange bravely compared their Champion steel to Reynolds 531 showing a yield stress at 48 tons per square inch compared to 45 for the Reynolds

Ishiwata rationalize their chromoly series and initiate exports (growing to about 35% of production). Technical sheets list all the diameters, wall thicknesses (butted values), lengths, and tube weights under their alpha-numeric collections (later only the numbers will be used).

These will be Innovative years for Ishiwata. They introduce their "Exactus" process of stress disbursement allowing thinner, lighter tubing. The also introduce their "EX" and "EXO" tubes that use this process. Later, it will be applied to their renowned 019E tubing. Ishiwata is producing one million pieces per month (tubes, forks, and stems combined) however they will fall into receivership within a decade.

KAISEI STEEL TUBE MANUFACTURERS, LTD.

KAISEI

1972

1973

World Championship victory taken by Freddy Maertens on Ishiwata tubing, again in '76.

1980

The Soviet Olympic Cycling team acquires 90 sets of Ishiwata tubing in order to build team bicycles for summer Olympic games held that year in Moscow.

1982

In 1981 Ishiwata introduces "Mangy-V" tube a manganese, vandium, niobium steel alloy that improves "weldability" at higher temperatures.

1993

Ishiwata ceases operations and all tooling and assets are assumed by controlling partners and associates. Newly formed company is named Kaisei (meaning "good weather and cloudless skies").

1998

Standards for chromoly tubing are established by SAE International (originally, Society of Automotive Engineers). Specification goes under reference 4130. (Standard—AMT6736). Principal element ranges are: Chromium at .8–1.1%, Manganese at .4–.6%, Carbon at .28–.33%, and Molybdenum at .15–.25%.

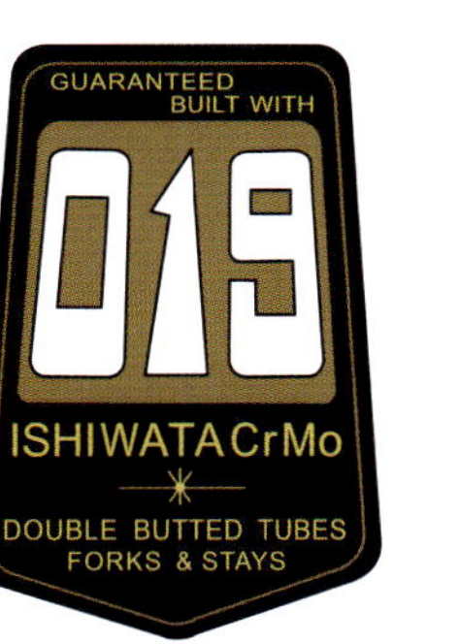

.8mm .5mm

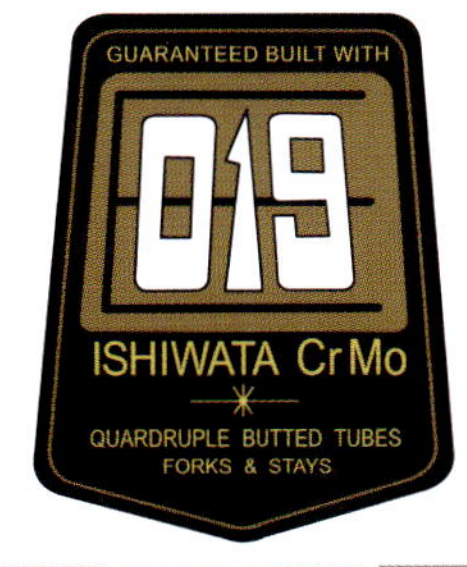

.8 .5 .4 .8

GUARANTEED BUILT WITH V MAGNY TRIPLE BUTTED TUBES ISHIWATA

1.0mm .7mm

.9 .6 .5 .8

1.0mm .7mm .8mm

.8mm .5mm

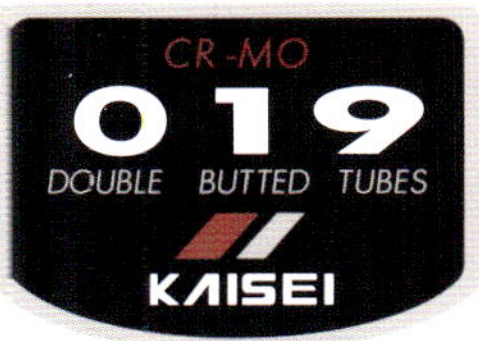

.8mm .5mm

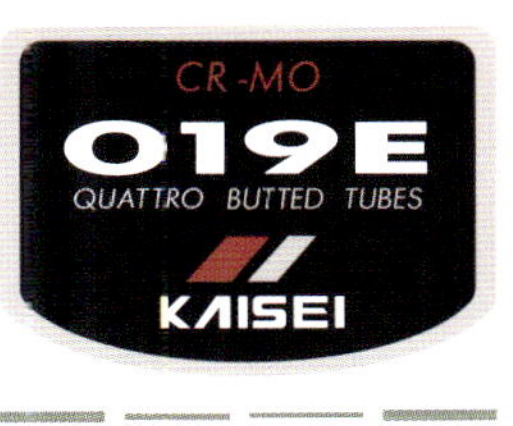

.8 .5 .4 .8

CR-MO 4130 DOUBLE BUTTED TUBES R KAISEI

.7mm .5mm

NiCR-MO 8630 DOUBLE BUTTED TUBES R KAISEI

.7mm .5mm

(prior to brazing). They initially offered heavier sets (*No. 4* and a *No. 5*), but the three lightest sets: Pro, No. 1, and No. 2. earned excellent, well deserved reputations.

Panasonic consistently specified their top-tier models with Champion No. 1. However, in a bid to build what would be considered the finest production bicycle models in the world, Panasonic turned to Columbus SL for several years. Scott Johnson tells an interesting story regarding this production decision: when his shop was visited by some of the Panasonic engineers in the very late 1980s, they were incredulous that buyers were willing to pay more for what they claimed was tubing produced to a lower manufacturing tolerance, "from every set of 100 tubes from Columbus we build 92 bicycles; from every set of 100 tubes from Tange we build 100 bicycles" they claimed. Regardless, when Tange introduced their heat-treated *Prestige* a new level was attained. Panasonic's *PR6000,* their last high specification road export bicycle of the 1990s (exported to Europe, not the USA), used Prestige. Tange (Taiwan Region) still manufactures all the top line specification tubes.

Initially, Ishiwata both named and numbered their tubing sets. The numbers related to the near-hectogram weight of a full eleven-piece ensemble. The lightest set was *Alpha 015*, their most robust was *First Light 026*. When Ishiwata developed their *Exactus* heat tempering process in 1982, one of their lighter weights of tubing, the *Glories Victory 019* became a show-stopper. Bridgestone and Fuji both cited its outstanding properties. Bridgestone noted 019E was, "equal to any chrome-moly in the world." When Kaisei (the only remaining tube maker in Japan) assumed Ishiwata's facilities in 1993 they continued production of both 019 and 019E It's truly a testament of quality that the finest Japanese steel of the 1980s is not forgotten, but still being produced for discriminating enthusiasts today.

1906 • FUJITA, SADDLES
1908 • ARAI, BRAKESETS
1910 • NITTO, HANDLEBARS
1914 • HOSHI, SPOKES
1914 • IZUMI, CHAINS
1914 • KASHIMAX, SADDLES
'16/'41 • SOYO, TIRES
1919 • DNB, DERAILLEURS
1919 • MITSUBOSHI, TIRES
1919 • UKAI, RIMS
1919 • WING STAR, SPOKES
1921 • TOKAI, RIMS
c.'22 • TAKAHASHI, SADDLES
1926 • INOUE RUBBER, TIRES
1931 • BRIDGESTONE, TIRES
1933 • DAIDO KOGYO, CHAINS
c.'31 • YAMASHITA, COGS
c.'34 • SAKAI, HEADSETS
1944 • ISHIWATA, TUBING
c.'45 • ARIAKE, SADDLES
1945 • HATTA, HEADSETS
1946 • ALPS, HANDLEBARS
c.'46 • CHERRY, BRAKESETS
1960 • MIKASHIMA, PEDALS

JEX GROUP

JEX, the Japan Bicycle Parts Manufacturers Export Association, was the trade group that included Suntour. This group established a non-compete arrangement between all the members.

"KANSAI 6"

1922: MAEDA INDUSTRIES, Ltd. **MAEDA SUNTOUR** DERAILLEUR SYSTEMS; FREEWHEELS & COGSETS

1910: SUGINO CYCLE INDUSTRIES, Ltd. **SUGINO** CRANKSETS & CHAINRINGS

1930: YOSHIGAI KIKAI KINZOKU Co., Ltd. **DIA-COMPE** CALIPER BRAKESETS

1916: HOKOKU CHAIN Mfg. Co., Ltd. **HOKOKU** CHAINS

1924: NANKAI TEKKO., Ltd. **NANKAI** COASTER BRAKE SYSTEMS

JBM GROUP

JBM, Japan Bicycle Parts Makers, was also established when Japan Sports Cycle Association was concluded. Shimano was the leader of JBM, but the arrangement allowed for open competition.

"KANSAI 5"

1921: SHIMANO INDUSTRIAL Co., Ltd. **SHIMANO** 333: DERAILLEUR SYSTEMS; CRANKSETS & CHAINRINGS; FREEWHEELS & COGSETS

1903: ARAYA INDUSTRIAL Co., Ltd. **ARAYA** RIMS

1920: TANGE INDUSTRIES, Ltd. **TANGE** FRAME TUBES & FRONT FORKS; HEADSETS & BOTTOM BRACKET SETS

1945: SAKAE RINGYO Co. Ltd. **SAKAE RINGYO**

(CORPORATE LITERATURE GIVES VARYING FOUNDING YEAR)

1897/1904: TAKAGI INDUSTRIES, Ltd. **TAKAGI** CRANKSETS & CHAINRINGS

1931: KYOKUTO MANUFACTURING Co., Ltd. **KYOKUTO** PEDALS; TOE CLIPS & STRAPS

The first post-war Japanese bicycle exports shipped to Korea in 1946. Manufacturing for this effort fell under the supervision of the "GHQ" (MacArthur's General Headquarters, the centralized governing restoration entity). Decades later, as the bicycle boom was heating up, the industry was long since fully privatized. But Japanese government and industry planning methods were still strongly infused in the corporate culture. *Competitive cooperation* was the established business practice, but there would be skirmishes upon the field as the new business methods vied with the old ones.

As the export market began to boil, the parts-making industries were set up in a manner that would minimize internal, national competition. This allowed for just-adequate profitability so exporting was seen as a good way to boost theses profits. Looking back upon the 1960s parts manufacturing landscape, it certainly *feels* as if the suppliers were orchestrated according to component categories. There were three derailleur manufacturers, three crankset fabricators, three chain makers, and so forth… Admittedly a generalization, but it was seemingly so.

For a company to find a niche (or have it assigned) and not directly compete across product lines had many benefits. Parts makers could openly share technology, pricing, and marketing plans because this would not directly enable reciprocal competition. Nearly all of the manufacturers were part of *The Bicycle Industry Association* (tracing its roots to 1930 and having establishing quality standards).

As the bicycle boom flowered (but more so, when it faltered) this collective approach would prove a hindrance. SunTour and Shimano would become internationally recognized brands, while groupsets (*ital. gruppos*) would became increasingly mandatory. (Thanks to Campagnolo's lead.) Consumers were drawn to the technology, the logic, and the visual appeal of groupsets. In short,

Note: The company names and product lines in the main timelines above were those in effect when Japan Sports Cycle Association, [JASCA], broke into the two main component trade groups: Japan Bicycle Parts Manufacturer Exports Association, JEX, and JBM: Japan Bicycle Parts Makers. Members of these groups were within the Kansai region, and would be known as the Kansai groups.

Two other, lesser promoted, regional trade groups existed: the "Tokyo-8" group and the "Chubu-6" group. Some of the companies listed at the top of this page (displayed at a diagonal) were part of these. Taskhashi and Daido where originally members of JASCA but did not continue into either the JEX or JMB groups. (Inclusion within the groups tended to be slightly fluid.)

A wealth of parts makers were poised for growth as the bicycle boom began to unfold. Trade groups promoted these companies and minimized competition. JASCA, Japan Sports Cycle Association, formed in 1963 with twelve original members. Six years later JASCA was dissolved into two groups JEX and JBM.

JEX was led by SunTour while JBM had Shimano as its principal member. Each of these would take divergent business strategies over the ensuing years. With the advent and continual importance of groupsets, parts makers were faced with two options. One approach was to vigorously compete within their niche, as did Nitto and Araya.

The other strategy was to continually expand the line toward a full groupset status, this is the strategy that Shimano, SunTour, and (after separation from the JBM), Sakae Ringyo took. Shimano created the first comprehensive Japanese groupset, the Dura-Ace line, through in-house development and engineering. SunTour's groupset, Superbe, would leverage other members within the JEX group. Sugino would also develop a group in partial conjunction with JEX members called "75."

Color key:
JASCA
JEX Group
JBM Group
Independent or affiliated with other groups

1963: JAPAN SPORTS CYCLE ASSOCIATION ESTABLISHED
1969: JASCA ENDED JEX & JBM GROUPS FORMED
SUPERBE
1992: JEX GROUP ENDS
SR SUNTOUR SOLD BY MORI INDUSTRIES
SunTour INTRODUCES THEIR GROUPSET: LATE 1976
75
SUNTOUR ACQUIRED BY MORI INDUSTRIES
ON THE OCCASION OF THEIR 75TH ANNIVERSARY SUGINO CREATES THE "75" GROUPSET: 1985
SANSHIN MATSUMOTO (SUNSHINE BRAND / HUBS) REPLACES HOKOKU
KUSUKI MANUFACTURING (WIN BRAND / HANDLEBARS) REPLACES TAIHEI
TAIHEI 1954: TAIHEI INDUSTRIAL Co., Ltd.
SADDLES; SEATPOSTS; PANNIERS
DURA-ACE
1984: JBM GROUP ENDS
...IPER, DISC & COASTER BRAKES; HEADSETS; HUBS & MULTI-SPEED REAR HUBS; SPOKES — SHIMANO INTRODUCES JAPAN'S FIRST GROUPSET: 1973
TANGE ACQUIRED BY TANGE SHENZHEN
SAKAE RINGYO ACQUIRED BY MORI INDUSTRIES
...ANKSETS & CHAINRINGS; HANDLEBARS & STEMS; SEATPOSTS
SAKAE RINGYO SEPARATES FROM JBM GROUP
TAKAGI ACQUIRED BY SHIMANO

a recognized brand meant more and more. Brand-neutral efficiencies were becoming antithetical to marketing.

Trade groups established competitive balance. But when such brands directly competed, as did SunTour and Shimano, belonging to the same promotional entity became unwieldy. The *Japan Sports Cycle Association* (established in 1963) could not easily serve two masters, so, six years it was replaced with two trade groups. One of these would be led by SunTour, one by Shimano. This created a tale of two nations—a tale of old Japan and new Japan.

One of these rallied around SunTour, establishing a *non-compete arrangement* along "old school" lines. Initially, this was a very effective strategy. When the SunTour Superbe line was released in late 1976, Sugino (cranksets), Dia-Compe (brakes), and Mikashima (pedals) all contributed to the group. But the non-compete meant that no one could effectively expand their product lines to address new industry developments, or fulfill more ambitious corporate strategies. SunTour became vulnerable and was purchased by Mori Industries (Japan) and then merged into their earlier purchase of Sakae Ringyo. SunTour's group was rendered effectively defunct. In 1992, the combined firm, SR SunTour, was sold to a Chinese concern.

The group led by Shimano took a new-school approach: sometimes cooperate, sometimes compete. Shimano introduced the Dura-Ace groupset in 1973. Everything was engineered and produced by Shimano. Compete became the only option. As bicycle parts became more mechanically sophisticated and non-interchangeable with other brands, deeper engineering and broader manufacturing capabilities would become essential. The Dura-Ace line is the vanguard of new world technology. But look closely, you'll see that Shimano's components embody the spirit, and history of all the parts makers that came before.

Chronology of the Dura-Ace series and groupset as shown in Shimano catalogs:

- 1972: FIRST DURA-ACE PARTS
- 1973: DURA-ACE TRACK ENSEMBLE
- 1976: FRONT DERAILLEUR ADDED
- 1977: DURA-ACE 10 FOR TRACK
- 1978: REAR DERAILLEUR ADDED
- 1980: DURA-ACE EX INTRODUCED
- DURA-ACE 10 BECOMES 7000
- ROAD SERIES BECOMES 7100
- EX SERIES BECOMES 7200
- DURA-ACE AX 7300 (AERO)
- 1984: TRACK SERIES BECOMES 7500
- 1988: NEW DURA-ACE 7400 SIS
- 1990: DURA-ACE TRACK 7600
- 1993: DURA-ACE 7400 DCL
- 1996: DURA-ACE 7410
- 1998: DURA-ACE 7700
- 2004: DURA-ACE 25th ANNIV.
- 2008: DURA-ACE 7800
- 2009: DURA-ACE 7900
- 2012: DURA-ACE 7970 E
- 2016: DURA-ACE 9100
- 2021: DURA-ACE R9100
- DURA-ACE R92000

TABLE OF ORIGINALITY & OWNERSHIP

46 bicycles (plus one cut-away frame) were photographed for this book—we were very focused on originality. A great deal of effort was expended to procure the smallest part, at significant cost, from a faraway place. Most of the examples, therefore, are represented to near-factory specification. Despite our best efforts some modifications were necessary, and these are listed below. Also, very special thanks to Nick for selling so much of his collection in order to acquire the bicycles I sought.

	Bicycle	Owner	*notes and modifications*	NEW OLD STOCK [NOS]—"TIME-WARP"	MOSTLY ORIGINAL (SEE NOTES)	MODIFIED (NO LONGER TO FACTORY SPECS.)	HIGHLY MODIFIED OR CUSTOM	
Araya	82 Aero 821	Nick Ozerov	*Araya aero wheel, period modifications*			●		*restoration work by Allan Wanta*
	82 Aero 821	Nick Ozerov	*original Shimano show bicycle, newer tires*		●			*sourced from Garth Braithwaite*
Bridgestone	72 Super Speed	Kate Bevington	*earlier Kyoitsu Airbike saddle, later cables*		●			
	81 Diamond Sports	Hank "TK" Blumenkranz	*replacement saddle, Christophe toe clips & straps*		●			
	82 Diamond Formula D	Jeremy Hinsdale	*Fujita NuBuck saddle, toe clips & straps*		●			
	84 Gran Velo 2000	Daniel McMartin	*non-original tires, bar tape and plugs*		●			
	94 RB 1	Nick Ozerov	*NOS frame factory equipped SunTour Superbe*				●	*facilitated by Robert Broderick*
Centurion	73 Professional	Nick Ozerov	*fully restored & repainted to original specification*		●			*restoration and repainting by Alan Wanta, facilitated by Steven Baine and prepared by Krister Katsogiannos*
	76 Semi-Pro	Nick Ozerov	*non-original tires, maintenance modifications*		●			
	77 Pro-Tour	Nick Ozerov	*non-original tires, maintenance modifications*		●			
	78 Semi-Pro	Nick Ozerov	*period tires, Mikashima adjustable toe clips & straps*		●			*sourced from Todd Grantham*
	84 Turbo	John Goodman	*non-original tires, maintenance modifications*		●			
Nishiki	72 Professional	Charles Bevington	*replacement, period wheels, later Soyo tires*		●			*sourced from Kevin Kruger*
	79 Superbe	Nick Ozerov	*NOS frame built to near-factory specifications*	●				*NOS frame sourced from Ralph Carnevale*
	80 Ultimate	Daniel Clark	*3rd owner, updated tubular tires only*	●				
	81 Comp II	Nick Ozerov	*NOS, never ridden, pulled from carton*	●				*NOS bicycle sourced from Ralph Carnevale*
	83 International	Nick Ozerov	*Fujita Seamless No. 215 (quilted) saddle, wheels*		●			*sourced from the author*
Panasonic	82 Professional 7000	Nick Ozerov	*non-original tires, period Mathauser brakepads*		●			*facilitated by Robert Broderick*
	82 AR 6000	Nick Ozerov	*refurbished to factory specification*		●			*preparation by Krister Katsogiannos*
	85 Team Europe	William F. Goodman	*correct specification, but some replaced parts*		●			*preparation by John Stanwood*
	86 Team Japan	Nick Ozerov	*very minor maintenance updates*		●			*sourced from Todd Grantham*
	90 PR 6000	Nick Ozerov	*not NOS, but completely original specification*	●				*sourced from Jacob Hartog*
Miyata	82 Team	Nick Ozerov	*non-original tires, maintenance modifications*		●			
	83 Aero	Nick Ozerov	*non-original tires, maintenance modifications*		●			*sourced from Rick Kendrick*
	84 1000	Paul Romaldini	*non-original tires, maintenance, bar wrap*		●			
	85 Team	Nick Ozerov	*non-original tires, maintenance modifications*		●			*sourced from Mark Koepke*
	87 1200	Nick Ozerov	*non-original tires, cosmetic modifications*		●			
Fuji	71 Newest	Nick Ozerov	*NOS never ridden, original tires*	●				*sourced from the author*
	73 S10-S	Nick Ozerov	*replacement wheels and tires*		●			*sourced from the photographer*
	74 Ace	Steve Hall	*non-original tires, minor maintenance modifications*		●			
	76 Professional	*author's collection*	*Fujita Professional Super saddle, Fujita barwrap*		●			
	77 Pursuit	Steve Hall	*as custom built in 1977*	●				*as acquired by author from Gene Ritvo estate*
	77 Professional	Steve Hall	*as custom built in 1977*	●				*as acquired by author from Gene Ritvo estate*
	81 Professional	*author's collection*	*SunTour Superb brakeset upgrade, tires*		●			*author is original owner*
	83 Opus III	Steve Hall	*mildly restored to factory specification*		●			
	85 Touring Series V	Steve Hall	*NOS never ridden, original tires*	●				*sourced from the photographer*
	85 Prof. Super Record	Steve Hall	*replacement rims, tires to factory specification*	●				*no period photos known to exist*
	85 Design Series Gorski	Steve Hall	*with SunTour Superbe track groupset*	○				*sourced from author, sold as frame only*
	87 Team Sante	Nick Ozerov	*NOS never ridden, including original tires*	●				*sourced from Scott Johnson of Scott's Cyclery*
San Rensho	Custom	Nick Ozerov	*as purchased from trade show*	●				*all four of the SanRensho show bicycles were built by Yoshi Konno and acquired by Ralph Carnevale from the Long Beach, California, Bicycle Dealer Show*
	Custom	Nick Ozerov	*as purchased from trade show*	●				
	Custom	Nick Ozerov	*as purchased from trade show*	●				
	Custom	Nick Ozerov	*replacement parts to spec., and new tires*	●				
Lotus	84 Aero Super Pro	Nick Ozerov	*updated tires, bar wrap, and pedal mods.*		●			*sourced from Bradely Woehl of American Cyclery*
	86 Unique	Nick Ozerov	*replacement tires*		●			*facilitated by Denise Niewinski*
Fuji	73 T.F. Special	*author's collection*	*customized recreation of original build*				●	*with thanks to Waylo at City Plating in San Antonio, Texa*

the original Fujita leather bar wrap installed on this, and other bicycles, supplied through the courtesy of Hank "The King" Blumenkranz.

SOME SOURCES

No matter how confidently one construc's a timeline and unfurls stories, there are bound to be errors. Original sources are the best bulwark against such blunders, but much must be conveyed by memory. Below are a small fraction of what guided me and often saved me from inaccuracy. Where I have fallen short, factual-wise, the blame is entirely mine.

In addition to back-issues of contemporary magazines, such as *Bicycling* and *Bike World*, current periodicals, principally Jan Heine's *Bicycle Quarterly* proved invaluable.

Today, many online bicycle-focused forums, and enthusiasts sites are populated with generous, informative, history-savvy individuals. They've proven to have a great sense of humor as well as decisive insight. Truly, a double bonus and terrific resource.

The majority of hard facts for this volume come from period corporate literature. Although expectably biased to their own brand offerings, key specifications and dates are generally very trustworthy and provided useful departure points.

Simultaneously pragmatic and beautiful, in an info-geek kind of way, are the *Japan's Bicycle Guide* volumes (annual publications initiated in 1951 by *Japan's Bicycle Industry Association*). These contain a wealth of both general information and minutiae—they lasted into the early 1990s. Another trade resource, *Japan Bicycle Press* was a constant go-to for very specific reporting. (Their first issue was not until September, 1980. I wish they had been formed around ten years earlier).

Two fascinating and extremely useful documents that helped set the stage for the time I cover are Tatsuzo Ueda's *The Development of the Bicycle Industry in Japan After World War II*, and Tsuneyoshi Takeuchi's *The Formation of the Japanese Bicycle Industry: A Preliminary Analysis of the Infrastructure of the Japanese Machine Industry*. Both of these publications were produced under project co-coordinator Dr. Takeshi Hayashi for The United Nations University. *Bicycle Design*, by Tony Hadland and Hans-Erhard Lessing (The MIT Press) and *No Hands*, by Judith Crown and Glenn Coleman (Henry Holt and Company) were amazing sources.

In this table (left page), bicycles are classified as original, or modified. We referred to a limited number of the most original as "time-warp candidates" if they met certain criteria.

At first we considered a (production) bicycle as a "time-warp" machine only if you unboxed it from the factory carton in which it was originally packed, and, as with a newborn, brought the subject into light. That was too extreme, so we extended the honor to any machine with every original part, including the tires that it came with. This is obviously very rare. However, some readers are restorers and these details matter.

The majority of the machines photographed we considered mostly original; for these, perishable parts (tires, brake-pads, bar tape, brake and derailleur cables, etc.) do not have to be "as it left the factory." Bicycles under the mostly original category will look like factory bikes from a short distance.

(There is always that conundrum of absolutely perfecting a bicycle to factory specification and then being disinclined to actually ride it! But for collectors this level of accuracy is welcome.)

The other categories, modified (and custom) should not be used as references for a build, but they are all period correct. The only exception is the tires. We photographed some extremely original, or rare machines with flat tires and after a while we did not like doing that… so we made the tire exception.

The best possible thing in the world is to find the most original bicycle you can and learn how to care for it on the mechanical (maintenance) and chemical (preservation) levels. Then modify the bicycle to make it a street worthy companion. Put those original parts you swapped-out in a secure box with proper identification – and, go, riding.

PHOTOGRAPHY & PRINTING

During the early design and presentation phases for this book, the photography was shot via traditional film camera and digitally scanned; the author used a Leica R8 with Fujifilm 160-C. Scott originally debated as to whether to go film or digital, but after testing our options the decision was decisively made: digital. Scott never looked back, but he certainly looked at a lot of beautiful bicycles!

All of the bicycles featured in this book were shot at *Milk Street Studio*, located in Essex, Massachusetts. The studio is purpose-designed for photographing modes of mechanical transportation: bicycles, cars, or motorcycles.

Every photograph was taken by Scott Ryder.

Lighting schemes designed and provided by John Hurley. Profoto studio strobes with various light modifiers were used to create the detailed lighting scheme specific to each of the bicycles.

Each image was baselined to 1/160th of a second.

Images were captured using a Canon EOS-5-DS with a:

Canon EF 100mm f/2.8L Macro IS USM lens.

Images were converted from 60mbg. raw files to .tiff format.

The book was printed in China.

All images printed on 157gsm matt-coated art paper.

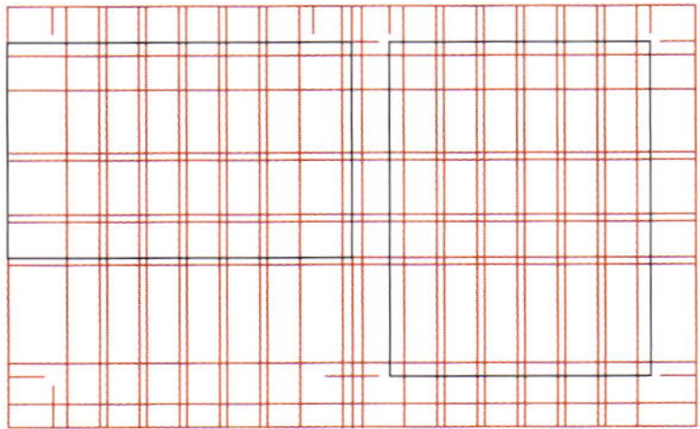

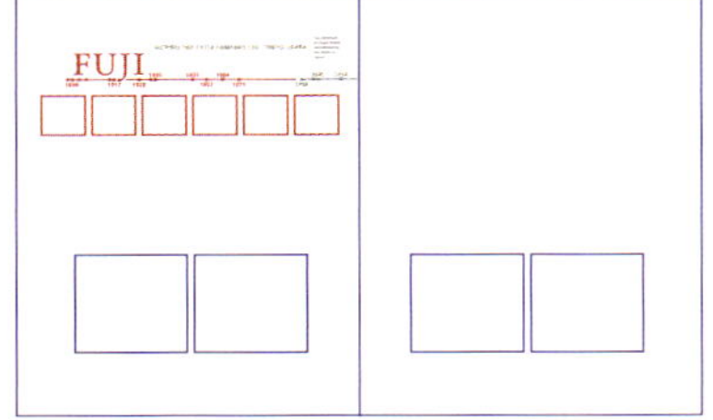

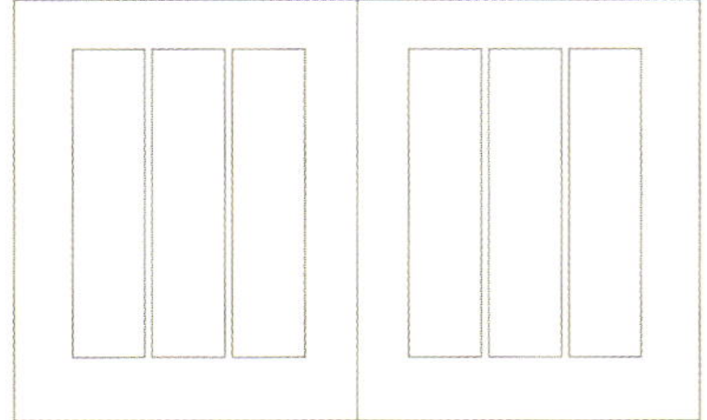

DESIGN & TYPOGRAPHY

This book was designed by the author. Siu Chong-Basdeo, principal of Spire Integrated Design, served as design consultant. I am grateful for her talent and steadfastness. In the realms of design and typography I must also thank my many students, from years present and distant: what an amazing collective of talent and optimism—my daily inspiration.

The layout for this book was composed through the use of a multi-layered grid system.

The *photography grid* permitted innumerable choices for sizing, cropping, or bleeding (extending to the edge of the sheet) the bicycle images. Despite this flexibility, all full-profile photographs are of the same size and location within the page. This follows a design principle of juxtaposing consistent elements against a series of variables.

A *timeline and title grid* is used for chapter openings, as well as for the informational pages presented in the frontmatter and backmatter of the book. Four typefaces are incorporated within these densely designed areas. The main (large) titles are in **Berthold Garamond.** This typeface was designed by Günter Gerhard Lange in 1972, and is derived from the classic forms of Claude Garamond's work of the 16th century. The supporting titles are set in **Frutiger 87** (87 is the 'black-condensed' variant within the Frutiger family). Adrian Frutiger designed the original version of this typeface in 1968 for the Airport Roissy (later renamed Charles de Gaulle Airport) in Paris. The years along the timeline are also in Frutiger 87, but the captions are set in **Myriad Italic.** Myriad was designed for Adobe Systems Incorporated by Robert Slimbach and Carol Twombly in 1972. Special 'call-outs' are set in News Gothic #2. The first font in this family was **News Gothic #2 Thin.** The original was commissioned by Leonard Battipaglia c. 1984, but Linotype Corporation completed the type family over the ensuing years. News Gothic was originally designed by Morris Fuller Benton in 1908.

The two-column (per page) *body copy grid* uses **Frutiger 45** in a consistent location through the book, while the three-column *caption grid* uses **Berthold Garamond Italic** in a flexible manner, aligned as necessary to the photography and period art.

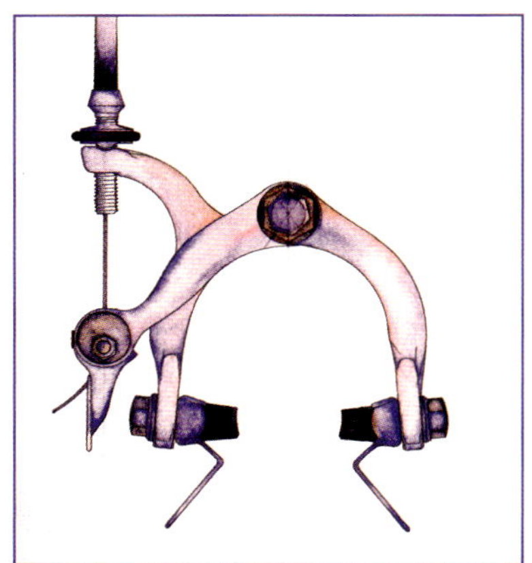

I once had a dream to draw every bicycle part of merit and bind these into a book of technical watercolor paintings. Alas, teaching and design-project obligations lured me from the task. I only finished a handful; decades later I undertook 'Japanese Steel.' I wish to expressly thank everyone at the Classic Fuji Collaborative, for not letting me off the book until I finished.

ACKNOWLEDGMENTS

All worthy books cost more in time and expense than first imagined, but I'd still be toiling at this volume today if it were not for the dedication of Scott Ryder and the perseverance of John Hurley. I add to these the hospitality of Kate Bevington, my sister, and Margaret M. Scheffs, her partner, who kindly let me withdraw to their loft in Long Island City, New York, as my sequestered writing retreat.

I wish to thank Jessica Fuller and Jacob Lehman of Rizzoli; Jessica for setting me upon the road, and Jacob, my endlessly supportive editor, for getting me to the finish line.

I met marvelous individuals on my junkets to Japan and must particularly thank two remarkable men: Masayuki 'Mike' Hasebe, Director of the Bicycle Museum Cycle Center in Osaka, and Toshio 'TT' Tsutsuji, President of Akibo Corporation, also in Osaka.

On the home front, many persons extended kindness with both their time and their knowledge, but of particular generosity were Patrick Cunnane, President, and Karen Bliss, Chief Marketing Officer, of Advanced Sports International.

When it came to procuring all the bicycles, the thank-you list is nearly endless; I insult many by listing only the tireless Nick Ozerov and the fastidious Stephen Hall. Preparing the bicycles for photography was another project unto itself; in this regard I extend a wrench of gratitude to Michael Monaco and Shawn Stehling. And then there was shipping; not one bicycle was damaged, not one ball bearing lost—I attribute this to BikeFlights, who were always there for us during every logistical adventure.

I am grateful to those who reviewed developing sections of the book, providing their valuable insight and corrections. The two individuals of incomparable thoroughness in this regard were Kurt Bodden and Nick Ozerov—both adept at wordcraft and passionate about bicycles. Last, love most inestimable to my daughters, Caslon and Lindsay, for always being there (even when you're far away.) To both of you, I dedicate this book.

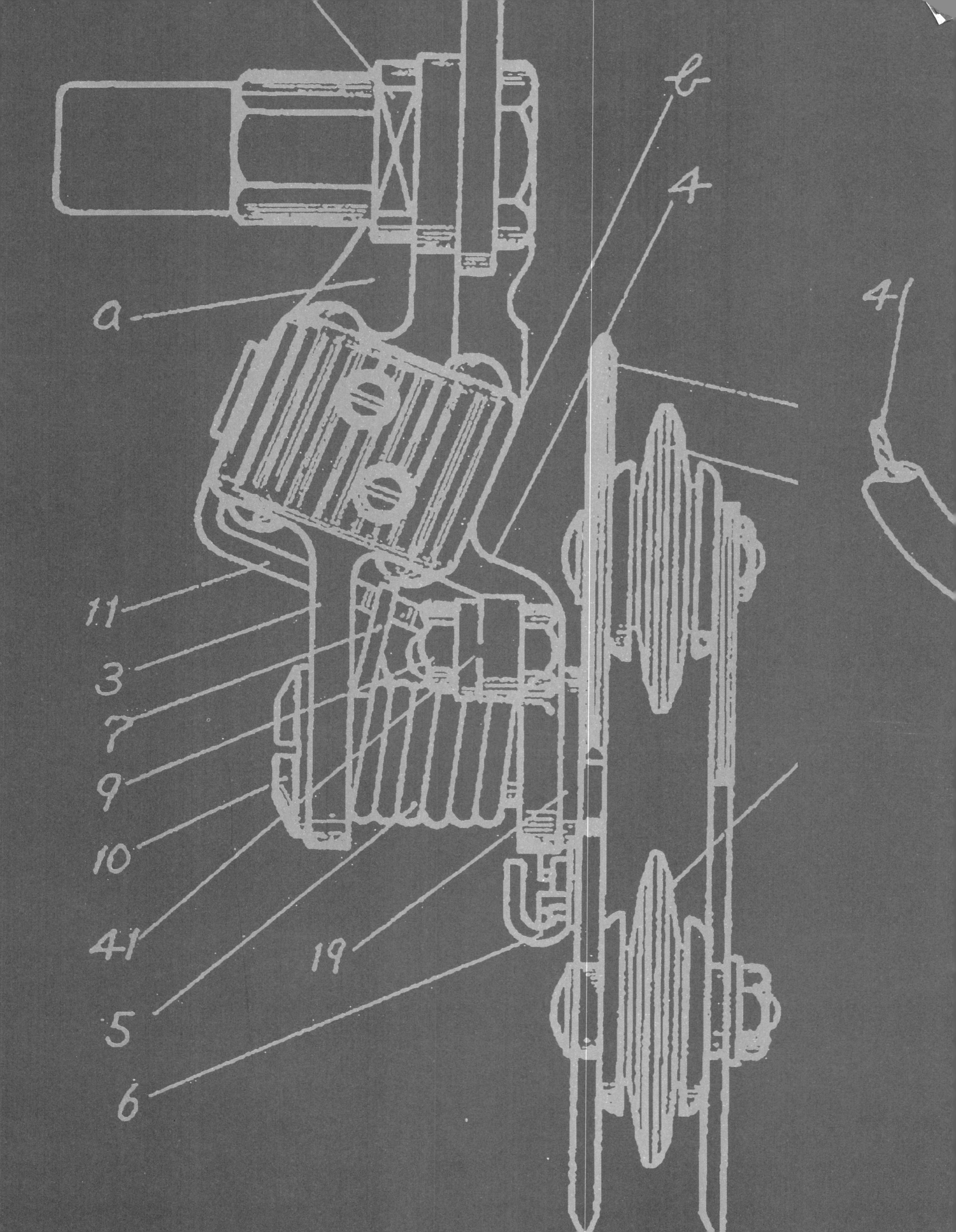

b
4
4
a
11
3
7
9
10
41
19
5
6